THE MOTHER
NEXT DOOR

THE MOTHER NEXT DOOR

MEDICINE, DECEPTION, AND MUNCHAUSEN BY PROXY

Andrea Dunlop and Mike Weber

ST. MARTIN'S PRESS
NEW YORK

First published in the United States by St. Martin's Press, an imprint of St. Martin's Publishing Group

www.stmartins.com

The Library of Congress Cataloging-in-Publication Data is available upon request.

ISBN 978-1-250-28427-3 (hardcover)
ISBN 978-1-250-28428-0 (ebook)

Our books may be purchased in bulk for promotional, educational, or business use. Please contact your local bookseller or the Macmillan Corporate and Premium Sales Department at 1-800-221-7945, extension 5442, or by email at MacmillanSpecialMarkets@macmillan.com.

First Edition: 2025

10 9 8 7 6 5 4 3 2 1

We dedicate this book to the many survivors of
Munchausen by proxy whose stories are as yet unheard.
We believe you.

AUTHORS' NOTE

The names of children who appear in this book have been changed to protect their privacy, as have those of individuals who did not participate in interviews, with the exception of public officials and both convicted and alleged perpetrators.

CONTENTS

Introduction   xi

PART 1: THE CHEMIST

1. Meet Hope   3
2. Saving Sophia   17
3. Meet Mike Weber   24
4. The Investigation Begins   33
5. A Family Divided   49
6. Poison   58
7. The Interview   73
8. The Arrest   92
9. Aftermath   100

PART 2: THE COPYCAT

10. What Happened to Alyssa?   111
11. Fooling No One   125
12. "Unable to Determine"   132

13. The Turn   143

14. The Trial   153

15. Reason to Believe   163

PART 3: THE UNRAVELING

16. After the Fall   171

17. When Mary Met Doug   178

18. Jane Justin   183

19. Turning Doug   189

20. "Nurse" Mary   196

21. A Tangled Web   205

22. Minnesota   224

23. A Seismic Shift   230

Conclusion   248

Acknowledgments   265

Notes   269

Introduction

It was a rainy night in Seattle in July 2019. The global pandemic that would reshape life as we knew it was still several months in the future, but my life was in its own dramatic state of flux. I was a first-time mom trying to navigate the exhausting back-and-forth of being a working parent. My daughter, Fiona, was eight months old and I was launching my third novel, *We Came Here to Forget*, at one of my favorite local bookstores. It tells of an Olympic skier whose relationships and career are turned upside down by a family catastrophe. Book publications—with their touring demands, media pushes, endless social media shilling, and alternating waves of excitement and dread—are always draining, but this one was like nothing I'd been through before. The book was fiction, yes, but it was heavily based on events that had destroyed *my* family. I'd never written anything that made me feel so vulnerable.

Overall, the launch was not going especially well. If you are lucky enough to publish more than one or two books in your life, as I have been, you are sure to have at least one where everything goes wrong: this was mine. For one thing, my beloved editor had left the publishing house some six months earlier, leaving me orphaned. Since then, there had been so many staffing changes that no one who had worked on my previous books was still in place by the time this had come out. Worst of all, instead of spending publication day trying to relax before the launch event that night, I had spent it alternating phone calls with my lawyer, agent, and therapist.

The cause was an eleventh-hour cease and desist I had received from my sister, Megan, attempting to halt the publication of my novel and insisting I stop discussing my personal connection to one of the central themes of the book: Munchausen by proxy. Megan had always denied the abuse allegations, and now her lawyer was demanding that I retract previous statements to the media and cancel my tour. In essence: she wanted me to shut up and go away.

I wrote the majority of *We Came Here to Forget* while I was pregnant with my daughter. I always knew I'd write about my sister eventually—writers are prone to working out their traumas on the page. When motherhood came into the picture, it suddenly felt necessary to write about the tragedy that had devastated my own family. Some book ideas take forever to coalesce, while others—like this one—arrive fully formed and feel so urgent that you ignore them at your own peril.

My life was in a good place when I wrote the book, but you don't get over becoming estranged from your only sister, especially when that separation is due to something as terrifying as suspicions of child abuse. At best, it's a wound that changes over time—and just when you think it's closed, it splits right open again. For me, the experience of becoming a mother brought my history with my sister to the surface in a way that I was no more prepared for than anything else about new motherhood.

I feel the loss of my sister particularly acutely during life milestones. I always imagined she'd be the first person I'd call when I found out I was pregnant. Even now I can imagine the conversation vividly; I can hear her telling me how excited she is, soothing all my fears, and talking me through the endless list of pregnancy dos and don'ts. She used to work as a nurse in an OB-GYN clinic, so she would have been the perfect person to ask about my dreadful morning sickness and all the paranoias that accompany a first pregnancy. It would have given me an opportunity—increasingly rare as we grew into adulthood and our lives took different paths—to feel close to her again. She would have been so great on that call.

But she wasn't there on the other end of the line to take that call. Just as she wasn't there to celebrate with me when I got my first book deal. She wasn't standing next to me on my wedding day. She wasn't holding my hand in the delivery room. Her absence has fundamentally altered the life I thought I would lead. I was sure we'd raise our kids together. I took for granted that she'd be there to help me cope as our parents age, when they inevitably pass away. I imagined us having lunches together as old women, comparing notes on our grandkids. As it stands, I can't imagine she'll ever even meet my children, much less their children. Her absence has hardened into a permanent thing that feels like a death, only less complete.

In July 2019, I hadn't seen my sister in almost a decade. And as the years had gone by, what once seemed unimaginable felt increasingly likely: that I would never see her again.

Until that rainy night of the book launch.

Thankfully, a dear friend, humorist Geraldine DeRuiter, was moderating the event, so I didn't have to sit alone at the microphone after being rubbed raw by the emotions of the preceding days. As she finished introducing me, I smiled, trying to appear calm as my eyes scanned the room. This was my hometown event, so there were lots of familiar faces in the crowd. My parents and my husband and daughter were sitting in the front row, along with some other family members. One face in particular moved me so deeply that I almost lost my tenuous composure right away: Stephanie was my sister's best friend growing up, and a second big sister to me. We'd only recently reconnected, but she was there, heavily pregnant with her second child, sitting with her own mom.

Between these friends and the subtext of the book, it felt like my sister's ghost was hovering in the front row as well: the ghost of the sister who should have been there. For a moment, I let myself imagine her, somewhere on the edges of the store. All day, a small part of me had wondered whether she might try to disrupt the event, but when I didn't see her in the audience, relief washed over me.

Most writers share an alternating fear and fantasy about our books drawing people out of the woodwork to see us triumphant in our success. Maybe the crowd will part and an old lover will try to win you back, or your high school bully will approach, chagrined and apologetic. When I'd launched my previous books, I confess there was some small part of me that hoped my sister might show up, full of pride that I'd accomplished what had always been my lifelong dream. But this was before I ever went public about her. On that night, I knew that wherever she was, she wasn't feeling anything close to pride.

Regardless of what she thought, I didn't write *We Came Here to Forget* to settle a score. I wrote it because I needed to. And the reason I went public about my own connection to Munchausen by proxy—also known as medical child abuse, wherein a parent or caretaker fabricates, exaggerates, or induces illness in their child—was that I wanted to authentically portray a family coping with its specter. The media pays little attention to this topic, and when it does, it sensationalizes it. At the time of my book launch, I had never spoken to a single other person who'd navigated the bizarre, lonely waters of an investigation. Back when my family was imploding, it would have meant so much to me to talk to someone who could understand. It would have helped to see the story reflected with empathy and dignity, rather than as grisly fodder for true crime drama. My third novel could be my chance to live that adage: write the book you want to read. I wanted to be that voice for someone else.

A FEW DAYS after my book event, I had lunch with Stephanie at a pub on Seattle's Eastside. Stephanie is so deeply entwined in my history that her voice feels familiar to me in the way a family member's does; more of my memories growing up include her than don't. It meant so much that she and her mom came to the event and that she read my book. I filled her in on the surrounding legal drama, eager to talk to someone else who'd known—and loved—my sister. "I was up there just waiting for her to burst in and disrupt the event," I finished, now able to laugh at my paranoia.

Stephanie's eyes got big. "There's something I have to tell you," she said slowly. "I didn't want to say anything the night of, but I went to the ladies' room right before the event started." She paused. "Meg and I walked right by each other."

I froze. My sister had not just been a ghost in the room. I was instantly grateful I hadn't seen her and also deeply spooked that she'd been there watching, no doubt waiting for me to misstep, to say something that she and her lawyer could use against me. She could have been inches from my baby and husband, who would not have recognized her.

Like everyone who once knew Megan—every member of our family, each friend from her formerly tight-knit circle—Stephanie hasn't spoken to my sister in years. That night, the two women who had been inseparable as girls didn't say a word as they brushed past each other.

When I got home from lunch, I told my husband that Megan had been at the event, and I watched his face go white. He had never met my sister, yet she was an inescapable presence in our lives, looming large in her absence. In that moment, I could see in his expression that the horror story of my past had suddenly become real.

That night marked the beginning of the next phase of my complicated forty-year journey with Megan. We'd been sisters. Then we'd been strangers. And on this night, we'd morphed into something new, something I had been fighting to avoid, but which suddenly felt inevitable. Now we were enemies.

I FIRST MET Detective Mike Weber at a Munchausen by proxy (MBP) training in January 2020—mere weeks before the Covid-19 pandemic would make the idea of sitting in a room full of unmasked strangers in a hotel ballroom all day unimaginable. I was attending the American Professional Society on the Abuse of Children's annual conference in San Diego at the invitation of Dr. Marc Feldman, an author, professor, and psychiatrist who is one of the world's foremost experts on Munchausen by proxy and other factitious disorders in the world. A quick search of his name produces hundreds of interviews with him on the subject, as well as his significant contributions to the literature—including four books[1] and innumerable research papers. He and I had been introduced by journalist Dvora Meyers after she'd interviewed both of us for her excellent *Longreads* piece "The Disease of Deceit" about a friend who'd faked having cancer. Marc and I became fast friends and began pairing up on interviews. He asked me to come to San Diego to meet with APSAC's MBP committee, a cross-disciplinary group of child abuse professionals who represent the only cohesive effort to combat a form of abuse so taboo and misunderstood that even many of the most hardened social workers, detectives, and psychologists want nothing to do with it.

By the time I met with the committee, I was an experienced public speaker. Yet as I paced my hotel room, inhaling the ocean breeze and trying to find serenity in the waves that crashed just beyond a line of palm trees, I was nervous. Previous attempts to tell this story hadn't gone well. And I didn't know what to expect from the committee: I wasn't sure how receptive a group so packed with advanced degrees and professional accolades would be to a novelist whose sole qualification in the arena was her own sad story.

In the hotel's conference room, I was immediately met with warmth and appreciation as the group gathered around the big table with hotel pastries and hot coffee; it felt like a meeting of old friends more than stuffy academics. In the rare instances when I'd tried to explain to someone what had happened in my family, I had been met with dropped jaws, wan faces, and, occasionally, tears. I had never encountered nodding heads and knowing looks. It was the first time I understood that what I'd witnessed in my family was not a bizarre outlier, but part of an eerily consistent pattern of behavior. I'd been utterly alone with this story for almost a decade, then all at once, I wasn't.

This feeling deepened the next day as I sat in the front row listening to Mike Weber and Sheriff Bill Waybourn unpack the case of Brittany Phillips—which we'll cover in this book—for a rapt audience. I'm not a religious person, but sitting in that nondescript hotel ballroom, I was overcome by the powerful sensation that I was exactly where I was supposed to be.

Bill Waybourn and Mike Weber are straight out of central casting. Whatever comes to your mind when you think "Texas sheriff," Bill embodies it. He stands a towering six feet four (not counting the additional inches of his signature ten-gallon hat) and sports a glorious moustache and a gleaming belt buckle. I could imagine him being intimidating under the right circumstances (likely a job requirement) but he also exudes warmth. When I first introduced myself after his presentation, I asked if I could give him a hug and found myself fighting tears. Bill was the first person I'd ever met who'd had a case of Munchausen by proxy in his family. His story had left very few dry eyes in that crowd. His was also the first story that gave me any hope.

Mike hadn't been present at the committee meeting, but I knew he was a member and Dr. Feldman had spoken highly of him. Tall with a flattop haircut, in a no-nonsense suit and tie, Mike was an endearing combination of tough and humble. I complimented him on his presentation and his response was an "Aw shucks, just doing my job" mumble that I've come to expect from him, and that belies the truly remarkable work he's done over the course of his career. I quickly discovered that Mike has an extraordinary capacity to run headlong into the hornet's nest of cases that make other seasoned detectives run for the hills. I told him I was an author and he mentioned, bashfully, that people were always telling him he should write a book. He'd structure it around the three cases that had stuck with him the most: the ones that gave him a full understanding of the complex issue he'd just spent several hours educating the audience about.

"You *should*," I said, and meant it.

"Oh, I don't know."

I explained to Mike that I'd worked in book publishing for almost twenty years, and a great many people had told me their book ideas. "They're almost never good," I emphasized, "but this one is *good*."

Mike's serious detective exterior cracked as he let out a full belly laugh.

By the time I met him, Mike had worked on approximately thirty medical child abuse cases and secured more convictions than anyone else in the country by leagues. But these three women's cases made such a deep impression on him that they forever shaped his understanding of this abuse: Hope Ybarra, Brittany Phillips, and Mary Welch. These were the ones that introduced him to what

Munchausen by proxy could look like: how it could masquerade as love; how it could manifest online; and how a case could fall apart in the hands of the wrong official, no matter how strong the evidence.

Hope Ybarra was Mike's first full investigation into medical child abuse. He'd never seen anything like her: a con artist so committed to her version of reality that it went on for the better part of a decade before anyone caught on. The facts of the case were so chilling that he realized *nothing* was off the table when it came to these types of offenders. But if he was expecting every perpetrator to be a master manipulator, Brittany Phillips—a person who fooled exactly no one—would prove him wrong. Brittany brought home for Mike how important an offender's digital footprint could be. The phenomenon of social media has exacerbated Munchausen by proxy in unimaginable ways, and in the early 2010s, when Mike investigated Brittany, it was only beginning to emerge how dramatic the coming shift would be. And with Mary Welch, Mike would see just how inept the systems around medical child abuse truly are, and how money and the soft power of charm and beauty can blur all the lines. Mary was the archetypal perfect upper-middle-class mom, impossible for many to view as a criminal.

At first, I'd planned to help Mike with a book proposal, introduce him to some agents, and then bow out. But before I knew it, I'd gone through the looking glass, too, and offered to write it with him. I'd spent years trying to avoid analyzing what happened in my family, but by the time I met Mike, I was deep into the process of trying to understand it and to hopefully help others do the same. It was a fateful meeting that would launch not only the creation of this book, but my podcast, *Nobody Should Believe Me*—which, as of this writing, has been downloaded more than five million times.

———

BEFORE WE GO any further, some lexicon.

The disorders underlying what are colloquially known as Munchausen syndrome[2] (factitious disorder imposed on self) and Munchausen by proxy[3] (factitious disorder imposed on another) are grouped together under the umbrella of "factitious disorders" and are characterized by intentional deception around medical issues for the purposes of attention and sympathy.

"Munchausen syndrome" was first coined by Dr. Richard Asher in *The Lancet* back in 1951, after Baron Munchausen, a character from a 1785 novel who told tall tales about his exploits. Munchausen behaviors do not always lead to Munchausen by proxy abuse, but they are certainly considered a risk factor by every expert I've spoken to, and we will see ample evidence of both disorders in this book. It's worth noting that, on its own, the Munchausen phenomenon is baffling and complex and causes very real harm to the people it ensnares, even as the risks are less horrific than child abuse.

Consider one example: In 2015, Australian food blogger and author Belle Gibson caused a national firestorm when it was revealed to be a hoax all along that she'd "cured" numerous forms of cancer with her diet. The cascade of fallout included a fraudulent claim that she had donated $300,000 to various charities. Belle was ultimately convicted in the Federal Court of Australia for breaching consumer laws and was fined more than a quarter of a million dollars (which as of this writing, she still has not paid).[4] According to news reports, numerous people came forward with their stories of forgoing traditional treatment for their very *real* cancer diagnoses in order to follow Belle's regimen. In a disquieting interview with Australia's *60 Minutes,* Belle maintains she believed her diagnosis to be real and that she was fooled by unscrupulous doctors—another claim that was swiftly proven false—and evades taking responsibility for her actions.[5]

But even in more quotidian cases than Belle's, the damage done to those involved is often deep and long-lasting. The story of Sarah Delashmit—a woman who falsely claimed to suffer from a host of ailments including muscular dystrophy and breast cancer—was chronicled first by Sarah Treleaven for *Elle*, and then further explored by the podcast *Sympathy Pains*, which focused on the emotional, financial, and psychological fallout for her primary victims. No one who is ensnared in such a lie is ever the same. Delashmit was ultimately sentenced to eighteen months in federal prison after pleading guilty on several counts of fraud.[6]

It's important to understand that factitious disorders are characterized by *deliberate* deception and are not cases of someone who is simply anxious or even having outright delusions about illnesses. It feels very worth noting here, too, how enmeshed this all is in our deeply flawed and often biased medical system. People *do* suffer from ailments that can be difficult to get to the bottom of, and if someone feels they are not getting adequate care, they have every right to continue to seek help and move on from doctors who aren't listening to them or treating them properly.

"Medical gaslighting"—the phenomenon of doctors wrongly blaming a patient's symptoms on psychological factors or denying their symptoms entirely—is especially prominent with female patients, due to age-old biases in the medical community about women and pain. Medical misogyny is real, and I don't know a single woman—myself included—who hasn't experienced it, who hasn't been brushed off or had their experience of their own body questioned at least once by someone in the medical establishment.

Add in any other marginalized identity and the problem gets worse: Black people receive worse care (the mortality rate for Black mothers in the US is nearly three times what it is for white women[7]); as do fat people, who are routinely denied care because of their size;

and trans people, who face innumerable barriers and biases to receiving care.

Most doctors get into the profession to help, but they are still human beings with biases, and they're operating within a system originally designed to serve the needs of cis white men first, with everyone else as an afterthought. We are still in the nascent stages of re-forming those ideas. Take, for example, the body mass index (BMI), developed two hundred years ago by a Belgian astronomer and mathematician (*not* a physician) as a way to determine the "average" (white, Belgian) "man," which he considered a social ideal. Despite its problematic history, this metric is nonetheless trotted out for bodies of all genders and races and used as though it is an infallible metric of health. Or consider that women were generally excluded from clinical trials until the 1990s,[8] based on an earlier medical ethos that they were just men with "boobs and tubes." Black Americans have a particularly horrifying history with the medical system, including the 1932 "Tuskegee Study of Untreated Syphilis in the Negro Male"[9] wherein Black male participants were not told they had syphilis and treatment was intentionally withheld. The study went on for forty years until an Associated Press exposé put a stop to it. There is also the grim history of Dr. J. Marion Sims[10]—the so-called father of gynecology—who conducted gruesome experiments on enslaved women, forgoing anesthesia.

These examples are the tip of the iceberg in terms of why *many* people have a rightful mistrust of the medical system and find themselves needing to be dogged about receiving care—perhaps even to be a bit more dramatic about their symptoms than they'd prefer.

But Munchausen is not seeking a second opinion, or even hamming it up a little bit to make sure the doctor takes you seriously: it's a pattern of deliberate, often extremely well-researched deception, perpetrated for the intrinsic reward of sympathy, attention, and, to a degree, the sheer thrill of fooling people.[11]

These same motivations and behavior patterns underpin Munchausen by proxy, but because it involves child victims, who often cannot speak for or defend themselves, the consequences are far more severe.

The term "Munchausen by proxy" was first coined by the British pediatrician Roy Meadow in 1977. MBP has never been used in either the *International Classification of Diseases* (*ICD*) or the *Diagnostic and Statistical Manual of Mental Disorders* (the *DSM*). In fact, the term "MBP" is used descriptively rather than diagnostically: it encapsulates both the act of deliberately falsifying, exaggerating, or inducing illness in a child *and* the underlying psychopathology of the caregiver who does so.[12] This confusion over terminology is at the heart of our immense cultural bewilderment over the issue itself.

One of the questions Mike and I get asked most frequently is whether Munchausen by proxy is a crime or a mental illness. The answer is both. MBP is used interchangeably to describe the act of "medical child abuse"—a term coined by child abuse pediatrician and nationally recognized expert Dr. Carole Jenny in her book so titled, published by the American Academy of Pediatrics in 2009[13]—and "factitious disorder imposed on another," which is the official *DSM* diagnosis for a caregiver who subjects a child to unnecessary medical care for the purposes of attention, sympathy, and emotional gratification. We'll be using all three terms throughout this book, but "MBP" is still the most widely used, including by doctors, the legal system, and experts.

Mike—who had worked in crimes-against-children units for years when he got his first medical child abuse case—has a helpful way of cutting through the confusion that arises here. "Munchausen by proxy" is used the same way "pedophilia" is often (incorrectly) used: to describe both the act of child sex abuse and the *DSM* diagnosis of pedophilic disorder, which are related but separate. I find the comparison helps those new to the topic, both in understanding the relationship between mental illness and actions, and also in grasping the seriousness of what's happening. In both cases, children are being victimized by abusers who, though they may struggle with their mental health, are still culpable for their actions and understand the difference between right and wrong. More study on offenders is sorely needed, but what we do know about the profile of MBP offenders paints a complex and challenging picture from a mental health perspective, as there is a high rate of comorbidity (i.e., coexistence) with certain personality disorders—borderline, narcissistic, and histrionic—as well as high rates of severe depression.

The mental health of offenders is fascinating and worth exploring, so long as we never lose sight of the safety of the victims. When we discuss MBP offenders, we're not talking about overly anxious parents or those who are suffering from delusions. We're talking about parents who knowingly deceive others and put their children's well-being—and often their lives—at risk in doing so.

These two unspeakable crimes of child sex abuse and medical child abuse form a sort of dyad in our cultural conception of child abuse. In cases of child sex abuse, the vast majority (88 percent)[14] of perpetrators are male; in cases of medical child abuse, an even more overwhelming majority (96 percent)[15] are women. There was a time when society believed child sex abuse to be extraordinarily rare, but with the myriad scandals surrounding organizations ranging from the Catholic Church to the Boy Scouts of America, we've undergone a reckoning that it is far from unusual, and that it is most frequently committed not by some menacing stranger but by someone known to the victim. Medical child abuse is equally damaging and even more intimate, as most perpetrators are the mother of their victim: the one person we're meant to be able to trust above all else. In both cases, abusers seek the cover of a trusted position in the community: Who is going to question that nice T-ball coach all the kids love? Who would be so cruel as to question a mom of a child with cancer?

Yet millions of dollars are dedicated each year to the worthy cause of preventing child sex abuse. The resources dedicated to medical child abuse? There is some support given to individual hospitals, CASA (court-appointed special advocate) and GAL (guardian ad litem) programs, or community care–based organizations that certainly help. But in terms of organizations focused only on MBP, there is only one: Munchausen Support, the small 501(c)3 nonprofit that I founded in 2021. In the Tarrant County Sheriff's Office, where Mike currently works, there are four officers and a sergeant assigned to the human trafficking division. For medical child abuse, there's Mike, who works these cases in addition to a full load of physical and sexual abuse cases. And that's one more dedicated officer than anywhere else in the country: Mike is the only detective in the United States who has made this a focused area of expertise. This is why he's tapped by child abuse professionals nationwide, as well as the FBI, for direction on these complex investigations.

As author and actor Jennette McCurdy said in an interview with *New York* magazine about her 2022 memoir, *I'm Glad My Mom Died*, "With dads, everybody can flippantly say, 'Ugh, never mind him, you know how dads are!' There's so little acknowledgment and so much fear around saying anything negative about moms."*

Over the years, pop culture has made sporadic attempts to depict Munchausen by proxy on the big and small screen, beginning with *The Sixth Sense*, in which a little girl ghost portrayed by Mischa Barton takes the young protagonist of the film, Cole, to her own funeral. There, her mother sits weeping like a martyr despite having caused her child's death. In 2019 alone—the year *We Came Here to Forget* was published—a spate of prestige television dramas depicted fictional MBP narratives. These ranged from HBO's

---

* "How Jennette McCurdy Survived Child Stardom—and Her Mother" The Cut; August 9th 2022 https://www.thecut.com/2022/08/interview-jennette-mccurdy-memoir.html

Sharp Objects and Netflix's *The Politician* to *The Act*, which depicted the sensationalized story of Gypsy-Rose Blanchard, a victim who conspired to murder her abusive mother. There was also an HBO documentary on the Blanchard case—the more responsibly made production, in my opinion—*Mommy Dead and Dearest*.

In terms of real-life cases, few have captivated the public's imagination like Gypsy Rose's, with its unbelievable twists and turns and just plain bizarre characters and details. When she was released from prison in December 2023, Gypsy Rose's social media followers ballooned to millions in a period of days. Gypsy Inc. was in full swing with a book and a Lifetime series and a slate of press appearances already in place. It was an unprecedented moment of visibility for a survivor of Munchausen by proxy, but it was treated like an entertainment story, with Gypsy Rose as the Roxie Hart of it all.

For those of us who work with MBP in the professional sphere and those who've been personally impacted by it, this was both a welcome moment of interest and a precarious balancing act as we watched one traumatized young woman become a monolithic representation of survivors in the public's imagination. Even more incredibly, Gypsy's release from prison came directly on the heels of the Maya Kowalski trial—in which the Kowalski family won an unprecedented quarter-billion-dollar verdict against Johns Hopkins All Children's Hospital (the hospital denies the charges and has filed an appeal). The Kowalski family alleged that the hospital had unjustly kept Maya from her mother due to suspicions of medical child abuse. Unlike the Gypsy Rose case, this time the public's sympathy largely fell with the suspected perpetrator, Beata Kowalski (who died by suicide before an investigation could be completed), with the media positioning it as a case of "medical kidnapping."

The innumerable chilling parallels between the two cases have been largely obfuscated in the popular imagination, but for anyone paying attention, there was a moment of whiplash as the public demanded to know why Gypsy's doctors didn't intervene to stop the abuse, even as those who *did exactly that* in the Maya Kowalski case now faced reputational ruin and fiscal punishment. Whether this confusion is a sign of our profound dissonance that some mothers are capable of doing unspeakable things to their children or the messy beginnings of a cultural reckoning on this type of abuse remains to be seen.

In general, any media coverage on MBP tends to fixate on the medical horror and to sensationalize the deranged nature of the perpetrators. Viewers could be forgiven for walking away from these stories with the comforting assurance that this could *never* happen to anyone they know. Only a monster could be capable of such crimes, and of course we'd readily recognize such a monster if we met her. The heavy gothic horror of *Sharp Objects* and the outlandish portraits of Dee Dee Blanchard and her eccentric Southern relatives suggest this abuse would never happen in an ordinary family, that decades of trauma and dysfunction must precede such behavior. In fact, in most of the cases I've researched, the opposite is true: the mother at fault appears not just normal, but especially warm and devoted to her children and, as often as not, the family she comes from is as loving as one could hope for.

Horrifyingly, MBP cases tend to make the news only after a child has died, as was the case with Olivia Gant* and Garnett Spears.† But this abuse is believed by many to have one of the highest death rates of any form of child abuse, at around 9 percent.[16] These gaps in both cultural awareness and media coverage leave us less room to look at how systems might be improved, to study cases where the child *was* successfully protected, to examine what the system looks like when it does work.

---

* Olivia Gant was killed in 2017 by her mother, who needlessly placed her in hospice care and removed her feeding tubes.
† Garnett Spears was poisoned by his mother with table salt, finally dying in 2014.

Yet there is such a place: Tarrant County, Texas.

Detective Mike Weber is a big part of why children in this *one* county may currently be safer than anywhere else in the country. But he's not working in a vacuum: several key people—some of whom you'll meet in this book—play a role in making Tarrant County a microcosm that can show us how common medical child abuse might really be, and can instruct us on how to fix it.

THE SOCIETAL ISSUES intertwined with Munchausen by proxy could hardly be more contentious than they are in this moment. I was holding my nine-day-old son when, in June 2022, the Supreme Court's *Dobbs* decision overturned the decades-old precedent set by *Roe v. Wade*. Strict abortion laws in numerous states have currently made it next to impossible for the women who live there to receive necessary obstetric and gynecological care—leading to a flood of doctors moving elsewhere. What has always been fraught territory has now become explosive.

Likewise, the intertwined systems of the criminal courts and the police are the subject of voracious debate, much of which is beyond the scope of this book. Mike and I have different politics— rare for friends and collaborators these days—but we are in alignment on issues surrounding medical child abuse. And however I may feel about the criminal justice system in our country, I have nothing but respect for Mike's work: he's worked for decades in crimes against children, and has taken many reputational hits in order to do the right thing where others are unwilling.

Many of Mike's cases have impacted him, but these three particular women, Hope Ybarra, Brittany Phillips, and Mary Welch—and their interactions with three of our most essential institutions: the medical system, social services, and the courts—gave him a thorough education in what it takes to protect a child from this kind of abuse.

They also illustrated how, even with the best efforts of all involved, the systems that we count on to take care of us can fail.

These three cases go back more than a decade, yet very little progress has been made within the organizations that handle child abuse. If anything, public awareness is moving in the wrong direction, as dramatic stories of so-called false accusations make headlines and the conspiracy theory of "medical kidnapping"—the idea that child protection teams that work with hospitals are snatching children away from their parents, for mysterious motivations—is going mainstream.

NBC journalist Mike Hixenbaugh's expansive 2020 series *Do No Harm* lambasted doctors for their role in separating children from their parents and insisted that they wielded too much power.[17] Lehigh Valley Health Network in Pennsylvania is currently the subject of an investigation that claims to have uncovered "systemic overdiagnosis" of medical child abuse.[18] Yet what Mike has found in over a decade of working these cases, as I have found in my years of research for my podcast, is that this abuse is *far more likely* to be underreported, underinvestigated, and underrecognized than the opposite. If any one place has what might be viewed as an overabundance of cases, it's much more likely that it's just the only one actually catching it. Like Tarrant County.

The women at the center of this book are ostensibly very different from one another: they're from different types of families and different social classes, and they have different backgrounds and professions. (Though these three cases concern white offenders, no expert I spoke to felt there was any correlation between MBP and race.) But despite their distinctions, the parallels between Hope Ybarra, Brittany Phillips, and Mary Welch are staggering, from their overall patterns of deceit, to the extremely specific details about the alleged medical issues their children suffered. I was struck by the sense that there was some sort of playbook for these offenders, that they were learning from each other. It would turn out that suspicion was more accurate than I could have imagined in the Brittany Phillips case.

Unfortunately, these same details echo throughout both my experiences with my sister and the documentation I've uncovered about her case, which I discussed in detail in the second season of my podcast. Since *Nobody Should Believe Me* hit the air in fall 2022, I've been overwhelmed by the responses from listeners. People pull me aside at parties and book events to tell me about their aunt, their friend, that one lady on Facebook who's always posting about her kids being sick. I've received hundreds of messages from survivors and family members reporting their shock at hearing their own story reflected back to them in someone else. These messages have a common theme: "I thought I was the only one." In my experience, once people see the pattern of MBP abuse, once they accept that it's real, they cannot unsee it. And they shouldn't, because children's lives *depend* on us seeing it. So, as we take you through these harrowing stories, we ask of you one thing:

Open your eyes.

PART 1

THE
CHEMIST

1

Meet Hope

In early 2009, Hope Ybarra and her husband, Fabian, prepared to have the most difficult conversation of their lives. After an eight-year battle and two remissions, Hope's bone cancer—a rare and aggressive form called Ewing sarcoma—had returned for a third time, and there were no treatment options left. Now the couple had to tell their three children that Mommy was dying.

The Ybarra family had been through a lot over the past few years. Not only had Hope been battling cancer, but their youngest child, five-year-old Sophia, had already spent much of her short life in the hospital after being born extremely prematurely and subsequently diagnosed with cystic fibrosis. As he sat down with Hope and his children, Fabian wondered how he'd handle working full-time and raising them without her. Hope had always been a devoted mother, going above and beyond to take care of Sophia in particular. Amy Newsome—a child life specialist from Cook Children's Medical Center in Fort Worth, where Sophia was being treated—was also with the Ybarras that day. She was experienced in supporting families dealing with grief and loss.

Amy—who had worked with the Ybarra family for years and

knew them well—remembers the day Hope told her that her cancer was back. She'd noticed that Hope was walking with a limp and that one of her eyes was twitching. Hope said that her cancer had spread to her hip and the orbital area of her brain, tearfully explaining that she wasn't sure how long she had to live. Amy asked if she'd told her children yet. Hope said no, that she couldn't bear the thought of making them sad. Concerned, Amy explained the necessity of discussing it with them to prepare them for what was to come, and Hope asked if she would come to the family's house to help her and Fabian deliver the news.

Amy sat with the kids as Hope explained that her cancer was back and that the doctors had tried all kinds of treatments, but there was nothing more they could do. Sophia was too young to truly understand anything beyond the idea that sad news was being delivered. She put her arms around Hope. "I'm going to miss you, Mommy."

The two older children—then nine and twelve—were better able to process what their mother was telling them, and grew increasingly distraught as Hope explained that she didn't have much time left. Amy led the family through a conversation about grief and a therapeutic exercise to help the children cope with the many emotions she knew were besieging them in that moment: sadness, anger, guilt, anxiety, and confusion.

Amy noticed that though he would sometimes hold Sophia on his lap, Fabian remained completely silent throughout the discussion. Fabian had always been stoic during Amy's interactions with him at the hospital. It was Hope who took complete command of the issues regarding Sophia's health: smart and knowledgeable, Hope held a PhD in chemistry and had worked in a pharmaceuticals lab until her cancer had forced her to quit.

For the past several years, Hope had chronicled her own health trials on a blog she'd created to keep family and friends updated on her near-decade-long cancer journey. After the sit-down with their kids, Hope wrote a new post about how they'd broken the news to close family and friends; she included loving notes to the children she would soon leave behind. "How I wish I could carry your burdens for you," she wrote to her youngest, Sophia, who would face the hardest road without her mother and primary caregiver. "You are such a brave little girl, and I am so very proud of you. You keep fighting this monster and NEVER give up. . . . When God calls you to join me, I will be waiting for you with open arms. I will reserve a garden of butterflies for you to play in."[1]

THE OLDEST OF four children, Hope Ybarra was born to teen parents in Houston in February 1976. Growing up, she went to church, played clarinet in the band, and always had lots of friends. "She was just an overall good kid," her father, Paul Putscher, recalled. A good-natured sixtysomething with a wry grin, Paul has a prosthetic leg, replacing the one he lost in a motorcycle accident when he was a teen. "She was always in groups at school, in band, doing volunteer stuff. She was fun to raise, too." High school pictures of Hope reveal a pretty teenager with long shiny hair, sparkling green eyes, and a smile that lights up her whole face.

Paul and his wife, Susan, had their first two children—Hope and Robert—as teenagers and then waited seven years to have their second two, Robin and Nick. The family was tight-knit, fun loving, and raucous, with Paul as the ultimate prankster and Susan a devoted, hardworking mom. Nick and Robin idolized Hope. For them, she was the perfect big sister and set a good example for her younger siblings; the age difference put her in a parental role in their busy household, and she was warm and encouraging. She was an A student and had a big group of friends. She was musical and talented, spending long hours at the piano at home with her mother and playing the saxophone in her high school's jazz band and the clarinet in the marching band.

Hope had some health issues during high school, beginning with seizures that the doctors couldn't get to the bottom of. Then, one day early in her senior year of high school, Hope fell out of bed and hurt her back so badly that she couldn't walk, and was confined to a wheelchair. Doctors could find no explanation for the pain, but Paul and Susan dutifully rolled her from one office to the next. That year, the high school football team made the playoffs. Paul has a potent memory of his boss—at the time, he was a salesman for a corporate pool manufacturer, where he was much loved—wheeling Hope onto the field so she could join the rest of the marching band. "The vice president of this large company," Paul said, "and he's pushing her. . . . We were doing wheelies and everything."

Hope set a goal to be able to walk across the stage at her high school graduation. Miraculously, she recovered just in time to stand and collect her diploma. The family was relieved. It wouldn't be until many years later that they would look at this series of events in a different light.

The summer after she graduated high school, Paul and Susan packed Hope up to take her to Sul Ross State University in Alpine, Texas. She was the first in the family to attend college, and she blossomed there. She received a band scholarship and was passionate about studying science, with the initial goal of becoming a veterinarian. For fun, she took up jujitsu, where she would meet the man who'd eventually become her husband, Fabian Ybarra.

But one night during Hope's freshman year, Susan Putscher got a terrifying phone call: her daughter had suffered a seizure in her dorm room and been found on the floor. Flinty, smart, and bighearted, Susan Putscher was the ultimate matriarch. "I think she was happiest when she was taking care of somebody," Paul said of his late wife, to whom he was married for over forty years. When

Susan got the call about Hope, she rushed to Alpine to be with her daughter. The doctors checked her out and gave her the all clear. Soon, Hope was thriving again. Still, Susan visited frequently after that, braving the seven-hour drive to make sure her daughter was managing.

Fabian Ybarra is a handsome former high school quarterback who remembers Hope constantly hanging around the party house that Fabian shared with four fellow Sul Ross students. "She was a sweet kid. Hope was fun to be with." For Fabian, it wasn't exactly love at first sight, but when Hope told him she was pregnant, their casual fling became serious. The idea of disappointing his Cuban, Catholic family with an out-of-wedlock child was anathema to Fabian. He decided that committing to Hope was the right thing to do. Besides, she had a lot going for her: she was fun to be with, ambitious, and smart. Fabian also really liked Hope's family, especially Paul: "He's a joker, and he had the gift of gab," Fabian said. He liked that Paul was also Catholic, and he could tell how much he loved his family. Hope and Fabian were married shortly after their son Jacob was born in 1996, becoming parents while they were both still in college.

Despite the misstep of an unplanned pregnancy, Hope's future looked exceptionally bright. Her youngest brother, Nick Putscher—now a tall, charming thirtysomething with green eyes and a fashionable beard—recalled how much he looked up to her. Nick was in kindergarten when Hope left for college, but remembers deciding then that she would be his main role model. "I was always telling my parents," Nick said, "'I'm going to make at least a hundred thousand dollars a year. I'm going to take care of you when you retire.'" And Hope—who was still excelling in school even as a new mom—was the one who made him feel he could do it.

After Hope finished undergrad and Fabian completed his master's degree in education in 1998, Hope went on to get her PhD in organic chemistry from Texas Christian University, taking night classes twice a week as well as online classes to finish in record time. They were a promising young couple with their whole lives ahead of them.

Their second child, Amanda, was born in 1999. She arrived about a month before her due date, and faced immediate challenges due to cerebral palsy. She suffered developmental delays and walked with leg braces for the first few years of her life. In 2001, Hope, Fabian, and their two children were living with Susan and Paul while they prepared to move into a larger house that was currently under construction. Their family was growing again: Hope was pregnant, this time with twin girls. She was ecstatic.

But in September of that year, Hope mentioned to Fabian that she had discovered a strange bump on her arm. When she went to get it checked out, she received devastating news: it was Ewing sarcoma, a rare type of cancerous tumor that grows in the soft tissue around the bones. Hope faced an agonizing decision: her treatment could put the babies at risk, but if she forwent it, they could all die. She went ahead with radiation, and two weeks in, she was hit by another blow. She had lost the pregnancy.

The family was devastated: Hope had been almost six months along; she'd been showing off her pregnant belly and wearing maternity clothes. Robin remembers seeing ultrasound pictures of the twin girls, whom they had already named Alexandria and Alexia. When she lost the pregnancy, the family visited Hope in the emergency room. Robin would go on to name her son Alexander in memory of the lost little girls. Her eldest daughter is named Allison—Hope's middle name—a tribute to the sister she once feared might not live long enough to know her niece.

Hope ordered a special urn where she kept the babies' ashes along with memorial objects friends had given her, including a plaque from the hospital with her daughters' names and weights—a little over two pounds each—and special candles that she'd light each year on the girls' birthday. In the backyard she kept a six-foot-tall concrete angel dedicated to the twins' memory.[2]

Hope talked about these remembrances on a cancer survivors' forum where she began blogging in 2002, after being told in January of that year that the radiation had failed, and that the cancer had spread to her lungs and brain. The disease was already taking its toll: in addition to the pregnancy, Hope had lost her hearing. Ever the trouper, Hope became fluent in American Sign Language and, according to her mother, became deeply integrated in the local deaf community, even working with a Fort Worth deaf ministry.

At last, in 2003, the family got some good news: after an aggressive course of radiation and chemotherapy treatments, Hope's cancer was gone. And, as part of a medical trial, Hope received a cochlear implant—a device surgically implanted in her brain—which helped her recover her hearing. The family threw a party to celebrate her triumph over cancer, and a crowd of more than a hundred gathered to toast the lady of the hour. So many people were rooting for Hope.

More good news soon followed: Hope was pregnant again.

But it seemed nothing could go her way for long. Hope fell down the stairs of her parents' house in March 2004 and Sophia was born at twenty-four weeks—nearly four months premature, barely over the line of viability. She weighed a little over two pounds. Robin remembers this as an intense and harrowing time for the whole family. "They thought she was going to die," she said of her youngest niece. "They had a photographer come out and take the baby's last pictures. She was in the NICU for months."

Even after she went home, little Sophia struggled with reflux issues and couldn't gain weight. In early 2005, she had a gastric tube surgically attached to her stomach so she could receive formula that way. Hope also reported that Sophia was having trouble breathing, and after a series of sweat tests at Cook Children's Medical Center in Texas, the family received the life-altering news that Sophia had cystic fibrosis—a hereditary disease that affects the lungs and digestive system. The prognosis for cystic fibrosis patients has improved a great deal in the past several decades, but life expectancy remains short. Worse, Sophia had an aggressive and rare form of the disease. It appeared that, in all likelihood, her life would be difficult and brief.

2005 was a terrible year for the Ybarra family. Sophia required round-the-clock care: feedings with special formula and administering of medications every few hours via a central line placed in her chest. In May, she had a life-threatening anemic episode. Then, in the summer of 2005, Hope's cancer came back.

Around that same time, Sophia's beloved pulmonologist, Dr. James Harmon, moved to Birmingham, Alabama. Hope told her family that there was a clinical trial in Birmingham that she had been accepted into, and rented an apartment there so she could take part and so Sophia could continue to see Dr. Harmon. Five-year-old Amanda moved with her mother and sister, while the Ybarras' son, the eldest, stayed at home with Fabian. Despite her own ill health, Hope often made the ten-hour drive back and forth. She would do anything for her little girl, and Dr. Harmon was a rare find: young and dedicated, he developed a friendship with Hope. His wife, Laura, would even watch Amanda and Sophia while Hope was receiving her treatments as part of the clinical trial. This constituted something of a blurring of professional boundaries, but Hope had a way of making people want to help her.

Their sacrifices paid off when the Ybarras received the news in late 2006 that Hope had beaten the cancer once more. This time, the family held an even *bigger* celebration to commemorate the extraordinary milestone. "All the people that have been experiencing some of this with us came and had a big party at my parents' house," Nick recalled. Family came in from Houston; the Putschers' neighbors and even Paul's colleagues and friends attended. There was a massive crowd of loved ones present to watch Hope as she made an unforgettable entrance: soaring into the front yard via parachute, after skydiving from a plane above. Nick remembers that his sister looked happy and healthy that day, and he finally felt reassured that she was in the clear. If Hope was well enough to skydive, surely that meant the cancer was gone for good this time.

Home video of this moment shows a beaming Hope preparing for her flight. Her dad remarks that not too many people get to drop in on their own party. "Not too many people get to fight cancer for three, four, five years in a row. So yeah, I think I earned it," Hope replies. Soon after the party, she crossed another item off her bucket list when she got a large tattoo covering her back: angel wings. Between the wings, snaking down Hope's spine were five red stars—one for each of her children, including the twin girls she lost during her radiation treatment.[3]

In addition to fighting her own cancer battle, Hope had become a beacon for other families of sick children. She was the volunteer coordinator for the Take My Hand Foundation—an organization dedicated to helping children with cancer—and joined the parents' advisory committee at Cook Children's, where Sophia was receiving treatment. She worked with the local chapter of the Knights of Columbus to raise money for local families. All of the Ybarras got involved, with Hope's older children, Jacob and Amanda, selling teddy bears to benefit the Cystic Fibrosis Foundation. In March 2007, Hope and Sophia were the subject of a profile in the *Dallas Morning News,* which introduced Hope to their readers as a devoted mother who put her sick toddler first.

"Hope Ybarra," the article begins, "doesn't spend her days worrying about the cancer that potentially remains on her brain. Every waking moment is concentrated instead on helping her daughter with her own illness." The article was a portrait of a mother heroically resigned to the reality of her daughter's disease: "We realize she will never likely see a cure," Hope tells the paper. "When her day comes, we'll have no regrets. We tried our hardest to bring awareness. And we will spend the rest of our lives trying for other families." The article details the fundraising Hope had done for the Great Strides 5K walk to benefit the Cystic Fibrosis Foundation, and the reporter describes an energetic Sophia bouncing around the local coffee shop where they meet. Meanwhile, Hope tells him how her little girl spends at least two weeks every other month in the hospital receiving treatment, and that her last visit had lasted five weeks. "We can only hope there is a greater purpose for her suffering," says Hope. The piece ends with a quote from Sonya O'Brien, a mother whose nine-year-old twins suffer from cystic fibrosis and who heads up the committee behind the Great Strides 5K. "God put it on my heart that she should be our campaign child," O'Brien told the reporter about Sophia. "For all that poor little baby has been through, she is always so full of life. We can't sit back and hope (a cure) will happen. We have to make it happen now for children like Sophia."

Shortly after the piece ran, Sophia suffered another harrowing episode of anemia, a chronic issue for her. Then, the iron dextran treatments she was given sent her into anaphylactic shock, signaling a life-threatening allergic reaction.

IN LATE SPRING 2007, Hope summoned her siblings to her house. Robin was heavily pregnant at the time, but made the trip down from Washington State anyway; Hope was being elusive about the news she had to share, and Robin feared the worst. Nick remembered the four siblings gathering in her sitting room. Hope, subdued, opened the conversation in an odd way, saying, "Recnac." The three siblings were baffled by the riddle but eventually discerned that this was "cancer" spelled backward; it was as if Hope couldn't even bear to say the word.

Hope had convened her three siblings to announce that this would be the end of the road for her; she wasn't going to fight it this time. The three sat there in shock: The last thing anyone expected of tough, determined Hope was for her to throw in the towel. She had always been such a fighter. Nick was heartbroken. His grief curdled into anger at his big sister for giving up. "Why are you being so selfish?" he asked her. "You've got kids, you've got a family!"

Hope tearfully told them she couldn't bear that she'd become such a burden: her journey had been so long and so painful, it was just too much. She tried to help her baby brother cope, giving Nick a copy of *The Last Lecture*, the memoir by computer science professor Randy Pausch about his diagnosis of terminal cancer. Nick—a numbers guy who wasn't much into books—read it cover to cover. Hope had always seemed invincible to Nick, especially after beating cancer twice. Now he had to accept that they were going to lose her.

For Hope's parents, the blow was even worse. They'd been steadfast in their support of Hope through her cancer and now they faced every parent's worst nightmare: burying their child. Paul struggled to process the grim reality. It wasn't until the family was celebrating Christmas—the one they were certain would be Hope's last—that it finally began to sink in that he was losing his daughter. "That Christmas day, I remember going out behind the barn and hollering and screaming at God," he said.

Hope had been sick for eight years by now. With all of Sophia's medical bills, the family was in bad shape financially. So when the owners of the house the Ybarras were renting—a quaint yellow Craftsman with white trim—told them they were putting it on the market, Hope and Fabian couldn't afford to make an offer. On top of everything else, they would now have to move.

Hope recounted her sad story to a local news station, which featured her in an armchair with blankets over her lap, little Sophia snuggled to her side. The anchor told viewers the family was in dire straits, explaining Sophia's condition, and Hope's eight-year battle with cancer, as well as the twins pregnancy she'd lost as a result of her treatment.[4]

Hope had also recently lost her job at Neos Therapeutics, where she'd been the lead chemist, and the family's savings were depleted. Now they were being evicted. "I just want to die at home," Hope said. "That's the hardest part." She didn't want her children to have to lose their house and their mother at the same time. The emotional news segment offered a link where viewers could donate to the family.

The Putschers were worried what would happen to their three grandchildren once Hope was gone. She'd earned a six-figure salary working as a chemist—first at a food manufacturer, then at Neos—and Sophia required intense, time-consuming care. The Putschers decided that they couldn't let Hope and Fabian lose their house. A close friend of Paul's helped them organize a blowout fundraiser at a local golf club: an auction and golf tournament that raised almost $100,000 for the Ybarra family. Paul's colleagues and clients and even strangers made donations, played in the tournament, and contributed auction items. Nick remembers how the community rallied around his dad: "A lot of people that he's really close with come from his business. . . . They were all there helping support us through all of this." He remembers taking out the golf carts and doing donuts with his uncle, Paul's brother, in the middle of the course—how it felt like one of those strange moments of joy that can come at you in the midst of a tragedy. "It was just such a fun day. . . . The whole day was just about supporting the family, supporting Hope."

Still, it was clear that Hope was nearing the end. A priest came to read her last rites. The Ybarra family moved in with the Putschers so that Susan could care for her daughter while Fabian worked and looked after their kids. They set up a hospice room for Hope.

The Putschers began seeing a grief counselor and Susan dutifully drove around with Hope as they chose her coffin—rose stainless steel with a white interior—and cemetery plot. Hope purchased five adjoining plots overlooking the Trinity River. She told Susan it was a place she could imagine her children visiting her and finding some measure of peace.[5] Hope asked for the twins' ashes—which she'd kept in an urn on the mantel—to be buried with her.

Then, in April 2009, Susan Putscher received a phone call that changed everything.

Though Hope had wanted to die at home with her parents, her pain had become so bad that she'd transferred to the hospital to receive palliative care. The oncologist treating her called Susan to enlist her in finding some information about Hope's care team. Did she know whom her daughter had previously seen? Susan couldn't recall the names of Hope's doctors off the top of her head so she mounted a search throughout the house, looking for prescription bottles or paperwork that would list the names and numbers of her doctors. Hope had been staying with her for weeks, so her stuff was everywhere—but Susan couldn't find a single thing relating to her treatment. Bemused, she called Fabian and asked him if he could share the login for the family's insurance so she could look it up that way; he gladly complied. When Susan logged in, what she discovered shocked her to the marrow of her bones. Though the recent insurance records contained pages and pages of information about Sophia, there was nothing about Hope. Susan dug deeper, and looked back through years of records. There wasn't a single entry about Hope's cancer treatment.

For eight years, the Putscher family had lived with the devastating fear that their beloved daughter and sister was battling terminal cancer. For months, they'd been preparing for her death. But in that moment, a new horror was dawning: for nearly a decade, Hope had been lying.

2

Saving Sophia

The same day the Putschers discovered that Hope was lying about her eight-year-long battle with cancer, Paul's entire extended family was on its way to Fort Worth to be with them in their darkest hour. One of his brothers had arranged the visit, unbeknownst to Paul, when Hope had—allegedly—gone into hospice care. "Susan had told them that she's fixing to die," Paul said. "So, my mother, my brother from Houston, my sister from New Mexico, my sister from Philadelphia and their mates . . . everybody came and they were ready to go to the hospital with us. That's the day we found out."

Unable to grasp the significance of what they were being told, Paul remembers he and Susan were mostly elated and relieved that their daughter wasn't going to die. Their entire life had just done a 180. Hope's cancer had dominated their lives for so long that they had no idea what to do next. So they went bowling.

Various family members arrived at the bowling alley to find the Putschers in a very unexpected celebratory mode. Susan and Paul didn't know how to even begin to explain to their family—which had flown in to be by their sides for a death—that there wasn't going to be one. "The general consensus for that evening was, It's good news. She's not dying. We'll talk more tomorrow," Paul said.

Nick remembers being so baffled by the discovery that his sister didn't have cancer that his mind seemed unable to process the information: "I've never experienced it before and never experienced it since. It was like this white light. Like my head is just not fathoming what's going on." For months, Nick had been struggling to accept that his sister was going to die. He'd had a large cross tattooed on his right forearm and he'd recently added angel wings to match the huge ones that covered his sister's shoulders: a way to keep her with him when she was gone. But now he knew the truth: Hope wasn't going anywhere.

Though their initial feeling had been relief, as the Putschers awoke the next morning, Hope's actions started to sink in. Now they all had to face the truth, including Hope. Susan and Paul drove to the hospital to confront Hope, who—realizing she had no other choice—immediately confessed. All of it had been made up; all the details of her diagnosis and treatment had been fabricated. Paul remembered feeling a sudden tear in the fabric of his reality: "One minute your child is dying. Now your child's a really confusing character." When they asked her *why* she had lied about having cancer for the past eight years, Hope tearfully told them that it was the only way she felt she could get the attention of her husband, Fabian, who was always busy with work.

The Putschers ran through their own memories, trying to square them with the truth. With the new facts in front of them, everything looked different. They realized that Hope had never let anyone go with her to chemo, always insisting that it would be more helpful if they did other things, such as watch the kids while she was in treatment. But where had she been going, if not to the hospital?

Robin remembered how Hope had seemed like such a star cancer patient. "Everybody who met her was astounded at what she had been through and how she maintained her faith and her composure and her ability to carry on with life, with a zest for it. She never appeared to be overwhelmed by it. She would talk about it freely: like, this is just something I'm going through. She always seemed to come out ahead. She lost her hair, but it was okay. 'Look at these great wigs I have and look at these hats!'"

But now that whole era of Hope's life looked completely different. Hope *had* been bald and she'd had no eyebrows, but looking at pictures of her from that period, Robin realized she'd never lost her eyelashes. It hadn't fazed her at the time. But with the information they now had, a hundred incongruous details came rushing back at the Putschers.

At first, Susan—who had a background in mental health services—thought her daughter must suffer from a delusional disorder, that she must have *believed* she was actually sick to have so convincingly played the part of a patient for that many years. Yet the truth would turn out to be even more disturbing.

At the doctor's behest, Hope was transferred to a psychiatric ward, where she was diagnosed with major depressive disorder and Munchausen syndrome.

There is a separate disorder known as "malingering" wherein a person feigns illness for *primarily* financial benefit*; however,

---

* People *do* sometimes seek medical treatment for illnesses they don't have, because they're suffering from delusions, but this isn't the case with Munchausen. There's also a critical distinction between Munchausen and malingering: the latter is when someone fakes illness for a tangible benefit such as financial gain, or dodging work or military service. The reason for feigning illness is crucial to understanding the disorder. "In Munchausen phenomena," Dr. Marc Feldman explains, "the person is after emotional gratification: attention, sympathy, care, support that they feel unable to get in any other way."

Munchausen cases also frequently involve fraudulent fundraising, which is usually how the exorbitant medical costs racked up by perpetrators are financed. Hope was on the extreme end of this. The benefit that the Putscher family had organized for Hope had raised more than $100,000. Now, the Putschers realized with horror, they'd have to find a way to return it all—and to explain to everyone that Hope wasn't actually sick. She'd *never* been sick.

The Putschers began the daunting task of telling the people in their lives who'd supported their daughter for nearly a decade that they'd been victims of a massive hoax. Both Paul and Susan's careers took a drastic hit. Many of Paul's largest clients had donated big-ticket items or money for Hope, and Susan's colleagues had also participated. The Putschers tried to explain to baffled friends and family a situation that they barely understood themselves. And far from sympathizing with Paul and Susan, many people held them responsible. "We had maybe fifty percent of the people who understood that we didn't know, and the other fifty percent thought we knew and were doing this for the money." Paul was asked to resign from the job he'd held for over twenty-five years. He and Susan would eventually be forced to leave the dream house they thought they would spend the rest of their lives in, because of the financial fallout.

But the drama surrounding Hope's cancer hoax soon took a back seat for the Putschers. Now that they realized Hope could carry out a detailed, physically intensive, almost-decade-long manipulation, an even more horrifying question emerged: What else was she lying about?

Robin remembers that her family began to question everything in the weeks following the revelation of Hope's cancer hoax. It felt impossible to square the degree of deception with the sister she'd known and loved for so long: "As we're finding out that all of these things are lies . . . that's still your sister and you still have love for her.

It was my mom's child. You don't want to believe that they've made all of this up. You also don't want to believe that you allowed that to happen; there's a certain amount of guilt with that. We spent years knowing Hope as dependable and reliable. That doesn't change overnight."

A horrible thought occurred to Susan: What if the twin babies that Hope had lost—allegedly because of her chemo treatments, which she'd never undergone—weren't even real? "I remember the look on her face," Robin told me. "She was starting to break apart the events that happened, about that pregnancy. She goes, *I was at the hospital, it was real.* And then my dad asked her, *But did you see them?* And she goes, *No, I didn't see them.*" Had they been mourning grandchildren who never existed? Susan asked Hope, who assured her that she'd been lying only about her cancer. The pregnancy had been real. But for Susan, the matter would not be fully settled until she finally worked up the nerve to check the urn that held the twins' ashes. It had been stored at the Putschers' house, among Hope's things. Susan opened it and turned it upside down. Empty.

Alexandria and Alexia—in whose honor Robin's eldest child was named, whom Hope had memorialized in numerous ways including with the urn, the stone angel, and her elaborate tattoo—were a fiction. But if two of the five stars on Hope's back represented phantoms, what of her other three very real children? What about little Sophia, who had spent most of her young life in and out of the hospital? Sophia, who also had a terminal illness—at least, according to Hope.

FABIAN DOESN'T HAVE a clear memory of learning about Hope's cancer; when he thinks back on this time, that revelation is simply overshadowed by everything that happened next. He recalls only the numbness and confusion of trying to make sense of his wife's deception. At the time, like Susan, he understood it as a sort of supercharged hypochondria. This is a common misconception. Most important, Munchausen and other factitious disorders are characterized by *intentional* deception—whereas hypochondriacs are abnormally anxious about their health to the point of believing they're really sick. In Hope's case, whenever she left the house saying she was going to radiation treatment, when she was shaving off her hair and eyebrows to mimic chemo-related hair loss, when she was saying her dramatic goodbyes to her family . . . Hope understood that it was a fiction. She never believed she was sick.

Meanwhile, increasingly concerned about Sophia, Susan called her granddaughter's pulmonologist and told her about the revelations surrounding Hope's cancer. She explained that she was concerned that Hope could also be lying about Sophia.

On the afternoon of April 10—a few days after she was released from the psych ward—Hope and Fabian brought Sophia to Cook Children's to have a sweat test done to determine whether she really had cystic fibrosis (CF). Fabian remembers Hope becoming anxious as they prepared to take Sophia in for the simple, noninvasive test, claiming she couldn't drive herself to the hospital because she feared she might have a seizure on the road. But whether Hope actually ever suffered from seizures was an open question—no one in her family had ever actually witnessed one of these episodes.

Amy—the child life specialist who had sat in on the heart-wrenching conversation with the Ybarra children informing them that their mother was dying—was asked to be there for Sophia's sweat test as well. This time, rather than supporting Hope, she'd be watching her like a hawk to ensure that she didn't interfere with the test. A sweat test is a diagnostic tool used to detect the amount of chloride in a child's sweat; the chloride level in a child with CF will be dramatically higher than those without. The test is administered by placing a sensor on a child's skin and then having the child run around enough to produce sweat. Sure enough, Amy caught Hope fiddling with Sophia's bandage, claiming she was "just fixing it." When the nurse who was administering the test briefly left the room, Hope turned to Amy and asked if she could take her daughter to the bathroom so that Sophia could "have a meltdown." It was bizarre. Amy explained to Hope that she could not allow her to be alone with Sophia.

A short time later, the results of the sweat test came back.

Negative.

Sophia didn't have cystic fibrosis. For almost any parent in the world, the news that their child didn't have a terminal illness would have brought tears of relief. But upon hearing the test results, Hope broke down in tears for a very different reason. She'd been caught.

3

Meet Mike Weber

Mike Weber was born on a blazing mid-August 1964 day in Atlanta. His father had grown up poor on a farm in Wisconsin and gone to school on the GI Bill, meeting Mike's mother while he was still in the service. They moved to Fort Worth when Mike was a year old, along with his two older brothers, Bill and Bob.

Mike had an idyllic childhood, his feet thickening with calluses as he ran around barefoot from sunup to sundown each summer, his dad loading his three boys up in the truck camper to head to Colorado for weeks of rustic camping and fishing.

Mike attended the oldest high school in Fort Worth at the beginning of the eighties and spent his summers with his buddies cruising Camp Bowie Boulevard and trying to get their friend Tom—who looked mysteriously middle-aged—to buy them beer. At six feet four and 160 pounds soaking wet, Mike was a bit awkward and no hit with the ladies. His chronic inability to focus made him a painfully average student. He graduated high school at seventeen, a gangly, shy boy. Unlike Mike, his dad had always been academically inclined—he'd received his bachelor's degree from Georgia Tech and a master's from Southern Methodist

University—and knew his youngest wasn't ready to go straight into college. His frugal Depression-era father wasn't about to tap into Mike's college fund until he was ready to take it seriously.

Which meant Mike was a happy-go-lucky youngster in a Fort Worth where the drinking age was nineteen and keeping a roadie in your truck's cupholder was both acceptable and perfectly legal. Just fine putting off school, he took a job working as a stock boy at Larry's Shoes & Boots. He spent his days sweating it out in a warehouse in the Texas heat, and his evenings drinking beer with his friends and cruising around in his POS Gremlin that had no reverse gear, trying (mostly unsuccessfully) to pick up girls.

Mike was nineteen when a friend of his from the warehouse, Billy—twenty-three with a Corvette and plenty of dating stories—strutted into work crowing about getting out of there: he was off to the police academy at the local junior college.

"Why the hell do you want to be a cop?" Mike asked. He wasn't going to stay at his crappy warehouse job forever, but police work sounded stuffy.

"Well, cops don't give other cops tickets," Billy said.

That was something, Mike thought. He was a speed demon and was constantly paying low-rent lawyers to have his tickets dismissed. But Mike also saw the change in his buddy after he enrolled: suddenly pulled together and with a sense of pride about his place in the world. And the pay was certainly better than warehouse work.

Soon after, Mike enrolled in the police academy, where he was given six months of training. He had to have his dad buy him his first gun (you have to be at least twenty-one in Texas to buy one). Mike's mom was worried about her baby boy becoming a cop, but his dad was just glad to see his distractible youngest take some initiative. Mike kept working at the warehouse during the day and went to the academy in the evenings, proud of the fact that he was able to contribute financially to his own education. He learned about procedures and penal codes, and a few defensive tactics, all the while chuckling at his more gung ho gun-nut classmates. For him, being a cop was just a job, not a calling.

Two months shy of his twentieth birthday, Mike was given a badge and tasked with protecting the community of Kennedale, a small town on the outskirts of Fort Worth. Thankfully, these weren't exactly mean streets, so Mike was able to get his bearings as a police officer at a comfortable pace: handling traffic enforcement and domestic disturbances, and hauling a mostly harmless local oddball they affectionately called Weird Al back and forth from the station on charges of public nudity.

But soon Mike grew bored with his small-town beat-cop gig. In January 1988, he decided to go back to school to get an accounting degree. It seemed like a nice, stable choice, plus he'd always been decent with numbers. His chief in Kennedale, encouraging, let Mike stay on part-time as a police officer while he went back to school, working one weekend a month.

Mike moved himself into the dorms at the University of North Texas in Denton, a charming college town with an iconic bustling main street, located thirtysome miles north of Fort Worth. He played rec basketball with his roommate and had a string of none-too-serious girlfriends, all while keeping his weekend gig as a cop. Unfortunately, accounting was tougher than he anticipated, and Mike quickly learned that he liked the partying and socializing part of school more than the actual *school* part. He switched his major to physical education, imagining a future in sports management somewhere down the line, living out his career under the Friday night lights.

Mike remembered one particularly brilliant and colorful instructor of anatomy/physiology, Dr. James Lott, who kept the attention of his dreamy young students by using memorable phrases such as "stands out like a pregnant nun" and "sweating like a whore in church." His classes were tough, so Mike pulled all-night study sessions just to squeak by with a C. At the end of the year, Dr. Lott threw a pool party at his apartment complex for those who passed his class, complete with kegs. Mike asked if he was worried about getting in trouble for giving underage kids beer. The professor looked him dead in the eye and said in a deep Texas drawl, "Son, fuck 'em, I got tenure." Oh, the eighties.

When his postgraduation dream job in a college athletic director's office didn't materialize, Mike went back to working full-time in Kennedale. His onetime chief, seeing Mike's potential in police work long before he did, set him up on a Tarrant County narcotics task force as an undercover detective. Mike sported a serious mullet during his *21 Jump Street* phase.

By 1992, Mike had left the Kennedale PD and joined his buddy Jon in nearby Mansfield, where both were back on patrol. Jon was an incredibly smart guy who was about Mike's age, who taught himself Spanish—a useful tool in his community-facing work—and would later go on to be a deputy chief at the Irving Police Department, also in Texas. Mansfield was a small town spread across huge parcels of land and, not long after he joined, Mike got distracted trying to answer a call from dispatch on a winding country road. He hit the brakes going fifty on a sharp turn, sending himself and the patrol car through a barrier and into a field, demolishing his brand-new cruiser. As he waited for help on the side of the dusty road, Mike was sure he'd be fired. But when Jon—who was now his sergeant—showed up, he just chuckled and said, "Where is your car, Mike?"

The incident summed up Mike's career as a young officer. Jon later laughingly relayed a comment their city manager had made to the police chief about Mike: "His heart was in the right place but he wasn't thinking with his brain." Chief Martin replied, "His brain was in his head and his head was up his ass."

Mike worked at the Mansfield PD for three more years before better pay and benefits lured him to the Arlington PD, in a much larger town in Tarrant County. Mike worked patrol for several years before doing a four-year stint in narcotics, this time rocking frosted hair tips and two earrings to help him blend in. Narcotics was good training ground, and Mike began to take his career more seriously as he learned about search warrants and how to interview suspects and witnesses. These were the days before the Mexican cartels' involvement in the methamphetamine trade made working narcotics more dangerous, before the opioid and meth epidemics laid waste to small towns throughout the nation. Mike felt like he was fighting the good fight: trying to keep drugs out of vulnerable communities so those folks could live their lives in peace.

In 2004, after a year back on patrol, Mike saw a job posting for a detective in the crimes-against-children unit. He jumped on it. He wished he could say he felt some lofty calling to help kids, but he mostly liked the idea of working out of the county nonprofit Alliance for Children offices, meaning there'd be no sergeant two desks over breathing down his neck.

Mike quickly discovered that he had signed up for the most challenging police work imaginable. Child abuse cases often have no physical evidence and rely solely on the word of a child, yet the stakes couldn't be higher. One of Mike's first big cases was a local college professor who'd been serially molesting children—including his own granddaughter—for more than twenty years by the time it came across Mike's desk. After photo evidence was discovered on the professor's computer, Mike's investigation helped put him away for life. This case drove home for Mike how offenders who prey on children not only affect their victims, but devastate entire communities; it seemed like the most valuable work he could do as a detective. This sense of purpose was essential when he spent his days looking directly at the worst aspects of humanity.

It was in this role that Mike Weber first met Assistant District Attorney Alana Minton, who would go on to become a close friend and ally. When a position at the DA's Office opened, Mike immediately applied. Working crimes against children had sobered Mike; he'd left his Peter Pan side behind. He knew by then that he was more motivated and better equipped than the average cop to take on tough cases, and it was meaningful, if exhausting, work.

When he started in the DA's Office in 2008, Mike was forty-four and just out of a three-year relationship he'd been sure would end in marriage; the breakup had sent him into something of a spiral. When he'd looked into his future, he'd always seen himself as a father, but by the time he met his ex, Laura, at his fortieth birthday party, he felt the opportunity had passed him by. Many of his friends had married young and had kids who were already in high school or heading off to college, and he didn't think new fatherhood was in the cards for him. Laura had two young girls, and Mike relished being a part-time dad. Mike tried to stay in the kids' lives after his amicable split with their mom, but it didn't make sense. Losing them had compounded his heartbreak.

Sick of frontline work, he was ready for the more cerebral second-line job at the DA's Office, where he could see himself staying until his seventies, finishing out his career.

It was only in retrospect that Mike would understand the impact of his decision to leave the Arlington PD: If he'd stayed with Laura, he'd have stayed in Arlington, a jurisdiction with no children's hospitals—which meant he never would have encountered a medical child abuse case. Maybe it was all coincidence, but after twenty years as a detective, Mike didn't much believe in those anymore. His time working sex offender cases and seeing the overlap with organized religion had put Mike off regular church attendance, but he remained a man of faith, and he had to believe that his journey was taking him in the right direction.

Mike moved to a beautiful little lake house an hour south of Fort Worth in Granbury and purchased a boat and a jet ski for his new bachelor paradise. He was quickly learning, however, that as idyllic and lively as it was in the summer, his new home was sleepy and isolating in the winter. After tourists abandoned it, Granbury was essentially a retirement village.

His new boss, Alana Minton, was a brilliant prosecutor whom Mike had gotten to know during several high-profile child abuse cases they'd worked on together when he was with the Arlington PD. A mother of two in her early forties with auburn hair and soft green eyes, Alana was the kind of down-to-earth person who was as comfortable talking to people in a trailer park as she was talking to lawyers and judges. The Texas Tech grad was a dream boss, prioritizing team building and keeping an eye on the truth, rather than on the politics of a case. Mike felt the leadership at his former job had too often put what was right for the organization over what was ethically right, and it sat poorly with him. Alana had a big heart and strong moral compass, and absolutely no time for bullshit. If she needed to tell someone how the cow ate the cabbage, she'd do it.

Mike was three months into working as an investigator for the DA's Office when the bizarre case of eight-year-old Ethan crossed his desk. Ethan's mother had brought him to nearby Cook Children's after relocating from Ohio. When Ethan arrived at the hospital, he was in a wheelchair and receiving TPN (total parenteral nutrition), which provides nutrients intravenously through a central line, a last resort when all other interventions have failed. Born premature, Ethan had a long history of feeding issues. He'd previously been fed via a gastronomy tube—a G tube—that went through a surgically placed port in his stomach. When he'd mysteriously continued to fail to gain weight, the Ohio doctors recommended the TPN.

His mother was trying to get him admitted to hospice at Cook

Children's, and gave the attending physician, Dr. Wentworth, a laundry list of diagnoses that made no sense. Dr. Wentworth observed allegedly wheelchair-bound Ethan running up and down the halls when the mother wasn't present. When he called the referring physicians at Cleveland Clinic Children's, they reported that Ethan had tested negative for all the food allergies his mother claimed he had. When his mother refused to reduce Ethan's medications by even a minuscule amount, Dr. Wentworth reported her to child protective services (CPS), which intervened and removed the child. Once Ethan was separated from his mother, it quickly became apparent that he could walk perfectly well without a wheelchair and could eat normally without the assistance of either a gastric tube or TPN. As he was weaned from his various medications, Ethan emerged as a perfectly healthy child. His mother—it appeared—had been making it all up.

Mike was baffled. Ethan had undergone innumerable medical treatments, including invasive surgeries to put in a central line and the G tube in his stomach. Why would any doctor do this if it wasn't necessary?

Mike went to Dr. Jamye Coffman—Cook Children's board-certified child abuse pediatrician, a doctor with special training and skills in evaluating children who are suspected victims of abuse—for some answers. Dr. Coffman explained that a patient's medical history is a doctor's most important tool for forming a diagnosis, especially as there are so many ailments where testing is wholly inadequate. In the case of pediatricians seeing young children, this history is always provided by the parent.

Of course, doctors can't go through thousands of pages of medical records to check for inconsistencies during the roughly twenty minutes they have to spend with each patient. Dr. Coffman stated flatly that if a caregiver presents a false medical history for a child, there will be a false diagnosis every time. She explained that this type of abuser was almost always a mother—95.6 percent of the time, to be specific.[1] She told Mike that perpetrators often present as competent, loving women in public but that they felt little true bond with or empathy for their children. She also emphasized that perpetrators are not delusional: they know what they're doing, and they know it's wrong.

Ethan's case had ultimately been referred to the authorities in Ohio, where the actual surgeries had been performed, for jurisdictional reasons. But the case stuck with Mike: this was a different, more subtle kind of offender than what he was used to. Early in his new job, he was also keen to make a good impression. Knowing how complex medical child abuse cases were, and always up for a challenge, he asked Alana to refer straight to him any others that came up.

"Sure," she'd told him. "But I've never seen another case here in eight years."

So Mike was surprised when, on April 13, 2009—seven months into his tenure at the DA's Office and only days after he'd finished the Ohio case—Alana approached him with a second.

"You busy?" Alana said, leaning against the doorway of Mike's office. "We've got another Munchausen by proxy case. This one is ours. You interested?"

"Of course," Mike told her, somewhat taken aback. Wasn't this abuse vanishingly rare?

Alana deposited the voluminous CPS report about Hope Ybarra on his desk. Mike had worked dozens of child abuse cases by this point in his life. He'd seen children subjected to unimaginable horror. He thought he had seen the absolute worst of humanity already. But nothing could have prepared him for what he was about to discover about Hope.

4

The Investigation Begins

The Putscher and Ybarra families were reeling from the dual revelations that Hope not only had been faking an eight-year-long bout with cancer, but appeared to have falsified cystic fibrosis in her five-year-old daughter as well.

After the sweat test debacle, the CPS investigator working the case instituted a safety plan that required Hope to leave the family home and have no contact with her three children outside of two-hour weekly visits, which would be supervised by CPS: standard procedure for child abuse cases where the nonoffending parent could safely take custody as Fabian had.

The fact that Sophia had spent most of her life in treatment for a chronic illness she didn't have was shocking, but it didn't necessarily mean a crime had been committed. Even if Mike could prove that Hope had knowingly interfered with the original tests, that wasn't a criminal act in Texas. It also wasn't a crime to lie to doctors, even if it led to unnecessary treatment. In order to charge Hope with injury to a child—the only charge serious enough to result in more than a slap on the wrist—he needed to show evidence of physical pain. By then, Mike had learned that the unsettling Ohio case he'd worked on had gone nowhere after being referred to authorities in that state. This was despite the child having been treated at the internationally renowned Cleveland Clinic. A child whose mother had falsely claimed he was close to death, but who had proved to be perfectly healthy.*

Mike was immediately struck by several similarities between the Ohio case and Sophia's: in particular, the presence of a central line for medications, the premature birth, and the feeding tube. On Sophia's long list of persistent problems was her inability to gain weight. She had had a G tube surgically placed in her stomach and a Nissen fundoplication—a surgical procedure that wraps the top of the stomach around the lower part of the esophagus to correct reflux—in 2005. But had any of this been medically necessary? And what else in Sophia's medical records might Hope be lying about? As Mike dug into the preliminary reports, he was astonished by just how many procedures the young child had undergone. There were well over fifteen thousand pages in the five-year-old's medical records. If her central diagnosis was false, was the rest of it as well?

Hope's case was already captivating the DA's Office, but it was about to become a subject of fascination for the whole community.

"I saw your girl on the news again last night," Alana said as she stopped by to poke her head in Mike's office. Mike scrambled to find the news clip online, wondering if Hope might have said something incriminating to a reporter, or if the segment might offer any leads in terms of witnesses he could speak to. The video from the local CBS affiliate replayed the original footage from just a month earlier of Hope, seated in a lounger and covered with a blanket, stating her wish to die at home. The segment was followed by an interview with Kristin Courtney, a family friend who helped

---

* This particular child ended up in the care of his protective father and had a good outcome.

organize the blowout fundraiser for Hope. Courtney recalled getting a panicked call from Paul Putscher, who told her, "Whatever you do, don't spend any of the funds." Paul had explained to Courtney that there had been a "change in diagnosis" and that they needed to move in a different direction.

Hope did not, the reporter revealed, have cancer after all. Courtney said she felt for Hope and was praying for her even harder now. Her tone was ostensibly forgiving, but if you've spent enough time around Southern women, you'll know that "I'm praying for her" is right up there with "bless her heart"—in other words, a uniquely regional way of being both exceedingly polite and absolutely brutal. A stranger who'd learned of the hoax after donating a small amount of money to the family had a more acerbic take, telling the reporter that the experience had put him off ever donating to charity again.

Next, a photo flashed of the Ybarras on their wedding day, Fabian in a tux and Hope in a giant confection of a wedding dress. The reporter explained in a voiceover that Fabian had confirmed that his wife suffered from Munchausen syndrome, which the anchor described as a "mental condition where people need to be seen as ill to get sympathy." He went on to say that they "often undergo unnecessary medical treatment and make circumstances seem dire." But then the anchor wrapped the brief segment with a startling statement: "Back in February we told you that Hope's daughter is sick as well. That girl's father confirms it *is* true."

Mike's ears perked up. He knew Fabian Ybarra had been sitting in the room when the most recent sweat test had been administered, the one that showed Sophia did not have CF. Fabian *knew* Sophia wasn't sick, so why was he claiming to these local reporters that she was?

Mike knew Fabian would be crucial to his investigation, but his lie to the reporter made Mike nervous, especially as all three Ybarra kids were now living with him. If he didn't understand that Hope was a serious threat, they wouldn't be safe from her. But Mike knew some spouses protected their partner no matter what they'd done.

Hope had taken Sophia to numerous hospitals over the years, including across state lines in Alabama, but she'd primarily been treated at Cook Children's, a fact that may well have saved her life. Established over a century ago, Cook's boasts a sprawling tree-lined campus in Fort Worth as well as numerous specialty clinics and study centers throughout the area. It's a welcoming place for kids and families, with its Build-A-Bear workshop, a meditation garden, numerous playgrounds, and even a salon where children and parents can go for pampering. They offer yoga for kids, help with schoolwork, and a team of trained therapy dogs for cuddling. But Cook's has something more important than any of these amenities: Dr. Jamye Coffman.

Dr. Coffman headed up Cook's CARE (child advocacy resources and evaluation) team, which was responsible for the medical evaluation of children referred for abuse and neglect. With abundant curly hair, green eyes, and a warm but authoritative demeanor, Dr. Coffman was ideal for her role, which required a nearly endless well of empathy and understanding alongside a steel constitution. Every pediatric hospital has some system for dealing with child abuse, but they vary greatly, depending on the hospital's size and staff—in some cases, it consists of a single pediatrician or nurse practitioner willing to take on the role. But in the case of Cook's—a well-resourced, well-run hospital—there was a team of physicians and nurse practitioners who worked on abuse evaluations full-time.

Mike had always been impressed by her, so as he dug into the Ybarra case, she was his first call.

Dr. Coffman was already busy reviewing the thousands of pages of medical records that detailed the history of Sophia's short life, so much of which had been spent in the hospital. Mike asked about all of the feeding interventions, intrigued that, like the Ohio case, this, too, had involved surgeries for the same issue.

"How do you determine when these kinds of interventions are necessary?" Mike asked Dr. Coffman.

"When nothing else is working," she explained, "and the caregiver is reporting that the child still cannot keep food down."

It made sense: doctors wouldn't have any other way of knowing what a child was or wasn't consuming. Mike didn't have kids of his own, but he could immediately see how much pediatricians' actions were dictated by what parents told them. But there was one issue Sophia had that *was* documented by much more straightforward test results: her multiple episodes of severe anemia. The bloodwork had been taken at the hospital, not reported by Hope.

Looking the numbers over, Mike felt a bolt of anxiety: What if Sophia really was sick after all? Mike knew better than to assume anything, especially so early in an investigation. He needed to follow all of the threads, wherever they might lead. Dr. Coffman suggested interviewing each of the pediatric specialists who had treated little Sophia.

DR. KAREN SCHULTZ was a young pediatric pulmonologist with a gentle manner who'd grown close with the Ybarras in the three years she'd been treating their daughter. She'd been the one to receive the unsettling phone call from Sophia's grandmother, Susan Putscher, about Hope's cancer hoax and their fears about Sophia. When Alana and Mike went to visit her, Dr. Schultz was extremely forthcoming and knowledgeable. It helped that this wasn't Dr. Schultz's first rodeo; the notorious Susan Hyde was her former coworker.

Hyde had not only been the mother of a pediatric patient at Cook's but worked there, pulling overnight shifts as a paramedic three nights a week.[1] Hyde claimed that not one, but two of her daughters—both also born premature—had cystic fibrosis, a massive statistical anomaly given that the girls had different fathers. Additionally, neither showed any genetic markers for CF, which didn't rule it out but made it far less likely. A look back through Hyde's history showed that she had brought all three of her children to the hospital repeatedly for a series of consistently inexplicable ailments, beginning shortly after the birth of her eldest daughter six years earlier. "It's usually when things don't quite add up," Dr. Schultz said, explaining when she begins to suspect abuse. "They [the caregivers] tell you about symptoms, and then your treatment plan doesn't work whatsoever. And you try a different treatment plan that, again, should work, and it doesn't work at all." Ultimately, after CPS brought a case against Hyde, her children were removed from her care; though Hyde's parental rights were terminated, no criminal charges were ever brought against her.[2]

Alana Minton, who had been the ADA at the time, was quoted in a news article as saying, "Our laws are not written to prosecute cases such as these. . . . It is a problem, and there should be some way to incorporate these cases in our laws to be able to protect children from situations such as this."[3] The experience haunted Dr. Schultz. Still, she knew how important it was not to jump to conclusions.

When Dr. Schultz first met then-two-year-old Sophia at Cook's pulmonary clinic, she appeared to be a very sick little girl. She had undergone numerous sweat tests at a Dallas hospital that confirmed she had cystic fibrosis, so there'd been no reason to retest her. Hope had also shown Dr. Schultz a copy of Sophia's genetic test confirming she was positive for CF. Her gastrointestinal issues were also well documented, and she already had both a feeding tube and a central venous catheter, which allowed doctors to administer medications and take blood draws without so much wear and tear on the toddler's tiny veins. The central line had been removed and reinserted on one occasion, after Sophia had developed a lung infection. Dr. Schultz explained that these infections are common in patients with CF. But once Dr. Schultz received the call from Susan Putscher that Hope did *not* have cancer—putting doubt on her daughter's diagnosis as well—the whole story of the little girl's life began to unravel.

Mike asked if doctors had ever tested Sophia for anything else.

Hope had initially reported to Dr. Schultz that Sophia also suffered from hearing loss and a swallowing dysfunction, but when she was tested, she didn't show signs of either. At the time, Dr. Schultz thought that Hope might just be hypervigilant for any issue, like so many anxious parents of sick children. On its face, asking for additional testing didn't raise a red flag—parents know their children best, and a gut feeling can be powerful. "A lot of our decisions are based on what parents tell us," Dr. Schultz said, echoing Dr. Coffman. "We can't be there all the time. We don't live in the house with the child. . . . We expect the family to come and tell us what is actually going on at home." It was pediatric procedure to take a caregiver at their word.

Mike asked if it would be possible to falsify a sweat test.

"Pretty easily," Dr. Schultz allowed, "if they were knowledgeable; you'd just have to find a way to place salt on the skin. The parent is normally allowed to stay with the child when they're undergoing a test like that." Mike remembered Hope's attempts to take Sophia into the bathroom "to have a meltdown" in her most recent sweat test, the one that had finally come back negative.

Was there anything else that hadn't added up in Sophia's records?

"Hope consistently reported that Sophia needed oxygen treatments when she was at home, but her levels were always normal when she was here," Dr. Schultz said. She remembered Hope making the conjecture that Sophia hadn't been off her oxygen long enough to cause a drop. At the time, Dr. Schultz believed Sophia had CF—which, as a pulmonary condition, affects oxygen levels—so it didn't raise a red flag; but in light of Hope's deception, this, too, did not fit.

Given her specialty as a pulmonologist, Dr. Schultz chiefly treated Sophia for CF, but she also recalled the terrifying episode of anemia Sophia had experienced, the one Dr. Coffman had mentioned.

"Is anemia common with cystic fibrosis patients?" Alana asked.

"There's no direct association. But it was such a problem I sent her to our hematology clinic. It was severe enough that they treated her with iron dextran. She was allergic and went into anaphylactic shock; fortunately they're equipped to treat that instantly."

Alana asked how serious a reaction like that could be.

"Very," Dr. Schultz confirmed. "She could have died."

Medical child abuse cases always shook up Dr. Schultz, made her doubt herself and lose sleep. She'd gone into pediatrics with the basic assumption that parents want what's best for their children; when a parent violated her trust, it tore her up inside. She cared deeply about her patients—especially ones like Sophia, whom she'd been with for years.

On their way out, Dr. Schultz asked Mike and Alana if they wanted to see a picture of Sophia. They looked at each other, perplexed, as Dr. Schultz produced a large poster featuring Sophia dressed in a white shirt and blue jeans, with a huge pink bow in her hair. The clear but unmistakable tubing from her oxygen line snaked beneath her button nose. The text read "Sophia Needs Our Help to Find a Cure for Cystic Fibrosis" and included the contact information for the Cystic Fibrosis Foundation.

Sophia—a child who had never actually suffered from CF—was a literal poster girl for it.

MIKE HAD BEEN hoping that Dr. Schultz, who'd known the Ybarras for years, might help him get a read on Fabian, but Hope's husband seemed equally mysterious to her. She'd described Fabian as passive, noting that he often didn't look her in the eye when she was speaking to him. It was Hope who ran the show when it came to Sophia's health. Mike was worried. He'd worked hundreds of child abuse cases by this point in his career so he knew how denial could overpower even the strongest evidence; at the end of the day, no one wanted to believe that they could have chosen a partner who would harm their child. He needed to know if Fabian was going to put his kids first.

On April 17, 2009, Sophia was getting ready to have her central line removed and be released from Cook's, so Mike posted up outside her room to try to intercept Fabian. While Mike was waiting for Fabian to arrive, he noticed that Sophia's nanny, Crystal, had come to visit her. He pulled aside the diminutive twentysomething and asked if she could take a few moments to chat.

He couldn't compel anyone to talk to him at that point; it was all voluntary. Fortunately, Mike is about as disarming as anyone who is six four and wearing a badge can possibly be. Television portrays investigators as full of tough-guy swagger, but it is usually the opposite tactic that makes a good detective: it helps to be a good listener, someone people actually *want* to talk to.

Crystal, her brown eyes bloodshot with worry, agreed to talk. Mike pulled a second chair next to him in the hallway and pulled out his notes. Crystal had been hired by the Ybarras just after Labor Day two years earlier, when Hope began working a demanding new job as lead chemist at Neos. Hope worked from home part of the time because of her alleged cancer, but she was still employed there full-time until the fall of 2008. Crystal, badly shaken by the situation, was forthcoming with Mike, her eyes intermittently filled with tears. Crystal was struggling to make sense of the fact that everything she thought she knew about her employer and onetime friend had been turned abruptly upside down. The two women had been close, so after Hope was ordered to leave the family home, she'd even crashed on Crystal's couch for a few days, until Crystal had grown uncomfortable with the arrangement and asked her to leave.

Like everyone else in her orbit, Crystal had understood both Hope and Sophia to be terminally ill, up until the shocking news of the past few weeks. She choked up as she recalled seeing pictures of Hope bald as a cue ball because of cancer treatments. She seemed more heartbroken than angry. "I just want her to get help," she said of Hope. "She really believes it all, I think."

Mike didn't correct her: he understood how this was a more comforting thought than the cold reality that Hope wasn't delusional.

Mike asked Crystal what she had been told was wrong with Sophia.

"Oh gosh," Crystal said, "so many things: cystic fibrosis, lactose intolerance, she's hearing-impaired because of being born so premature. Hope had this *huge* binder with all the information about Sophia's illnesses." She described Hope as both very knowledgeable and very obsessive about medical issues. "Hope is so smart," Crystal said. She reiterated that Hope had received a PhD from Texas Christian University—Crystal remembered seeing the school's purple bumper sticker on Hope's car.

"And how did Sophia seem to you? Did you see her having all these issues?" Mike asked.

"Well, her oxygen would fluctuate sometimes," Crystal said, as would be expected with a child with a pulmonary condition. "But 97 percent of the time it was normal." The strangest thing, though, Crystal said, was Sophia's eating habits. "She was on feeds all day," Crystal said, referring to the formula Sophia received via her surgically inserted G tube. "And that little girl could put down a six-inch sub, two bowls of cereal, she'd snack all day, but she was still losing weight."

Crystal had been told Sophia had a swallowing dysfunction—indeed, this was in her medical records—but Crystal never saw her have any trouble getting food down.

Despite some of these inconsistencies, nothing had been a red flag for Crystal. She frequently attended doctor visits with the family, and she only ever observed Hope doing what the doctors told her to do.

Mike asked about Fabian, how involved he had been in Sophia's care. Mike knew some spouses chose denial, but something even worse had recently occurred to him. The vast majority of people charged with medical child abuse were women, but for the few men who were included, it was almost always the husband, who was a conspirator.[4]

"He's not super-involved, because Hope won't let him be. And he works a ton: he's a high school teacher and he coaches football and wrestling. He's gone a lot." This dynamic was nothing out of the ordinary, Mike knew: mothers often take the lead on medical care for their children. The well-being of children is one of the few areas where our culture lets women have complete authority.

Mike could see Crystal struggling in real time to make sense of her relationship with Hope. She'd spoken to Hope the day prior, before deciding to cut off communication. Crystal explained that it just didn't feel healthy to remain in contact with her. In their final conversation, Hope had tried to convince Crystal that she shouldn't be separated from Sophia, saying, "I'm her primary caregiver, it's in everyone's best interest if I'm back home with her." Yet Crystal had seen with her own eyes how many of Sophia's issues seemed to resolve in the seven days she'd been kept away from Hope.

As Mike wrapped up his interview with Crystal, he saw that Fabian Ybarra was coming through the door, on his way to pick up Sophia. He thanked Crystal for her time and watched as she and Fabian exchanged a strained hello.

Fabian was a clean-cut athletic guy in his midthirties with an olive complexion and dark eyes that matched Sophia's. Mike tried to seem as approachable as possible, explaining that he was with the DA's Office and that they were really just gathering facts to see if an investigation was warranted: Could he talk to Fabian for a few minutes? Fabian mumbled his assent. Just as Dr. Schultz had described, he barely made eye contact and his answers to Mike's questions were almost inaudible.

Mike started off asking some background questions about their family history: when he and Hope had met, the ages of their children. But things took a rocky turn when Mike asked about their middle daughter Amanda's early diagnosis of cerebral palsy. Fabian seemed to blow off the question, saying that his daughter had never been officially diagnosed and insisting that Hope's mother, Susan, had actually been the one to blow it out of proportion. Indeed, there's no definitive test for cerebral palsy—it's a developmental diagnosis—and the only note Mike found in Amanda's records, which he'd subpoenaed, from the child's primary care provider, was that Hope had *reported* that Amanda had been diagnosed with CP.

There would have been no reason for Amanda's pediatrician to doubt this. Dr. Schultz had already explained how easy it was for a falsehood to get reproduced in medical records, especially if a patient has previously been treated elsewhere: they depended on notes from other specialists; it made no sense to retest patients for every diagnosis they came in with, especially young children. When pressed, Fabian did recall that Amanda had been given leg braces but said she only used them a handful of times.

Fabian walked Mike through the family's numerous moves across the state of Texas: from Alpine to Justin to Lake Dallas to Haltom to Grapevine and, finally, to Fort Worth. The last three residences were all located in Tarrant County, which was crucial for Mike's investigation. He knew from experience that jurisdictional issues could wreak havoc on a case like this. Fabian also confirmed that Hope had spent three months in Birmingham, where she'd gone with Sophia, allegedly to participate in a clinical trial for her cancer—and to follow Sophia's pediatric pulmonologist, Dr. Harmon, who'd relocated there from Dallas.

Despite Mike's warmth and calm demeanor, Fabian remained resistant to his attempts to establish rapport. His answers were detached, as though he were recalling the details of a television show he'd seen—a marked contrast to Mike's earlier conversation with Crystal, who'd sounded as though her heart was in her throat as they spoke.

Fabian recounted the period around Sophia's birth, when she'd arrived so terrifyingly early at only twenty-four weeks—a gestational age at which many babies don't survive. Fabian recalled her fitting in the palm of his hand. During her initial hospital stay, she'd undergone "tons and tons of tests," as was expected with a preemie, but she wasn't diagnosed with any issues other than those associated with premature birth. Yet before her first birthday, she was diagnosed with CF.

When asked how much of Sophia's care he was responsible for, Fabian said it was about a sixty-forty split between him and Hope. This was inconsistent with what everyone, including Sophia's doctors, had said about Hope's controlling nature when it came to her daughter's health.

Mike was still trying to get a read on Fabian, but he was willing to view this minor rewriting of history as understandable, perhaps an expression of how much Fabian wished he had been available rather than what had transpired.

"Listen, I get it," Mike told him. "A buddy of mine, he works one hundred hours a week, his wife does everything for the kids." Rightly or wrongly, Mike knew that a mother who took charge of the kids' welfare was the rule in most families, not the exception.

Fabian allowed that he was there as much as he could be with his schedule. Overall, he lacked a definitive grasp of the details of his daughter's health history, but none of his omissions seemed deliberate; he simply seemed lost in the baffling number of medical issues Sophia was plagued by, which assuaged Mike's fears that Fabian could be a fellow abuser. Though careful not to make accusations about Hope, Mike wanted to ensure Fabian understood the gravity of the situation. He was now the children's primary caregiver; it was imperative he understand just how serious the "no contact" order with Hope was.

Mike asked Fabian what he knew about Sophia's episodes of anemia. Fabian looked confused and replied, "Well, we thought she might be anemic."

"No, she *was* anemic," Mike clarified. "It's in the medical records. But it would clear up when she was admitted to the hospital and then reemerge when she was at home."

"I know where you're . . ." Fabian began, letting the sentence hang in the air, perhaps because it was too horrifying to complete. Mike let the silence take up space, patiently allowing Fabian to try to work through things rather than jumping in to supply answers. Like Crystal, Fabian seemed to be processing the unthinkable: that his wife had intentionally sickened their child, maybe even bleeding her to make her anemic.

Mike then brought up the news segment about Hope's cancer hoax from the day prior, and Fabian's assertion that Sophia *was* sick. Mike pressed him on the false claim, but Fabian said that it was the reporter who'd misspoken, that she didn't have her facts straight. Did the reporter get it wrong or was Fabian simply trying to minimize what happened, to protect his family from further media scrutiny? It was bad enough that the whole world now knew Hope was lying about her cancer—did they need to know that Hope lied about Sophia, too?

Mike tried another tactic. "You understand that your daughter doesn't have CF, correct?"

Fabian nodded.

"How did Hope seem to take the news that Sophia didn't have CF?"

"She was happy, relieved."

Mike shook his head. This was a stark contrast to reports from the nurse and the CPS investigator who'd been there in the room. According to them, Hope had wept with frustration and questioned the test numbers, a response that had appeared to gall Fabian, who was understandably relieved that his daughter wasn't ill. But now Mike feared Fabian might be again retreating into denial.

"Mr. Ybarra," Mike tried again, "I understand you're in a really tough position. You've got your kids who you love, your wife who you love. We really need you to be as honest with us as possible. You don't remember telling your wife: 'Who cares about the numbers? She doesn't have CF!'"

Fabian shifted uncomfortably in his seat. He allowed that if the CPS investigator said it, it was true. But in his memory, he and Hope were sitting on opposite sides of the room when they received the news, and there'd been silence. Memory can be an unreliable narrator, especially in times when we are as utterly overwhelmed as Fabian must have been at that time. Still, his reaction in the moment had been entirely appropriate—it was his reaction *now* that flummoxed Mike. Was he protecting Hope?

"The investigator told you there's no possible way it could have been a false positive on three separate occasions," Mike continued.

Fabian nodded, and admitted that he'd always found it odd that his daughter had a genetic disorder. "My family has really good genes. Both my grandmothers are centenarians. But it was what the doctors were telling us." He acknowledged that the test wouldn't have been hard for Hope to manipulate, that all she would have needed to do was put some salt on their daughter's skin where the sensors would be affixed for the sweat test.

Mike pressed him further: "Let me ask you this. Say Sophia had no contact with Hope and things progress to where she gets her feeding tube out. What would you infer from that?"

There was another lengthy pause.

"The kids are my first priority," Fabian finally said.

Mike could only hope this would prove to be true.

5

A Family Divided

As April wore on, five-year-old Sophia's health continued to improve. She was weaned off every medication on her lengthy list of prescriptions and her central line was removed. She showed no signs of the reflux Hope had described and her medical team scheduled the removal of her feeding tube. This was good news for Sophia, but it pointed ever more strongly to Hope's culpability. Mike knew this "separation test," as it's called, was crucial for his investigation.

Meanwhile, Mike scheduled one of his most important interviews, with Hope's mother, Susan Putscher. Susan was central to the case: she'd always been close with her eldest daughter, and she'd also been the one to discover Hope's initial lie about her cancer. Mike felt she'd shown remarkable courage in calling Dr. Schultz to report her suspicions that Hope's medical deceptions might be carrying over to Sophia, a reality no parent would want to grapple with. She'd done the absolute right thing without hesitation and it had cost her dearly. Her thirty-year-plus marriage to Paul was under considerable strain—at one point during the investigation, they officially separated and Susan moved out—and when Mike spoke to her, Fabian wasn't allowing her to see her grandchildren.

Susan met Mike in his windowless ninth-floor office in the crimes-against-children unit of the DA's Office. She was short and stocky with a mop of blond hair. In her early fifties, she had the gravelly voice of a smoker and the knowing expression of a woman who has seen a lot in her life. In contrast to talking with the inscrutable Fabian, Mike was able to develop an instant rapport with Susan, who was forthcoming and sounded both exhausted and resigned as she sat with him, trying to unravel decades of her daughter's deceptions and bizarre behavior. It was clear that Hope's cancer had put into question much more than Sophia's CF diagnosis. There had been the twin pregnancy—allegedly lost due to radiation, which Susan now realized was impossible, since Hope had never undergone cancer treatment; the cochlear implant Hope had allegedly received after losing her hearing (again, due to nonexistent cancer treatments), which had prompted Hope to supposedly learn sign language and become an active part of the local deaf community.* Not to mention every other strange health crisis Hope had faced, going back to her teenage years. The cochlear implant, Susan believed, was real—though she now understood it had been put in under false pretenses. It was one of the things she and Paul were arguing over. She said that she'd seen the scar but that her husband, Paul, never bought it. Susan told Mike that her husband was nervous about her speaking to the police, fearing that perhaps they might be in trouble as well. Mike explained that they weren't and that he appreciated her cooperation. He knew the family was going through hell.

Mike asked her if she'd had any contact with Hope since everything had blown up. "Whenever we communicate, she starts lying. I have to terminate the conversation," Susan said. "She's telling me now that she's having all of these procedures done in the hospital,

* Whether or not Hope actually knows sign language is yet another mystery.

but I know it's not true. She says she's had her gallbladder out, liver biopsies, all these tests done. Supposedly they don't know what's wrong with her." Mike also suspected that these newest health woes of Hope's were utter fiction, an attempt to distract from the suspicions against her and paint herself as the victim.

Mike asked Susan what Fabian was like. She told him the man was as much a mystery to her as he was to Mike. "They've been married ten years. They've lived with us on several occasions. I can tell you he has a mom and dad in the Central Valley, some really elderly grandparents. That's about it." And what about his involvement with Sophia's health issues? "All Hope," Susan confirmed. "He's gone a lot. And he's pretty passive. Well, except for now, when it comes to letting me see the kids."

Things had grown increasingly tense between Susan and Fabian. Susan explained that she usually took her middle grandchild, Amanda, to gymnastics on Tuesdays; that week, she'd gone to the gym to watch her granddaughter practice for two hours, but Amanda had been whisked away before Susan could speak to her. "But she knew Grandma was there," she said, becoming emotional. Amanda was a talented gymnast, Susan explained. Susan reiterated that Amanda had also been born prematurely and that her alleged cerebral palsy had magically resolved itself around the time Sophia was born. While an individual's symptoms of CP may change over time—some people even go on to become accomplished athletes, such as mountain climber Bonner Paddock—you don't simply outgrow it. It appeared Amanda's CP had been a lie from the beginning.

Susan said Hope seemed to accept her Munchausen diagnosis, though Susan insisted that her daughter would never knowingly harm her children.

"I asked if they'd diagnosed her with delusional disorder, because she's clearly delusional. She clearly believes these things she's saying," Susan said, perhaps trying to reassure herself as much as she tried to convince Mike. He knew that Susan would have to come to her own understanding about Hope in her own time.*

THE MUNCHAUSEN DIAGNOSIS was forcing Susan to also reevaluate a long string of incidents with Hope, starting with the seizures she'd had in high school and up through the "cancer." "I've spent the last year preparing to bury my daughter," Susan said. "Now I've lost my daughter in an entirely different way, a completely intangible way. This person is not the person I know. At all." The two had always been close and Susan had never perceived her daughter as especially attention seeking when it came to her myriad health problems. "She more wanted attention for her charity work and all the various positions she held," Susan said, ticking off the numerous organizations Hope had been involved with over the years: Great Strides, the charity walk benefiting the Cystic Fibrosis Foundation; the Knights of Columbus; the Take My Hand foundation; the deaf ministry; and the parents' council at Cook Children's.

Next to Hope, Susan was the family member who had spent the most time caring for Sophia. She told Mike the little girl had required round-the-clock care: monitoring her oxygen, administering medications, and supervising feedings all meant that when she was caring for Sophia, she'd be able to get only about four hours of sleep a night. "I never could figure out how Hope was keeping up with it all. Now I think I know. She wasn't doing it." Despite Sophia's

---

* Dr. Mary Sanders, a clinical professor of psychiatry at the Stanford University School of Medicine, and the nation's leading expert on treatment of MBP perpetrators, offered some insight into why these women can seem so utterly convinced of what they're saying in the moment, even though their deception is intentional. "One parent told me they were able to take the knowledge that they were actively harming their child and sort of put it in a little mental drawer and close it. They knew it was happening, but they could just not pay attention to that information."[1]

alleged trouble with eating, Susan reiterated the observation the others had shared of Sophia having a normal appetite.

Mike was beginning to wonder about Hope's education. Clearly, someone who was capable of this level of deception was very smart, but one lie seemed to lead to another: Was there any part of her life that her deceptions hadn't touched? Susan said that she'd attended Hope's graduation from Sul Ross, where she'd watched Hope get her undergraduate diploma. But Hope had told Susan there was no need to attend her graduations for her master's and PhD programs at TCU, and Susan had never actually seen a diploma for either degree. She knew, however, that a PhD was required for Hope's previous job. Susan dug out from her purse one of Hope's business cards from Neos Therapeutics and gave it to Mike. The card read: HOPE YBARRA, PH.D. DIRECTOR OF LABORATORIES.

"Do you think Hope will talk to me?" Mike asked.

Susan said she wasn't sure. "I can give you the password to her blog, if you want that?" she offered. Mike had heard about the blog, but as it was set to private, he hadn't yet read it. He was anxious to see how Hope described her situation in her own words.

Mike decided he would wait until Hope was out of the hospital to approach her for an interview. He also needed to wait for Dr. Coffman to finish the mammoth task of reviewing the medical records. And the longer Sophia was separated from Hope and thriving, the better it looked for the case.

In the meantime, Mike set out to get to the bottom of some of Hope's other tall tales, as he knew they could be helpful in establishing her as a pathological liar. He started with an easy one to verify: calling the registrar's office at TCU to see if Hope had ever been a student at the institution where she claimed she'd received two advanced degrees. Sure enough, they had no record of Hope enrolling in so much as a single class.

Hope's deceptions were a many-headed hydra, and Mike needed

to focus on something he could actually charge her with. He was curious about Hope's time in Alabama, and thought perhaps Dr. Harmon could help illuminate how the lie about Sophia's sweat test had been perpetuated for so many years.

Before accepting a position with the University of Alabama at Birmingham's Children's Hospital, Dr. Harmon had treated Sophia at Children's Medical Center of Dallas. He recalled that Sophia had always seemed sicker than the average child her age with CF. She was always on oxygen and constantly had trouble gaining weight, which wasn't part of the normal profile. When he told Hope that he'd accepted a new job out of state, she'd been distraught. Though he tried to refer her to another physician, she'd insisted on following him to Birmingham. She told him that she was participating in a clinical trial for her cancer there as well, and decamped to Alabama with Sophia and Amanda for several months. Dr. Harmon confirmed that his wife, Laura, had even stepped in to babysit while Hope was purportedly at the hospital receiving cancer treatment. It struck Mike as telling that Hope had so clearly worked to ingratiate herself with the doctor treating her child. Though not necessarily unethical, that degree of closeness between a doctor and their patient's family can be tricky and can cloud judgment.* This kind of boundary-pushing is so common in MBP cases that Mike knew it was a red flag for abuse.

Dr. Harmon never conducted a sweat test on Sophia, as she came to him with the CF diagnosis; he seemed shocked to hear it had been a lie. He even recalled seeing documentation from the Cystic Fibrosis Foundation that Sophia had received genetic testing

---

* Dr. Jamye Coffman, who kindly did a medical review of this book for us, had this to say about this situation: "From my perspective this is definitely a boundary issue and a line a treating physician should never cross. The only time I could see this sort of thing happening is in a small town where everybody knows everybody and you are the only doc in town."

confirming her diagnosis. This piece of paper would become ever elusive; Dr. Schultz had also recalled seeing it, but it did not appear anywhere in Sophia's extensive medical records. When Mike later subpoenaed records from the Cystic Fibrosis Foundation, there were none relating to Sophia. Mike eventually concluded that Hope had falsified a document that she'd then shown to both doctors; meanwhile, Dr. Harmon confirmed that the only explanation for a false positive genetic test was tampering.

The following day, Mike went to the Fort Worth Alliance for Children's Advocacy Center to observe the forensic interviews with Hope's two older children, Amanda and Jacob. After the reports of Amanda's cerebral palsy and subsequent miraculous recovery, he'd begun to suspect that she'd been Hope's first victim, a practice case before moving on to her younger, more vulnerable child. Mike watched from a TV monitor in a separate room as forensic investigator Lindsey Dula sat down with Amanda, a dark-haired, athletic-looking nine-year-old. Dula took her through some initial tests to show she was developmentally on target and capable of distinguishing between a truth and a lie. Amanda promised to tell the truth. Mike had seen plenty of forensic interviews as he worked on crimes against children, in sexual assault cases. He knew interviewers often focused kids on sensory details: what things looked, smelled, sounded like—to take them back to their memories. But this was new territory, and they were at sea.

"I know I'm here to talk about why my mom isn't home," Amanda told Dula. "She said Sophia was sick but she's not sick." She also explained that her mother had announced that she had cancer and was dying. Everything had snowballed so fast; Mike was unsure what Fabian and Hope had told their kids about the state of her "cancer."

"Who takes care of Sophia when you're at home?" Dula asked her.

"My mom, my dad, and Crystal," she said, referring to the family's former nanny. She explained that Sophia had a special vest that buck-led in front and forced mucus out of her lungs. Amanda said she had also worn the same vest when she was little because she had pneumonia a lot. She recalled once being hospitalized for eleven days. She also described having to use a walker and leg braces when she was little, because of her cerebral palsy. "I don't have to use them anymore because my muscles got stronger," she said. Amanda believed she still had cerebral palsy, but that it simply didn't affect her any longer.

"And what about Sophia's eating habits?" Dula asked.

Amanda said they were normal, only her sister couldn't eat soy.

Next, Dula interviewed the Ybarras' son, Jacob, two years older than Amanda. He also described the vest and said Sophia didn't like wearing it.

"She eats everything the family eats," he told Dula when asked about her diet. "She's always hungry. The only thing she can't have is milk, the doctors told her that, but a little bit ago, they said she wasn't allergic anymore." He said she had to take enzymes before each meal but that she had a big appetite and ate lots of snacks between meals. Jacob told Dula that Sophia had used a walker when she was little and hadn't learned to walk on her own until she was three, a full two years later than most children.

"What about Amanda?" Dula asked him. Jacob said Amanda never had any issues and had always been healthy. Perhaps he wasn't aware of the CP; or, as the eldest, was he cognizant that his mother might be in trouble for lying?

It was hard to know what to make of the children's interviews. Jacob was both the most aware of the seriousness of the situation, and also the most conditioned to believe his mother's lies. Kids often (and understandably) try to protect their parents; how to untangle the equally true fact that in medical child abuse, the kids themselves are the primary subjects of manipulation? If Hope had fooled doctors, what chance did her children have of seeing through the ruse?

Mike knew it was common for children who'd been victimized by their parents to feel intensely protective of them. Even though abusers didn't feel empathy or a real bond with their children, it didn't mean the reverse wasn't true. Children want their parents to be good. One of the things that makes MBP abuse so particularly difficult to accept is that it robs children of the one person meant to love them best of all, eternally and unconditionally: their mom.

6

Poison

Hope may have lied about her education, but she had worked for years as a very high-level chemist, including a two-year stint at a major pharmaceutical corporation. Mike couldn't shake the feeling that her work might be more integral to the case than it appeared at first glance. He called Margaret, the HR manager of Hope's former employer, Neos Therapeutics, to confirm that Hope had actually worked there—and if so, whether she'd been hired under the false pretense of having earned a PhD. But when Mike got Margaret on the line, she said something that took him aback.

"We'll cooperate however we can," she assured him. "We want to make sure no one ever gets hurt again." Mike hadn't said anything yet to Margaret about the nature of his investigation. What was she talking about? He didn't have to wonder long. Shortly after they spoke, Mike heard from Brian Angler, the head of Neos Therapeutics, who wanted to talk about Hope, too. What kind of hornet's nest had he just kicked?

Angler seemed eager to help. He told Mike that Hope had been fired for gross misconduct when a private investigator—hired by the company after colleagues became suspicious of Hope's credentials—discovered that she did *not*, in fact, have a PhD. A memo about the investigation revealed that when Hope was initially confronted with her false claim, she insisted it was a simple paperwork mix-up. But when asked to name some of the TCU professors she'd studied with, she was unable to, claiming memory loss caused by her brain cancer. When pressed with irrefutable evidence that she'd never attended TCU, she said, curtly: "I don't have anything else to tell you. What I told you is what I know."

A series of alarming incidents on the job had spurred the initial investigation into Hope, Angler told Mike. In October 2007, the microbiology supervisor reported that Hope had made an unauthorized purchase of two pathogens: *Pseudomonas aeruginosa* and *Klebsiella pneumoniae*, both in a form that was not used by the laboratory.

When confronted, Hope claimed she'd sent the pathogens out to another laboratory, Micro Lab, Inc., for "further study"—of what, Hope didn't specify—which was why she'd ordered them in a form different from what Neos usually used. But while there was a record of the pathogens being delivered to Neos, there was no record that they had been sent out. Hope told Angler that she'd taken them home and mailed them via her personal FedEx account.

To say this was unusual was an understatement. But the normally strict lab standards had already been bent for Hope. Because she had a gravely ill child at home, Neos often let her work off-hours and gave her extra flexibility—meaning she was frequently at the lab late in the evening when no one else was around.

"Is it possible she kept the pathogens she stole at home?" Mike asked Angler.

"She could easily grow them with a laboratory incubator," Angler grimly confirmed, "and store them in her freezer in pellet form."

There was something else. Margaret, the HR manager Mike had originally spoken with, had been the one to coordinate the investigation into Hope. During one busy day at work, Margaret returned to her cubicle and discovered her water bottle missing. After she returned from another errand later that same day, it was back on her desk. Margaret figured she must have just misplaced it and took a drink; a short time later, she became violently ill. When alerted to the incident, Angler confiscated the water bottle and sent it to the lab for testing. Sure enough, the bottle tested positive for *Pseudomonas aeruginosa*—one of Hope's ill-gotten pathogens.

"Why didn't you report this to the police?" Mike asked, aghast.

"No one saw her do it," Angler explained. "Lots of other people had access; we couldn't prove anything." Mike wanted to hit his head against a wall, knowing the lab should have left it to the police to find evidence. But it was moot now.

"You should talk to her other former employer, too," Angler said. He was sure that Hope had falsely presented herself to them as a PhD as well.

The conversation with Angler had provoked more new questions than concrete answers, especially: If Hope was capable of poisoning her coworker, might she also have done the same to her daughter?

Mike phoned Crystal, and sure enough, she recalled Hope receiving packages from work. "She went out of her way to tell me that Neos had given her approval to get the stuff at home. I remember seeing this thing—it looked like an aquarium light—that Hope told me was for work. It seemed strange that she had it at the house."

ANOTHER OF HOPE's previous employers, Noah Banks of Nature's Formula, also remembered her well. There, too, she had falsely presented herself as having a PhD in chemistry. The employees who worked under Noah were an especially tight-knit group, and when Hope told them she'd been diagnosed with Ewing sarcoma, they'd rallied around her. "Hope said they were having trouble covering the expenses for her treatment and the company wrote her a check," Noah said. The company had given Hope somewhere around ten thousand dollars in total, he told Mike. "Her daughter was also sick, so we really felt for her." Hope had worked for Nature's Formula in the early aughts, around the time of the original "cancer diagnosis." Sophia wasn't born yet, so Noah must have been referring to Amanda. Noah didn't remember the details of her daughter's supposed health trouble, but another employee who'd been close with Hope filled in the blanks.

Camila recounted a conversation she'd had with Hope in the summer of 2002 when Hope had told her that her daughter was terminally ill and described the girl's recent brush with death. "She told me that the doctors had taken her off life support and were preparing to harvest her organs for donation when they noticed that Amanda was breathing on her own." From that point on, Amanda had allegedly made a miraculous recovery. "I remember Hope telling me about a service dog they had; I think it was meant to detect if the child was about to have a seizure."

THE HOPE YBARRA case was quickly ballooning into one of the most complicated investigations Mike had ever worked. The medical record review alone ended up taking months, and Hope's multitudinous lies kept throwing new leads in Mike's path. Knowing how deceptive she was, he wanted to have as much information as possible to confront her with before interviewing her in person. At the same time, Mike was also busy with his regular job of assisting prosecutors with preparations for actual criminal trials. The legwork of this type of medical child abuse investigation was outside his job description with the DA's Office, which mostly involved so-called second-line work of helping attorneys in the office prepare for trial. But after observing how the Ohio case had failed, Mike knew it was unlikely that another detective would take on the work of a medical child abuse case. Either nobly or foolishly, he'd already volunteered to Alana to take on any that came in, assuming they'd be once in a blue moon.

Though it seemed like a shot in the dark, Mike emailed Dr. Schultz to see if Sophia had ever tested positive for *Pseudomonas aeruginosa* or *Klebsiella pneumoniae*. Her reply stunned him. Sophia had cultures from her lungs test positive for *Pseudomonas aeruginosa* on several occasions. At the time, this hadn't raised any red flags because the bacteria are a common form of pneumonia found in patients with cystic fibrosis.

And what about those without CF, which they now knew included Sophia?

"Exceedingly rare," Dr. Schultz told Mike in a follow-up phone call.

"Do you still have those samples?" Mike asked.

"The laboratory destroyed them, I'm afraid."

It hardly seemed a coincidence that a pathogen Hope had stolen from her lab had shown up in her daughter. Mike shared with Dr. Schultz what he'd discovered at Neos. The possibility that Hope had stolen pathogens from work in order to poison her daughter was a chilling one, but Mike didn't know how he could prove it with the samples long gone.

Thankfully, Dr. Schultz had some good news to share: Sophia's health continued to improve. "She's eating well and she's presenting like a healthy little girl."

But before they hung up, she tossed Mike one more curveball. "Have you talked to Dr. Ashford or Dr. Villarreal yet?" Dr. Schultz asked, referring to the two doctors who'd treated Sophia in the hematology clinic. "The episodes of anemia that Sophia had seem suspicious to me."

"I'll get on it," Mike reassured her.

THE NEXT DAY, Mike and Alana met with Dr. Ashford in his office at Cook's specialty clinic, for the pediatricians treating the hospital's more complex cases. Dr. Ashford was a friendly, round-cheeked white guy in his thirties, and his office was covered in family pictures. He started by giving them a basic primer on anemia, which is the lack of iron absorption by the body. "Sophia was a strange case because her levels were all over the place," Dr. Ashford explained. "Normal one week, then extremely deficient the next. We couldn't get to the bottom of it: there was no sign of internal bleeding; no blood in her urine, stool, or vomit. Whenever she was staying at Cook's, her levels would be normal only to plummet again when she went home. Even for a child with severe cystic fibrosis, it didn't make sense."

"What about for a child who doesn't have CF?" Mike asked.

"The only explanation in that case," Dr. Ashford said, "is someone intentionally bleeding her."

Mike had been holding this suspicion in the back of his mind—but to hear it stated plainly by the doctor was still shocking. Sophia's anemia had been caused by someone intentionally bleeding her. Moreover, her allergic reaction to the treatment for anemia could have killed her.

After Dr. Ashford agreed to provide an affidavit attesting to this, Mike and Alana left.

"The kid had a central line," Mike explained to Alana as they made their way back to the station. "Hope could have easily taken

blood out using that." Mike was still absorbing Dr. Ashford's shocking conclusion, that intentional bleeding was not just a *possible* explanation for Sophia's anemia, but the *only* explanation.

As they drove back to the office, Alana reminded Mike that a
canny defense attorney would point out that they couldn't *prove*
Hope had done the bleeding, since numerous people technically
would have had access to Sophia's central line. The only thing they
could prove with the evidence they had was that Hope was a liar,
though Mike was now convinced she was guilty of far worse.

Alana hoped the interview with the hematologist, Dr. Villarreal,
might be helpful and said she'd tag along for it. Dr. Villarreal, a
pretty, dark-haired hematologist who hailed originally from Peru,
recounted Hope bringing Sophia in with significant anemia. Her
memory of the incident seemed vivid, though it had taken place
almost two years earlier. Her experience with Hope had clearly left
a mark.

Dr. Villarreal told them that Hope had seemed like she was in a
hurry, which struck her as bizarre. Her daughter was pale, lethargic,
and breathing rapidly, in obvious distress, yet Hope seemed to be
rushing through the appointment, complaining to the staff that she
needed to go pick up her other kids. Sophia's anemia was serious
enough that she could require an intravenous iron treatment. Left
untreated, severe anemia can lead to heart failure, but Dr. Villarreal
explained that there is a strict protocol around this treatment—
which involves administering a tiny amount to begin with, before
progressing with the complete transfusion—because of the risk of
the patient going into anaphylactic shock. Still, Hope was both
pushing for this specific treatment *and* pressuring Dr. Villarreal to
skip the protocol, claiming it was unnecessary because Sophia had
received the same type of infusion many times at the Children's
Medical Center in Dallas and she wasn't allergic. Of course, Dr.
Villarreal refused Hope's demands—which was good, because the

moment the team began administering the test dose, Sophia went into anaphylactic shock.

Alana asked how serious the little girl's reaction was. Dr. Villarreal explained that Sophia easily could have died if there hadn't been an intervention. If Dr. Villarreal had forgone the protocol—as Hope had insisted—the chances of death would have been far higher.

The episode had alarmed Dr. Villarreal. For one thing, there was no way Sophia could have received this treatment previously, as Hope had reported. A child wouldn't suddenly develop a new allergy to the iron treatment. She'd immediately reported her concerns to Dr. Ashford, and while Sophia was being stabilized, Hope was placed in a room with covert video surveillance. Nothing of note happened while she and Sophia were in that room and, ultimately, Dr. Villarreal didn't feel she had enough evidence to report Hope to CPS.*

Back at the office, Alana and Mike agreed that this revelation was significant. Hope's actions during the iron treatment had led to a substantial risk of death, giving them a possible path to charging her with "injury to a child—serious bodily injury." This was a first-degree felony, punishable by up to ninety-nine years in prison, though sentencing would be left to a judge or jury. And since Hope

---

* Mike told me that it's his opinion—one shared by the American Professional Society on the Abuse of Children's MBP committee—that police should be notified by the hospital if suspicions of abuse are serious enough to warrant placement in a video surveillance room. But doctors can be understandably reticent to take such a step, and that's if they know enough to identify the abuse to begin with. Both Dr. Coffman and Dr. Schultz confirmed that doctors don't receive much training on medical child abuse, despite their crucial role in prevention. "It is something that you learn in theory about, and you might hear lectures about, but nothing on what to do if you suspect it or where to go or who to talk to," Dr. Schultz said.

had a clean criminal record, she could easily wind up with nothing more than probation.

Alana told Mike she was worried about how convoluted this indictment would be: they'd be charging Hope with withdrawing blood from her daughter, which caused anemia, for which she was given an IV iron treatment that caused anaphylactic shock, which—absent medical intervention—carried a substantial risk of injury or death. The bottom line was that Hope could have killed her daughter, but Mike knew the road to that conclusion was confusing as hell.

"I've never seen an indictment that read like that," Mike admitted.

Neither had Alana, and she pointed out to Mike that DAs were loath to set legal precedent. Both knew they'd be out on a limb with a charge like that. Mike knew he had a long way to go before Alana had any hope of making this case in court. Back in his office, he started paging through the synopsis Dr. Jamye Coffman had prepared following a detailed reading of the ten thousand pages of Sophia's medical records, looking for more clues.*

This record review is crucial, Dr. Coffman confirmed. "You can't make a diagnosis of medical child abuse without reviewing all medical records. And that's not just in your own institution because many of these perpetrators doctor shop and hospital shop." She emphasized just how thorough the review needed to be and how onerous it is for hospitals. "You can't just review the doctor's notes.

---

* The burden of the record review in cases of medical child abuse is significant, and Cook Children's is the one in the country with a dedicated employee to do it, though Rady Children's in San Diego has a multidisciplinary task force dedicated to helping with investigations. Sarah Vega, Shalon M. Nienow, Maria Z. Huang, and Laurie Bernard Stover, "Medical Child Welfare Task Force: A Multidisciplinary Approach to Identifying Medical Child Abuse," *Pediatrics* 141, no. 2 (2023): e2022058926.

There is so much within the nursing notes, telephone calls; all those things have to be reviewed. It's every single notation, and it can take well over a hundred hours to do all that. And, of course, insurance doesn't reimburse for any of that time."

Mike was looking for further evidence of possible poisoning, which he now strongly suspected Hope had done to her daughter more than once. Mike noticed blood cultures showing a range of positive tests over a period of about three years for various pathogens: the *Pseudomonas aeruginosa* in particular caught his eye, as this was the same pathogen found in Hope's coworker's water bottle, the pathogen commonly found in CF patients—and the same pathogen that Hope had ordered while employed by Neos.

Mike emailed Dr. Schultz, Sophia's pulmonologist, who sent him additional details indicating another *Pseudomonas aeruginosa* culture in October 2008.

"What about this positive test for salmonella and staph aureus in '07?" Mike asked Dr. Schultz. "Are those commonly found in CF patients?"

Dr. Schultz confirmed that the finding was unusual—that, in fact, studies have indicated that CF patients are actually *more* resistant to salmonella than the healthy population. Dr. Schultz said she'd never seen a CF patient test positive for salmonella and, furthermore, it was bizarre to discover it in a lung culture, as salmonella is usually found in the digestive tract.

Mike put in another call to Margaret from Neos Therapeutics—Hope's former coworker—to see if she could identify which other pathogens Hope had had access to. Mike had a strong hunch that there would be crossover with those Dr. Coffman had mentioned in her synopsis.

While he waited, Mike opened the link to Hope's personal blog, using the password that Susan had given him. Mike was curious to see how she described her and Sophia's illnesses in her own words.

The entries began in July 2008 and, knowing how many falsehoods they contained, Mike found reading them to be a surreal experience. The blog—which Hope had named Grace's Angels—featured professional-looking black-and-white photos of Hope and her three beautiful, smiling children. The flowery fonts and soft purple-and-green design gave it the feel of a Hallmark card. The header of the website, a quote from Psalm 23:6, read "Surely goodness and mercy will follow me all the days of my life. And I will dwell in the house of the Lord forever." The final entry was from March 2009, one day before Sophia turned five.

"My body is weak and my soul is trembling, I see the sadness in my loved ones around me," Hope wrote in this florid entry before sharing an allegory about an eagle plucking its own feathers out. Mike read on as the entries moved back through time. The previous entry detailed Hope's conversations with her doctor determining that she was ready for hospice care. Hope reiterated her wish to die at home with her family and not in a facility. She wrote how much she hated being in the hospital. Hope's tone was resigned and brave. She talked wistfully about watching Amanda practice her gymnastics and reminded her daughter that though she wouldn't be there to watch her compete that summer, she'd be cheering her on from above. An entry earlier that year referenced Hope's "terminally ill daughter"; another from that same period detailed the experience of her and Fabian sitting with their children and explaining that Hope was going to die. Hope talked about how she's now too ill to care for her daughter and that Fabian is having to learn to take over. Interestingly, the date of this entry coincided with a hospital visit during which Sophia had had a positive culture for *Pseudomonas*. Hope detailed her own cancer treatments as well, and the toll they were taking on her body.

In one of the earlier entries, around Christmas 2008, Hope recounted a touching episode wherein their nanny, Crystal, had nominated the Ybarras to be adopted by a local family via a local radio station. The Ybarras were sponsored to the tune of several thousands of dollars, paying for months of gymnastics lessons for Amanda and dance lessons for Sophia, and even gifting the family a weekend at the high-end Inn on Lake Granbury. Mike confirmed with Crystal that she'd solicited the support from KLTY, 94.5 FM, a Christian radio station that ran a campaign each year to help the underprivileged during Christmas. He also spoke to the family that'd sponsored the Ybarras. The husband explained that they'd grown close with the family, and that he'd been inspired to help after losing his sister in a car accident earlier that year.

He was yet another stranger who'd been roped into Hope's deceptions, whose goodwill Hope had manipulated and betrayed.

THE NEXT DAY, Mike received a call back from Neos's Margaret, who provided a list of nine pathogens that Hope would have had access to when she worked there. Mike's ears perked up as she listed them off. Four of the nine—*Pseudomonas aeruginosa*, salmonella, *Staphylococcus aureus*, and *Candida albicans*—had shown up in Sophia's blood cultures.

"I also found out that one of the pathogens she ordered—*Klebsiella pneumoniae*—isn't even something we use at Neos," Margaret told him.

Mike had also discovered that the lab Hope had claimed to send the unauthorized pathogens to—Micro Lab, Inc.—had never received anything from her. She hadn't shipped the stolen pathogens anywhere.

LATER, MIKE TOOK a drive past the Ybarra house and saw a black Suzuki SUV parked in the driveway. Mike felt a rush of alarm—wasn't that Hope's car? It was crucial that Hope not be at the house. Any unsupervised contact could compromise the investigation and endanger the kids. Mike called Susan Putscher to see if she knew anything about where Hope might be staying.

Susan confirmed that the car Mike had seen was Hope's. "Her friends have told me she's at the house during the day when the kids aren't home and that she's staying in a shelter at night." Mike called the CPS investigator and told her he was worried that the Ybarras were violating the safety plan. Mike fumed with frustration. Why would Fabian let her in the house?

The next day, CPS investigator Carla Clark called Mike and confirmed his fears. She'd been by the Ybarra house and discovered Hope inside. Hope told her she'd been staying at the house during the day the past two weeks but hadn't, according to her, had any contact with the children. Mike's heart sank: by now he felt certain Hope had poisoned Sophia, and here she was, alone in the house all day with access to the children's food, medications, toiletries: any number of things she could contaminate in hopes of "proving" her daughter was legitimately ill. If her daughter began showing symptoms again outside of her care, Hope would use it as vindication that she hadn't been the cause. She didn't have to be able to see her children face-to-face to be a threat to them.

Looking back, Mike would realize that their grandmother Susan Putscher—the family member who'd been the most proactive about stepping in—would have made the ideal placement for the kids as she seemed to understand the most clearly how dangerous Hope was. But for CPS in all states, family reunification is the mandate. And there were no perfect solutions, often only bad and worse options. Medical child abuse investigations can and do stretch on for years, and it's obviously *also* damaging to remove kids from a loving parent who is not the perpetrator.

Leaving the children with Fabian could well have jeopardized the investigation, but as fate would have it, it was a misstep that might prove useful. The discovery that the Ybarras had broken the safety agreement gave Mike probable cause to search the property, so with any luck, he might find evidence of the missing pathogens that had mysteriously ended up in Sophia.

On the afternoon of May 13, 2009, Mike, along with two special agents and an investigator from the Food and Drug Administration, showed up at the Ybarras' three-bedroom redbrick house with a search warrant.

Fabian was standing on the patchy grass of the front yard when they arrived at his home. After Mike explained that he had a warrant to search the home, Fabian calmly led him and the others inside and put the family's two large dogs in the backyard so they wouldn't be in their way.

"I have to take Sophia to her counseling appointment," Fabian said as his dark-eyed daughter cleaved to his leg, her older sister by her side. "Can you just lock up when you leave?" he said as though Mike were his regular housekeeper rather than a police detective.

At this point in his career, Mike had executed more than a hundred search warrants at people's homes. This was ordinarily one of the tensest moments in an investigation, so he was used to being met with hostility: people yelling at him, calling their lawyers, throwing things, or bursting into tears. At a minimum, they were usually very nervous. Mike was not flippant about searching someone's home and always tried to be as respectful as possible—regardless of what the person was accused of, he understood what an invasion of privacy it was to have police officers pawing through your underwear drawer. But Fabian didn't even ask what they were looking for or demand to see the warrant. He had the same detached manner he'd had in his interview: utterly inscrutable.

The home was tidy considering how many people lived in such a relatively small space. It appeared every bit the typical family home, with kids' toys and family photos scattered throughout. The agents seized several things, including several opened bottles of children's medicine and a bag labeled "biohazard" found near the dining table—which turned out to contain the port for the central line that had once been inside of Sophia. The items were logged as evidence and shipped off to the FDA lab.

Mike left feeling unsure that they'd found anything useful. He'd been hoping to find the leftover pathogens in the pellet form Brian Angler had suggested might be there. Mike wanted to have as much evidence as possible before he interviewed Hope, but he couldn't wait forever. It was time for them to talk.

7

The Interview

The question of when to interview Hope weighed heavily on Mike. The timing of interviewing a suspect was always tricky, and this was an extraordinarily complex case. Hope's lies had seeped into every aspect of her life and it was difficult to know which ones were worth chasing. There were benefits to waiting until they had as much evidence as possible to confront her with—but on the other hand, waiting gave Hope time to gather her wits and go on the defensive, even to hire counsel. Any halfway decent lawyer wouldn't allow Hope to talk to Mike without being present.

The evidence in the case might look unusual and a little hard to follow, as Alana had feared, but it had its strengths:* between Dr. Ashford's affidavit indicating that the *only* possible cause of Sophia's drastic anemia was intentional bleeding, and the tie between the stolen pathogens and Sophia's positive blood cultures, there was plenty for Hope to answer for. But there wasn't something

---

* There was a lot of what is called, in law, "extraneous bad behavior." Mike explained that in Texas, this type of bad behavior can be used when considering an offender's sentence, even if it doesn't relate to their specific charge.

so definitive that a jury couldn't ignore it—the proverbial smoking gun. As to the elusive CF diagnosis, Mike had spent countless hours tracking down the four sweat tests that had been performed on Sophia throughout the spring of 2005: the first had been inconclusive, the second had been labeled "interfering substance," and the third and fourth had been positive. Mike thought this Goldilocks pattern looked awfully suspicious. He asked the hospital's IT team to check to see how many sweat tests had ever come back with that "interfering substance" result. The team searched all the way back to 1993—there hadn't been a single one other than Sophia's. With that in mind, he hoped to get Hope to just cop to faking the test, which she'd clearly done.

THERE IS NOTHING more powerful for a jury than hearing an account of the crime straight from the perpetrator's mouth. But Mike knew that without any admissions from Hope, a defense attorney could easily turn the blame on the doctors. Mike also knew that suspects were more inclined to bury themselves in an interview than one might think. If he could get to Hope before she clammed up, it could make all the difference.

But Mike knew he needed to come at Hope the right way. If he called and asked her to come to the station, he feared her next move would be calling a lawyer. If he could catch her in the moment, play the disinterested civil servant just checking the boxes, maybe she'd be so convinced he wasn't a threat that she'd let her guard down. After all, Hope was an incredibly smart, accomplished liar who'd been fooling doctors and scientists for over a decade. She'd probably think a stupid, flat-footed cop was no match for her. Mike could play that game.

Mike asked CPS investigator Clark when her next meeting with Hope was and if he could try to intercept her. Clark said Hope was coming in to sign a medical release form on May 21 and he could wait for her in the lobby of the Alliance for Children building, making it look like a serendipitous encounter, rather than an ambush.

With the date set, Mike prepared for the confrontation. After interviewing so many people who'd been deceived and victimized by Hope, Mike knew what he was up against, and he didn't want to waste his shot. He put in a call to Dr. Marc Feldman—the well-known expert whose work was some of the first Mike had discovered in researching MBP—who explained how unlikely it was that Hope would ever completely confess to the behavior. It was part of the psychopathology, he explained: offenders had an overinflated opinion of themselves and often enjoyed fooling people in positions of power.

Mike decided his best bet was to just let Hope tell the story of her children's health in her own words. Between his interviews with the doctors, Dr. Coffman's medical record review, and Investigator Clark's reports, Mike knew their histories like the back of his hand, but Hope didn't need to know that. Given the opportunity, would she be able to resist telling more lies? Much as someone with a factitious disorder might seem to be in control, it's not easy for them to resist the impulse to deceive, Dr. Feldman explained. "There is a compulsive or addictive quality to gaining attention, even if it's under false pretenses," he said.

Mike prepared for his interview as though facing off against a champion poker player. He knew to present himself as a rube, but there was also the question of whether to bluff. This was a tricky conceit in a police interview. Detectives can lie to suspects in order to elicit the truth, but this comes with stipulations. He could not, for example, present Hope with false documents; he could, however, present himself as less interested than he truly was. Moreover, he could claim they had evidence of things they actually did not. Mike knew that the latter tactic was a dangerous one: it was legal, yes, but there was also the question of how it might ultimately play to a jury. A canny defense attorney could easily make Mike out to be a bully: a coercive cop who'd bamboozled a poor, unsuspecting mother. No matter that Hope was the mastermind when it came to bamboozling. He would need to pick his bluffs carefully and make sure that Hope gave him what he needed without leading questions: he needed her not only to say that she did it, but to explain *how* she did it.

THE ALLIANCE FOR Children in Fort Worth is a welcoming and friendly place, built to look more like a cozy home than a government facility. It would offer an altogether different vibe than interviewing someone at a police station or in the DA's Office.

Mike sat in the lobby, anxiously waiting for Hope to arrive for her appointment with Investigator Clark. As soon as he saw her, he called her name. Hope was fair-skinned and green-eyed and her brown hair was cut into a sensible bob. She stood at five feet four, and Mike towered over her. She looked every bit the unremarkable mother next door.

"Hey, Hope," Mike said, reaching out to shake her hand, "I'm an investigator with the DA's Office, any chance we could talk for a few minutes? I've got this pile of medical records I'm going through and I just can't make heads or tails of it, I was hoping you could talk me through what's going on with Sophia's health?" Framing it as a problem on his desk that he just wanted to go away wasn't such a stretch; after decades in the field, Mike knew there were plenty of lazy civil servants who would see this case as a headache.

"Sure," Hope said, her voice soft.

"Thank you so much," Mike said. "We can go use one of the rooms upstairs and chat for a few minutes." The Alliance for Children partnered with the Fort Worth Police Department, meaning they had rooms wired for video and audio recording.

"How's your day been going?" Hope asked as they made their way to the room.

"Not too bad," Mike said. He could see right away how Hope's warmth and openness could disarm people. Her green eyes were intelligent and alert.

The interview room was small and windowless with a round table and a couple of chairs. "Why don't you have a seat right there?" Mike said, gesturing to the chair with the clearest path to the door. He wanted to avoid anything that might make Hope feel trapped, to prevent a lawyer making any argument that Hope had been coerced.

"Thanks for coming to talk to me," Mike said. "And just so you know, you're not under arrest or anything like that. You can leave anytime. And no matter what you say here today, you're going to be able to leave at the end of the interview, okay?" These caveats were a bit of legal business Mike needed to take care of before they got into it. Any casual *Law & Order* viewer will be familiar with a suspect being read their rights—what's officially known as the Miranda warning—but this warning only needs to be issued if a suspect is in custody. By letting Hope know she could leave anytime, Mike had alleviated the need for any more alarming-sounding official language. This let Mike strike the more casual, unmotivated tone that he was going for. And as compelling as the evidence he'd gathered thus far was, he didn't have enough to arrest Hope yet. That was one thing he couldn't bluff.

"Okay," Hope said, agreeably, "I understand." She sat with her arms tucked to her sides, making her appear smaller.

Mike started by asking Hope about her educational and professional background. Hope immediately copped to the fact that she'd been in some trouble over lying about her own health and education. It occurred to Mike that she was getting ahead of these facts to make herself appear honest and forthright.

"And how about your kids, can you talk me through their medical history?" Mike asked.

"Our oldest, Jacob, has always been healthy. My middle daughter Amanda was born premature, so she had some normal preemie stuff. Then she had some sleep apnea and muscle stiffness when she was a toddler, but we took her into Cook Children's and they said it was nothing to worry about." Mike clocked the first lie; he had on record that Hope had told Amanda's primary care physician that she had cerebral palsy, and she'd repeated this to her mother as well as other family members, friends, and coworkers. There was also the more outlandish story Hope had told her former coworker about Amanda coming back from the dead.

But Mike just nodded and scribbled some notes.

Hope went on to talk about Sophia, explaining that she'd been born twelve weeks premature and had continued to struggle with her health well past her first birthday, but that her initial pediatrician was of no help.

"I took her to see the pulmonologist, Dr. Harmon, and he said she ought to be improving. He sent me to Dr. Sikh, that's who suggested we test her for CF." She explained that before that test was administered, Sophia had been diagnosed with "failure to thrive" because she couldn't gain weight and—after failing a swallow test—a feeding tube was placed.

"They gave her the sweat chloride test twice at Children's Medical Center in Dallas," Hope told Mike. "She came back positive both times."

Another lie.

"We ended up leaving Dallas Children's because we weren't happy with them. That's when we went to Alabama for a while."

"Anything else going on with Sophia's health?"

"She had some issues with anemia for a while. It got really bad around 2006, 2007. But it resolved on its own."

Mike and Hope quickly developed a friendly rapport. Hope seemed relaxed and comfortable relaying the litany of medical details of her children's lives: a well-worn track for her, the interest that had consumed her life for years now. She sounded every bit the caring, authoritative mom, and it was easy for Mike to see how an interaction with her wouldn't raise any alarms for a doctor.

"I just want my kids back," Hope said, after they'd been speaking for about an hour. "I miss them so much. I know I have a bit of an 'honesty problem' when it comes to my health but I've *never* lied about my kids' health. I'd never do that."

Mike nodded understandingly. "There's some concerns I have, okay? One of them—and again, please be honest with me here today—is that going through the history, I don't feel you've been honest about Amanda. Have you ever told people that Amanda has cerebral palsy?"

Hope's eyes widened. "I told . . . I told . . . yes."

"Who did you tell?" Mike asked gently.

"My family," Hope said.

"And who else?"

There was a long pause before Hope said, "I wish I could remember."

Hope was treading lightly, Mike thought, trying to see what he knew. He laid a card on the table.

"Did you tell Dr. Sikh?" he asked.

"Potentially," Hope responded.

"When she went for treatment there?"

"Maybe. It's a potential," Hope responded.

"Okay," Mike said. "But you know she doesn't have it?"

"Yeah."

Mike needed more from Hope than one-word answers: the more detail she gave, the more likely her words could be considered a full confession, which was what Mike was after. "You know that," Mike reiterated. "It's not just me telling you that. You knew for a fact she didn't have cerebral palsy."

"Correct," Hope replied. Her demeanor had changed dramatically in the course of a few moments. She looked like a deer in the headlights.

"You can see the concern when you tell people Amanda has cerebral palsy and she doesn't."

"Yeah." Hope nodded.

"When did you stop telling people that?" Mike asked.

"Probably when I told Dr. Sikh," Hope said, letting out a nervous giggle. "That would be my guess."

"How old was Amanda then?" Mike asked.

"I don't know." There was a long period of silence, which Mike allowed to hang in the air. "I've made some bad choices," Hope continued. "I've made some really bad choices, but I'm on the right road. I see what I've done and I know your concerns and I can understand." Hope's words opened a path forward in their conversation: he knew she'd never tell him the *whole* truth, but if she was invested in making herself appear honest, perhaps she'd tell him more than she'd initially planned. Sensing a window, Mike switched the subject immediately.

"Hope," he said, "there are some more concerns about Sophia just from what you told me here today, okay? One of the biggest is that Dr. Sikh told me that it was you who wanted the cystic fibrosis testing, not him who suggested it." Hope didn't respond. "Also, Hope, when I talked to Dallas about the CF tests, there were four tests done in 2005. The second test that was done was disregarded for interfering substance. Do you understand what I am saying?"

"Yes," Hope replied.

"Do you know what that's about?" Mike pressed, trying to get her to tell him what exactly that interfering substance had been.

"I have no idea," she said, shrugging.

"Again, Hope, the only way to get past this is to be honest."

"I have no idea," Hope repeated.

"How do you think someone could manipulate that test?" Mike asked.

"I don't know," Hope replied.

Mike took another approach. "You have a background in chemistry, correct?"

"Yes." Gone were Hope's detailed explanations. She appeared to shrink further into her chair, her voice getting meeker.

Mike made a split-second decision to pull out his first bluff. "Children's Medical Center has that second test with the 'interfering substance' and they're currently reviewing it to see what that substance is, so we should know in a few days." He paused, letting the implication sink in. Then he moved on. "Back to your work as a chemist. We received a list of nine pathogens you had access to in the lab at Neos and we found Sophia testing positive for four of them."

Again, Hope feigned ignorance.

"Well, we've got one of Sophia's blood tests with the *Pseudomonas* out for DNA testing," he told her, another stone-cold bluff.

"There was no *Pseudomonas* in her blood," Hope interjected. "They only found it in her saliva."

Mike was caught off guard, realizing he should have double-checked the details before bluffing. He decided to play dumb. "I must have it wrong. I don't know anything about medicine," he said, aiming for a sheepish tone. "But how did those pathogens end up in your daughter, Hope?" he continued.

Again, she said she didn't know. When Mike pushed her on what an improbable coincidence it was—that the pathogens she had access to, and that had gone missing from her lab, were the same ones found in Sophia—she suddenly became tearful.

"Are you ready to be honest, Hope?" Mike tried.

Hope sniffled and wiped her eyes as another long silence persisted.

"There was a time . . . maybe twice . . ." Hope paused. Another minute went by. "That I would, um . . ." Hope trailed off, choking back tears.

"I know this is hard," Mike said. Television cop dramas often show investigators getting aggressive with suspects, demanding to know the truth, but Mike knew better. Empathy and friendly rapport were what got people to make admissions. He had to make Hope believe he could see her side of things, that telling the truth was in her best interest.

"I had, um, put *Pseudomonas* in her sputum, in the cup," Hope said, referencing the saliva samples that were gathered at Sophia's medical appointments. "But never in her. I would give them the sputum samples and say, 'Here's her sputum.' She would spit in a cup."

Mike clarified. "Okay. You would put the *Pseudomonas* in the cup?"

"Yes," Hope replied, "but not *in* her. I put it in the cup, but never in my daughter," she echoed adamantly.

Clearly Hope was minimizing her behavior, but it was still one hell of an admission.

Mike switched gears again. "What about the original CF tests in Dallas?" he asked.

"I don't know. I really don't," Hope responded.

"The lady told me that the machine never stopped running for salt, it was so high," Mike said carefully. Whatever substance Hope had used to create a false positive, she'd overdone it, using something with such high salt content that the machine couldn't even get an accurate reading. There was a long pause as Hope seemed to contemplate which way to go.

"And when you put the *Pseudomonas* in Sophia's blood, was that at Cook Children's Hospital?" Mike asked, pressing forward before Hope would come up with another lie.

"Just in her cup, never in her blood," Hope responded flatly. "She wouldn't have had *Pseudomonas* in her blood."

Mike's theory was that Hope had introduced potentially deadly pathogens via the port in her chest. Hope would later admit to Deanna Boyd—who covered Hope's story in depth for the *Fort Worth Star-Telegram*—in a prison interview that she'd poisoned her daughter by introducing the pathogens via Sophia's nebulizer treatments. But in the moment, all Hope would admit to was tampering with samples. Even as she was making admissions, she was still minimizing her behavior.

"I meant in her body," Mike said, but Hope was silent.

"I still come back to the issue with the CF and that test in Dallas," Mike continued, trying again. At this point they had been talking for nearly three hours. He paused. "You know how it was altered?"

Hope said nothing for a full four minutes—a seemingly endless pause. Mike knew silence could be a powerful tool, one that most detectives were too impatient to take advantage of.

Finally, he repeated, "You need to tell me how you altered it."

Hope fidgeted with her bracelet, her face twisting in a nervous grimace.

"I know," Mike said, "you need to tell me." He needed the admission to come from Hope herself; it would be infinitely more persuasive than his conjecture.

Hope's eyes remained fixed on Mike's gaze. The moments that passed between them felt like hours.

"Did you alter it?"

"I tried once," Hope said softly. Mike tried to conceal his surprise. This was her biggest confession yet. "They told me they had a lab error and I figured I messed it up."

"How did you try?" Mike asked, stretching back in his chair, both to relieve the tension in the room and in an attempt to make Hope speak up. Her voice had become so quiet that Mike feared the recording equipment might not pick it up.

"Nose spray," Hope responded.

"And where did you put the nose spray at?" Mike asked.

Hope pointed to her forearm and said, "Inside her . . ."

In his excitement, Mike finished Hope's sentence: "Inside her patch?"

"Yes," Hope replied.

"Why nose spray?"

Hope responded simply, "Salt water."

Mike's bluffs hadn't been perfectly executed, but they'd worked. Hope was only willing to admit to things he'd told her he already had proof on. But there was still one last big area he wanted to cover. The intentional bleeding. This, more than anything else, seemed the most likely avenue to bringing charges on Hope.

"Let's talk about the bleeding that happened in 2007," Mike began. "What happened with that?"

"I don't know. I'm being honest with you," Hope insisted.

"She lost half a liter of blood. And she's little," Mike said gently. "That's half of one of those big one-liter coke bottles. Nothing was found inside of her to indicate any blood loss. So the blood had to go outside. You were there," Mike pressed. "You gotta tell me how that blood got out of her body,"

"I don't have an answer to that," Hope said.

"You do," Mike insisted.

"Okay. Can you tell me what it is?" Hope said, trailing off in nervous laughter.

Mike didn't take the bait; he was not about to lay out his theory only to be later accused of leading her into a false confession. He dropped his head and mimicked her laughter. "You tell me. I'm not going to tell you anything. You tell me. I know you have the answer. When I say that, I know, and you know."

It was bizarre in a way, the charade. By this point Mike understood that Hope was, and had always been, completely aware of her actions. This was not the behavior of a delusional or confused person. Mike was an experienced interviewer, and he had stamina on his side: he'd sit there all day if he needed to.

Hope's voice stiffened. "I did not take liters of blood out of her. When I accessed her port, I would take one syringe of blood out."

"What would you do with that?" Mike asked.

"I would discard it in the trash. That's what the University of Alabama, when they told me to access her port, that's what they told me to do, pull that bad blood out, discard it, and then flush it, and then put the heparin in it, and that's what I would do when I accessed her port," Hope said defensively.

"Then where did the rest of the blood go?" Mike said.

"I'm being straight with you," Hope said, but for the first time in the interview, she dropped Mike's gaze and looked away.

"I've done this a long time," Mike said. "I know when people aren't being straight with me." He softened his voice. "You have come so far, I mean from February, you have come so far. This is just another step along that road," Mike said, trying to tap into the story of progress that Hope was telling herself and anyone who would listen, reverting to the theme of her being "honest" and coming clean.

"At this point, I feel like I'm diving into a big hole is what I'm doing," Hope said wistfully.

"What do you mean?" Mike asked. Maybe Hope was contemplating the consequences of what she'd already told him.

"That's just how I feel," Hope replied.

"Well, you know, there is always accountability for one's actions, I'm not going to lie to you there, but there is always the chance to get better." Mike paused, kicking himself. He knew better than to mention accountability in an interview, a word that immediately brings to mind *consequences*—the last thing you want a suspect thinking about.

Sure enough, Hope slipped right back into denial, saying she didn't have anything to do with the anemia episode. Mike tried asking about the incident of anaphylactic shock at Cook's, when Sophia had been given a treatment of iron dextran. Hope recalled the incident but denied pushing for the iron dextran transfusion, or insisting that the team skip the safety protocols. She again claimed that an iron dextran transfusion had been performed in Dallas on Sophia with no side effects. A lie.

Mike could see that Hope was done admitting to anything. It was time to wrap up the interview, before things got hostile. The tactic worked—Hope agreed to meet again if Mike had more questions, then she quickly exited the room.

It wasn't a full confession, but she'd admitted to plenty. He knew Hope could be criminally charged based on what she'd told him. Mike stretched his legs and got himself some coffee and a snack, his stomach suddenly growling as he came up for air after the intense hours-long conversation with Hope. Mike returned to the office feeling good about his work, doubly so as he recounted to Alana every chilling word she'd said. He realized how damning Hope's admissions sounded to fresh ears.

On May 26, 2009, a few days after Mike's interview with Hope, he got a message from her mother, Susan Putscher, who'd made an alarming discovery. As she'd been cleaning out the guest room, she discovered a plastic storage bin under the bed, filled with items belonging to Hope: birthday cards, financial documents, and old mail. Among the clutter, Susan had discovered a plastic bag containing three petri dishes taped together.

"Leave them where they are," Mike told her, "and don't let any-one else in that room for now."

Two days later, along with agents from the FBI, Mike went to Susan's house to recover the dishes. Susan signed the consent forms and showed the agents to the back bedroom where they took pho-tographs and confiscated the bag containing the dishes. Once re-trieved, the petri dishes were sent to the FBI's lab for analysis. A Neos employee confirmed that these particular dishes had been recorded as being placed in the lab's "discard" bin, and that two of them had contained *Pseudomonas* and one had contained staph.

WHILE HE AWAITED results, Mike checked in with Dr. Karen Schultz about Hope's claims that she'd only ever introduced pathogens into her daughter's saliva samples, and that she'd not actually put them in her body.

Dr. Schultz confirmed with her staff that Sophia had only had a sputum sample taken once, the previous December, when she'd tested positive for *Staphylococcus aureus* and *Pseudomonas aeruginosa*. Dr. Schultz explained that they didn't take samples in that manner from children younger than five—understandable, given young kids' unpredictable cooperation in spitting on command—and that they relied on throat swabs instead. The three other times Sophia had tested positive for the pathogens in question, a nurse had taken cultures directly from Sophia's throat with a swab. Meaning Hope had indeed put the pathogens *in* her daughter, despite her adamant denials. She'd not simply tampered with Sophia's saliva samples, she'd poisoned her. Dr. Schultz told Mike that there was no way Hope would have access to the samples from the throat culture after they'd been extracted, as they were taken directly to the lab by the nurses.

Mike's instincts were confirmed: even as Hope had made admis-sions, they'd been laced with lies.

The lab tests of the petri dishes wouldn't be in for several more days. In the meantime, Mike called Hope back in. This time, there was no delicate dance of trying to catch her with her guard down—she knew she was in trouble.

On June 5, Mike met Hope for a second time at the Alliance for Children. Because he felt he *did* have probable cause to arrest her, Mike took the additional step of reading Hope the full Miranda warning. Though he wasn't planning on detaining her then and there, he wanted to ensure that whatever Hope said to him that day would be admissible in court. After his first interview, Mike was feeling confident; she'd given him a lot to work with. But today, Hope's demeanor was steely and serious.

Mike told Hope about the petri dishes they'd recovered from her mother's house and asked her if she knew what was in them.

"*Pseudomonas aeruginosa* and *Staphylococcus aureus*," she said confidently.

"And where did you get them?"

"From my work, from the Neos lab."

"Are these them?" Mike asked, holding up a photo of the dishes.

Hope confirmed they were.

"There's something you said last time that's not adding up," Mike said, "which is that you only ever put the pathogens in Sophia's sputum sample. But she tested positive for *Pseudomonas aeruginosa* on multiple occasions, and yet she's only had one sputum sample taken, back in December."

Hope continued to insist she'd never actually poisoned her daughter with the pathogens from the lab, instead claiming that she took saliva samples at home and brought them with her when visiting Sophia's doctors.

Mike let out a little laugh. "Hope, do you realize how ridiculous that sounds?"

She laughed nervously, before acknowledging, "Yes."

Mike could feel Hope circling the truth, but it was as though every time she came close, a defense mechanism kicked in and out came another lie. Lying was her comfort zone. Mike tried again to pursue the question of Sophia's anemia, but Hope didn't take the bait, saying that it hadn't even been an issue for a long while.

"There's something else I've been wondering," Mike said, changing tactics. "When that news station did that follow-up report about you, you told them Sophia had terminal cystic fibrosis, but you'd already had her retested by that point. You knew she wasn't sick. Why did you tell them otherwise?" The news had quoted Fabian rather than Hope, but Mike still assumed she was behind it.

"I don't know," she said meekly. They were about an hour into their conversation. "I need to take a God break," Hope said, abruptly. "I need to go home and speak to God about my daughter."

"Hope, I know there's more here than what you're telling me," Mike said.

Hope leveled her gaze at Mike. "That's why I need to talk to God," she said. "I need to find the right path."

"There's only one path," Mike said gently. "That path is the truth."

"I'll talk to you again in a week," she said. And with that, the interview was over. Mike needed to file for an arrest warrant before he took Hope in, and in the meantime, perhaps God would tell her to confess.

But that June day would mark his last conversation with Hope.

SUMMER 2009 WAS busy for Mike, who was still adjusting to the forty-minute commute from Granbury to Fort Worth, and had a full caseload supporting two attorneys from the DA's Office, with a heavy summer trial schedule. Meanwhile, he was still pulling together all of the records for the Ybarra case and following up with doctors and witness interviews. Unlike the tidy timelines of *Law & Order: Special Victims Unit* episodes, cases like this came together in pieces, and Mike knew the DA would want him to have as much evidence as possible before proceeding with an arrest. In early September, Mike finally met with Alana Minton to present what he had: the pathogens, the faked CF tests, and—though Hope had made no admission regarding bleeding her daughter—the affidavits from the doctors saying this was the only possible explanation. Mike had been working the case for months, going down innumerable avenues trying to unearth Hope's deceptions: medical, financial, and otherwise.

Mike knew he had to be as close to perfect as possible: this case would be precedent setting for the DA's Office, the first of its kind to be prosecuted. There was a previous case that technically fell in the same category, but there'd been actual video evidence of the mother suffocating the child. It was nowhere near as circumstantial as Hope's case.

Alana told Mike that they were close, but he needed to tie up every possible loose end. Alana and another ADA accompanied Mike to visit Dr. Schultz to hear some of the information about the case straight from her. Mike knew they trusted him, but the details were so strange that he also knew it would help to hear directly from a medical professional.

Mike understood the need to be thorough on such a sensational and bizarre case, but he was worried, too. Fabian—who still had the kids—seemed increasingly resentful of the investigation. He was impossible to read: Was he simply shutting down in the face of his life falling apart, or did he not fully believe Hope was guilty? No one wanted to imagine that their partner had been doing monstrous things to their children under their own roof. Mike worried that the longer Hope walked free, the more of a threat she'd become to her children. With both her central line and feeding tube re-moved and her false CF diagnosis in her rearview, Sophia was now a happy, healthy child. But would she stay that way?

By mid-September, Alana finally agreed that Mike had enough to warrant an arrest. But on the morning of September 17, he got an unexpected phone call from CPS investigator Danielle Smart, who'd taken over the case.

"You'll never believe this," she said, "but I just got a call from Parkland Hospital in Dallas. They admitted Hope. She's in a diabetic coma."

She was right, Mike thought. He didn't believe it at all.

8

The Arrest

Mike didn't buy for a second that Hope's sudden convenient health crisis was real. After all these months studying her closely, he knew Hope's playbook. With consequences looming, it was time to evade them once again—this time by going into a coma. Mike just needed to figure out how she was pulling it off.

Mike put in a call to Dr. Shi, the psychiatrist who'd officially diagnosed Hope with Munchausen syndrome following the discovery that her cancer had been a hoax.

"I'm just calling to see if the doctors who are treating Hope have been in touch with you," Mike explained. "She's supposedly in a diabetic coma, but I have my concerns about the veracity of the claim."

"Understandable," Dr. Shi said. "She did mention that she was diabetic, but I didn't see test results myself. And unless the doctors at Parkland put in a request for the records, they have no way of knowing. Hope would have to sign a release." Mike wanted to bash his head against a wall; patient privacy was obviously important, but it was also a convenient shield for someone like Hope, who used it to exploit the medical system. The only way a doctor could warn another doctor that the patient they were treating had Munchausen—meaning that they would likely lie about their health—was if that patient *asked* their doctors to share and exchange information. The same was true on the pediatric side, for any doctor suspecting Munchausen by proxy: a parent would have to consent to sharing their child's medical records.

The next day, Mike got a call back from a Dr. Kennedy, the attending physician who was treating Hope at Parkland. Given that Parkland was a teaching hospital, Hope's case information was likely passed on to Dr. Kennedy secondhand from a resident. The attending physician may not have even laid eyes on Hope. But Mike didn't realize this at the time.

"Hope was admitted with a brain injury," Dr. Kennedy explained. "We think her seizure disorder may have caused a stroke."

"You're sure she has an injury to the brain?" Mike asked.

He confirmed: "We've done an MRI and an EEG that show substantial damage to the brain."

A brain injury seemed impossible to fake, yet he couldn't shake the feeling that Hope had caused the incident. "Could something like this have been caused by an overdose?"

"It's possible," the doctor conceded.

"What's her prognosis?"

"Grim, I'm afraid," Dr. Kennedy said. "About a fifty-fifty chance of whether she'll ever be able to live an independent life again."

Mike put in a call to the hospital's legal team, requesting that they provide updates on Hope's condition. He could feel the case slipping away from him: Even if she'd caused her own injury, an incapacitated woman couldn't stand trial. After coming so close, justice for little Sophia felt further away than ever.

Three days later, Mike got a follow-up call from Samantha, the social worker on the hospital floor at Parkland where Hope had been transferred from the ICU. Mike explained to Samantha the entire sordid history of Hope's medical deceptions.

"How is Hope doing?" Mike finally asked.

"Not well," Samantha said. "I saw her this morning and she could barely lift her head."

The odds of bringing Hope to justice felt ever narrower.

"Call me if she makes a miraculous recovery," Mike said ruefully.

The next day, he resolved to keep working the case even with this latest wrench in the machinery. Sophia deserved as much, and Mike couldn't let it go. He was convinced that Hope had somehow found a way to fake a brain injury.

Sure enough, two days later, Mike got a call from Samantha. Hope had made amazing strides: She was suddenly able to sit up and even stand. In fact, her progress seemed suspiciously fast to doctors—this sort of leap in recovery was impossible with the type of injury Hope had allegedly sustained.

In addition, the MRI that had shown such serious brain damage? It didn't exist: Hope claimed she had a cochlear implant, something that prevented an MRI of her head. This confirmed Mike's growing suspicion that Dr. Kennedy had simply signed off on paperwork and hadn't taken his call very seriously. And the EEG that had been performed hadn't shown "substantial damage" at all—in fact, it had been inconclusive.

"YOU'LL NEVER GUESS who's feeling better all of a sudden," Mike said, leaning into Alana Minton's office doorway.

"You're joking," Alana said.

Mike shook his head and explained the whole convoluted story about the MRI.

"Mike," Alana said, "you've got to move on this."

"I know," Mike said. "I'm worried about those kids if Hope gets released."

They sat together going back over the details of the case so Mike could put together the arrest warrant. Alana determined that Hope's act of bleeding her daughter—which led to the anemia and IV iron treatment that could have killed her—could be charged under injury to a child. This was far from the only dangerous thing Hope had done to her daughter, but without a direct admission from Hope it was the straightest line, even if it was imperfect.

OVER THE NEXT two weeks, Hope was transferred to a rehab center and her condition continued to improve. She began to talk about wanting to go home to her children. Mike couldn't let that happen, but the DA's Office couldn't move forward with an arrest if she still required specialized medical care. At last, Hope was well enough that she could be treated by the facilities at the county jail.

On October 16, Hope's father, Paul Putscher, wheeled her out of HealthSouth City View Rehabilitation Hospital where they were met by two Tarrant County sheriff's deputies, who put Hope in handcuffs and booked her.

Hope sat in the county jail for months while she awaited trial. Her bond was set at $25,000, but no one was willing to bail her out. At last, on October 18, 2010—almost exactly one year after she was arrested—Hope accepted Alana's plea offer of ten years in prison. At the time, Mike was disappointed. Ten years seemed light for someone who could have killed her own child. But he trusted Alana's instincts, and she turned out to be right: a ten-year sentence was a massive win for a medical child abuse case where the child was still alive.[1] Furthermore, there were huge risks for both sides in going to trial. So much of this case depended on the overall picture of Hope's behavior: the faked cancer, the lies about her older daughter's health. On Hope's end, if a guilty verdict was reached, *all* of her extraneous bad acts could come into play in the punishment phase and land her with a stiffer sentence.

On November 17, 2010, Hope Ybarra was transferred to a women's prison, where she served every day of her ten-year sentence.

FABIAN YBARRA VISITED Hope in prison on one occasion, partly in an attempt to figure out what became of their once healthy savings account, which had by then been decimated. He eventually discovered that she'd paid for many of her innumerable doctor visits in cash to avoid them showing up on her insurance, like an addict hiding the evidence of their drug use. On this point—and with regard to everything else Fabian or anyone in her life has tried to confront her on—Hope simply told him she "couldn't recall" what had happened to the money.

"To this day, her favorite line is: I don't remember," Fabian told me, though he believes this to be an evasive maneuver and maintains that Hope remembers everything. "She's still the victim," Fabian said. "She will always be the victim."

When I sat down with Fabian in Fort Worth for an interview for the very first season of *Nobody Should Believe Me*, it had been more than a decade since Hope was sentenced. He seemed much different from the inscrutable man that Mike had encountered. He was affable and open, a father who's done his best under unimaginably difficult circumstances.

"He probably thinks I don't like him," Fabian said, reflecting on his interactions with Mike all those years before.[2] He's right on this count—until I spoke to Fabian, Mike was under the impression that Hope's ex-husband hated his guts. Fabian explains that at the time, he was flat overwhelmed trying to work and also care for three traumatized kids, and Mike's relentlessness was simply too much to take. He understands why Mike may have thought he wasn't ready to believe everything about Hope, but Fabian gave a different explanation when we spoke. He told me that not only had he been preoccupied with the issues surrounding their finances, but a lawyer friend had advised him to not show all his cards when dealing with the cops. Over a decade later, Fabian said he was grateful for Mike, and that he now understood that Mike had done what needed to be done to protect his kids.

The three Ybarra children are grown-up now and haven't had any contact with Hope since her arrest, other than the occasional letters she's sent them. Fabian told me that he initially held those letters back, but began sharing them with his kids on the advice of his daughters' therapist. Even though Sophia—who was five and a half at the time of Hope's arrest—was the victim of the worst of Hope's abuse, Fabian thinks it was even harder, in some ways, on his older kids, because they were more aware of what was happening and often had questions Fabian didn't know how to answer. "I had to go to therapy to figure this out, how to approach them," he said. "And now they can ask me anything."

Fabian doesn't hide the truth from his kids, but he also wants to give them time to grow up and sort their own lives out. "I think they're at a time in their life where they're okay. They don't need the disruption." Fabian leaves it to his kids if and when they want to reconnect with Hope, but he thinks that time is probably far in the future, if it ever comes.

Fabian eventually mended fences with the Putscher family, though he said it took time. "I was angry at everybody and I did blame them," he says, acknowledging how his relationship with his in-laws suffered during the investigation. "I shouldn't have blamed them. They were just as much victims as I was. It didn't come overnight," Fabian said of their eventual reconciliation, but he wanted his kids to have a family. "My sisters told me, just get as many people to love them as possible. Just because one player is out of the game, the other ones are still in there."

All of the Putschers told me what a great dad Fabian has been, and how much they admire him. They believe that Fabian was in an impossible situation and that he ultimately did the right thing. If rejecting the perpetrator seems like the obvious and inevitable choice for a father in this situation, it isn't. Many dads in similar cases stick by their wives, regardless of how much evidence they're confronted with, defending them even in the face of prison sentences and the death of their children.

When I first began researching this story, I sent a message to Susan Putscher's Facebook account, only to discover that she had passed away just months before Hope was released from prison. I was happy to learn that she ended up reconciling with Paul and that they spent the rest of Susan's days together. After she had a heart attack in 2017, Paul retired from his job to spend more time with her before she passed two years later. "I think it was God's gift to us that we had those two years," Paul said. The couple— married as teenagers by a justice of the peace for six dollars—had spent forty-four years together when Susan died, with Paul at her side.

Fabian also grew much closer to Susan in her later years, and he told me that her death had been hard on him and the Ybarra kids. He smiles remembering a cross-country road trip Susan took Sophia on several years earlier: "I still have pictures of them and they were so happy." Hope's three children went through an unimaginable ordeal, but with a protective family surrounding them—including Susan, who'd had to make the agonizing decision to report her own daughter—they'd survived, and had gone on to enjoy the healthy lives they were meant to have.

When it came to the Ybarras, the system ultimately worked as it was supposed to. But this was only Mike's second medical child abuse case. Little did he know just how rare this kind of outcome would be.

9

Aftermath

It was a warm summer day in July 2021 when my then podcast producer Tina Nole and I were driving a rental car across the arid, empty stretch of land that separates Boise, Idaho, from the tiny town where Hope Ybarra—now once again Hope Putscher—lives. I had been texting back and forth with Hope for months, and had become increasingly convinced that this meeting was never going to happen. Even though we'd messaged just that morning to confirm, I wasn't going to believe it until I laid eyes on her. If there's one thing we know about Hope, it's that she can't be trusted.

Hope did three televised interviews while she was serving her ten-year prison sentence, which ended in 2019. One was with Deanna Boyd, the reporter from the *Fort Worth Star-Telegram* who broke the story of Hope's case and did extensive interviews with everyone involved, including Hope.[1] The second was with a local news affiliate during the Christopher Bowen trial in 2019, a complicated medical child abuse case in which Christopher's father, Ryan Crawford, fought for years (with guidance from Mike) against a disbelieving system to finally get custody of his boy, who had undergone hundreds of unnecessary procedures at the hands of his abusive mother in the first decade of his life.[2] And the third was for the debut episode of a true crime program hosted by actor B. D. Wong of *Law & Order: Special Victims Unit* called *Something's Killing Me*.[3] It was during that final interview that Hope uttered the phrase that was emblazoned on my brain the moment I heard it, and eventually became the title of my podcast. The reporter asked Hope why he should believe what she was saying to him now, after she'd told so many lies. "Nobody should believe me," Hope said. These are perhaps the truest words she has ever uttered. It was this comment, along with the fact that Hope had been willing to be interviewed at all, that made me think that Hope could offer some insight on what this whole ordeal had been like for her.

BY THE TIME of my interview with Hope, I'd spent many hours with her father, Paul, and her siblings Robin and Nick. It had been a moving and healing experience for me. They were a warm, loving family who didn't deserve what Hope had put them through. We'd also been a warm, loving family; we didn't deserve what we'd been through. But the more time I spent with the Putschers, the more I wanted to talk to Hope herself. I'd come five hundred miles on that July day to ask the questions and say the things that I knew I'd never be able to say to my own sister. Hope was my proxy.

Tina and I pulled up at the burger joint and snagged a booth. The restaurant had a cheery fifties malt-shop aesthetic and was playing Motown music. Tina and I sat on one side of the booth facing the door. It seemed just as likely that Hope would never appear at that door as it was that she'd walk in any moment. When she did appear, I was flooded with simultaneous anxiety and relief that felt reminiscent of my single days waiting on some flaky boyfriend. Hope's hair was long now, halfway down her back, and she wore a tie-dyed T-shirt and loose orange trousers.

She was warm in person, friendly and disarming. In preparation for the interview, I'd been trying very hard to compartmentalize everything I knew about her case. The word "monster" had been used frequently in the news coverage about Hope, but I wanted to make every effort to see her humanity. Framing Hope, or any perpetrator, as a monster is utterly unhelpful. If abusers were monsters, inhuman aberrations, they'd be far less dangerous because they'd be much more obvious to us. The fact that Hope appeared every bit the compassionate, harmless mother next door was exactly what made her so terrifying. I'd spoken to Mike a lot in preparation for this interview and he'd told me that under no circumstances should I be alone with Hope. I'd kind of laughed in response, imagining myself in danger by simply sitting with the diminutive fortysomething Hope.

"Okay, Mike," I said.

"Andrea," he said, and paused. "I'm serious." Mike had spent countless hours looking into all of Hope's worst deeds. She'd poisoned her coworker, she'd poisoned her own daughter; there was no reason to think anyone was safe around Hope.

I didn't have to fake empathy for Hope, because by this point in my journey, I genuinely felt it. Once, she'd had an enviable life with a loving family, tons of friends, a handsome husband, three beautiful children, and a great career. After ten years in prison, all of that was gone, and she was living on the fringes of society; the only person from her old life who took her calls was her sister, Robin. Once a lead chemist at a pharmaceutical lab making a six-figure salary, Hope now told me about her new job as a greeter at Walmart. You can think what you want about what Hope deserves, but there's no question that she's paid a price for her crimes.

Hope was currently living with a boyfriend, whom she had met through a fellow inmate—he joined us about ten minutes in—and their Siberian husky, which she proudly showed me pictures of. At first, Hope spoke with the familiar speech impediment that she'd affected in her previous interviews. She explained that she was deaf and would throw in some occasional sign language. I knew this wasn't true, but didn't challenge her on it. I wasn't there to push Hope on the facts—that would be a fool's errand. Instead, I wanted to see what insights she might have after what she'd been through, to get some sense of what the world looked like through her eyes, to possibly begin to unravel the question that plagued me most about both her and my sister: Why would someone with so much going for them throw it all away? I was hoping to mine that little window of honesty she'd opened when she'd told the reporter that nobody should believe her.

After months of back-and-forth with Hope, trying to schedule this meeting, I'd expected her to be reticent with me. But once we were sitting together, it felt like the floodgates opened. She became tearful almost immediately.

"What I would say to all of them," she told me when I asked about her family, "is that I am so sorry for everything that I put them through. I was selfish. I love my family. Especially my children. More than anything on this planet. It was not fair, not right what I put them through. Especially Sophia. She was always my baby girl. And I have so much regret for hurting her, and then in the process hurting the other two as well. And I destroyed what was a wonderful marriage. And I will carry that guilt for the rest of my life for hurting all of them."

Hope's words echoed her tearful comments in previous interviews. It was moving to watch her appear to grapple with this as I was sitting with her. She *looked* like someone wracked with guilt, but as with everything with Hope, it was impossible to know what was real. "I don't think she was ever sorry for what she did," Fabian told me when I interviewed him on my podcast. "I don't think it's genuine." I know exactly what he means. Once someone has told a certain kind of lie—created an entire parallel reality that goes up in smoke—it becomes impossible to believe them ever again. Even if you want to.

I asked Hope what she wanted people to know about her.

"That I'm an individual," she told me. "I have feelings. I love my family, especially my children, more than anything on this planet, regardless of what I've done and the choices that I've made."

I admit: I've wondered whether someone who does the things Hope has done is even capable of love. The experts are certainly in agreement that an individual must have a profound lack of empathy to engage in this kind of behavior. But there is the separate question of whether Hope *believes* she loves her family. I can accept that perhaps she sincerely *believes* that she loves them, even if her version of love looks very different from mine.

"What do you think people have the wrong idea about with you?" I asked.

"Based on the results of my other interviews, their total focus was that I'm an attention seeker. And I'm not, that's the last thing I am."

If not attention, I asked, what does she think she was after?

"I wanted to feel loved. I wasn't looking for the attention to be focused on me. I wanted to feel loved, I didn't and I don't know why. I had a wonderful family."

I appreciate the nuance here because Hope is right: there's something about "attention seeking" that feels a little lightweight to describe the motivations of a Munchausen by proxy perpetrator. Love, on the other hand, is a deep and ancient human need that will drive people to all sorts of extreme behaviors. It's as if someone like Hope is unable to metabolize love in the normal way, so she did wild and destructive things to be able to *feel* loved, to feel less alone.

Hope described herself as a loner growing up. She's said in interviews before that she felt like an outcast as an adolescent, but I found this increasingly dissonant the more I learned about what she was like before any of this had happened. As I pointed out to Hope when we spoke, this wasn't how anyone who knew her in her old life described her. My producer offered to play some of the audio of what her little brother Nick had to say about how much he looked up to her. This led to one of the strangest moments in the interview as her boyfriend—who had jumped in throughout the interview with the occasional incomprehensible non sequitur—interjected to insist that Hope was deaf and it wouldn't work to play the audio for her.

It was as though everyone else at the table had forgotten about this ruse of Hope's: she'd begun speaking in a normal voice and had halted her sign language a few minutes into the interview. In that moment, I was genuinely unsure if the boyfriend *believed* she was deaf or if he was covering for her. Tina assured him that she'd turn the audio way up and that she'd explain what Nick was saying as we went. She played the tape and Hope was silent—though she became visibly emotional as she listened to Nick describing how much he admired his big sister, how she had inspired him to go to college.

It was clear in talking to her that Hope's interior view of her life does not match up with reality. Abusing your child is, by its nature, a desperate act. And, listening to Hope, it was evident that despite how good her life might have looked from the outside, she'd felt desperately alone. I asked her what advice she'd give to a mom who found herself in that same situation.

"Look outside the box," Hope replied. "Don't look internally because you are loved regardless. You may not feel that way, but you are, but you don't want to wait until you get to the other side of a bad decision to be able to see it. Don't wait until it's too late. That's what I did."

I ask Hope what she would do differently if she could go back in time, if she could return to the moment before everything escalated to the point of no return.

"I would have told my mom. Because I know she would have helped, and if she couldn't help, she would've found the right help."

Everything I've learned about Susan Putscher leads me to think Hope is right on this count. Susan was doggedly loyal and tough. I'm convinced that if she'd known what her daughter was struggling with, she would have done anything for her. Susan was sharp and knowledgeable about mental health, having worked as an occupational therapist for geriatric patients; if anyone could have figured out how to get Hope the support she needed, it was her.

Hope's reflection about her mom was the most poignant moment of the interview for me. It's as though both Hope and I can suddenly see those two paths diverging: what might have been if Hope had told Susan what she was going through, rather than continuing to deceive everyone around her. Susan would have rallied; that's who she was. And that's what mothers can be at their best: their child's most devoted champion, long into adulthood. The kind of mother that Hope's children will never have.

In one important way, my sister's story is very different from Hope's: She's never been charged with a crime, and she's never permanently lost custody of her children. She didn't go to prison or lose her husband. But she did lose us—or rather, we lost each other. I wasn't the one who decided to become estranged from her. When she was first investigated for medical child abuse, I wasn't willing to say I thought nothing was wrong. And for that, I was ousted from her and her children's lives, as were my parents, the rest of the family, and all of the many tight-knit friends she'd had for decades.

Maybe that doesn't feel like a loss to her—maybe she thinks she's well rid of the lot of us—but it's hard to imagine that's entirely the case. I don't think becoming estranged from one's entire family is a desired outcome for anyone. For me, the idea of what might've been with my smart, accomplished sister is always glimmering out there in a ghostly parallel reality. By the time the schism happened,

I believe she'd been suffering for a while, that she'd felt alone. What else could drive someone to do all that? I wished I could've helped her. I wish she'd ever asked.

And it's this moment in my conversation with Hope that gives me the opportunity to say something to her that I will never get to say to my own sister: I can help her if she wants it. I explain that, in fact, there is treatment available and that if she truly wants to have a relationship with her family again—especially her kids—there may be a healthy way to do so. I tell her that I'm on a committee with some of the top experts on MBP in the world, and that I've learned from my colleagues about how MBP perpetrators—the tiny percentage of them who are willing to be accountable and get help—can heal.

Mary Sanders, a clinical professor of psychiatry at Stanford and a leading expert on treating MBP perpetrators, explained to me the model they use. "What we found is that the most important aspect of treatment is being able to acknowledge that the abuse has occurred."[4] Of course, this is particularly challenging with MBP perpetrators, because "they tend to blame others, not take responsibility, and get their needs met indirectly using deception. It's very difficult for them to admit and acknowledge that they've engaged in these behaviors, not only to others, but to themselves." Treatment, she told me, is challenging and lifelong, requiring consistent reevaluation to ensure a person isn't slipping back into old behaviors. But I'd seen signs that Hope was capable of admitting her wrongdoing. Maybe she could be one of the rare success stories.

Of course, it isn't up to me whether or not Hope gets help, or whether she ever has a relationship with anyone in her family again. Hope said she understands that any relationship she has with any of them will have to be on their terms.

"I have to be okay with that, with my entire family," Hope said. "When I hurt them, I lost my terms."

I told her candidly that it would be an intense recovery process that would continue for the rest of her life. I repeated that if she was willing to put in the work, I'd help her.

"I don't shy away from hard work," she said. Hope told me she'd do anything to have her family back. When the interview was over, she and I hugged each other. I reminded her she had my number and that I was sincere in my offer to work with her to get treatment.

I never heard from Hope again.

PART 2

THE
COPYCAT

10

What Happened to Alyssa?

On August 23, 2011, a young mother named Brittany Phillips brought her three-year-old daughter, Alyssa, to the emergency room at Cook Children's. Alyssa was small for her age and adorable, with a heart-shaped face, green eyes, and a head of auburn curls. Her twenty-eight-year-old mom, Brittany, pale and round-faced, had stringy brown hair and a brash demeanor. During the visit, Brittany told doctors that her daughter had been constantly vomiting and was severely dehydrated. She gave a detailed health history for her toddler, who had spent much of her young life in the hospital after being born premature. After persistent trouble gaining weight, Alyssa had a G button—similar to a gastro tube—inserted in her stomach to help her get nutrition enterically, and had undergone a surgical procedure called Nissen fundoplication in order to correct the reflux that was thought to be inhibiting her ability to keep down food. Alyssa was below the fifth percentile in weight and height for her age: worryingly small.

The ER staff immediately found Brittany's behavior off-putting: she was abrupt and rude, a human bulldozer constantly complaining that "no one would tell her what was going on" despite the nurses and doctors spending ample time at her daughter's bedside. Brittany said she was worried about swelling in her daughter's limbs and high blood pressure, though testing revealed neither. The nurses noticed that when Alyssa complained she was hungry, Brittany insisted that she couldn't eat because it would make her sick. A nurse brought her some cereal at one point, and when she went to check on Alyssa, the otherwise cheerful three-year-old began screaming not to take her Trix away. The startled nurse reassured her that she could have as much as she wanted, only for Brittany to interject that no, she couldn't, it would give her diarrhea and ulcers. When Alyssa told a nurse that she was thirsty, she offered her something to drink, but Brittany wouldn't allow it, claiming her daughter had trouble swallowing and could aspirate. Another nurse saw Brittany give Alyssa a quarter of a graham cracker as she wailed from hunger. Brittany insisted to the nurse that she would get sick if she had more and, besides, "She's not hungry, she's just tired."*

Two days into their stay, Brittany's behavior took a distressing turn in the middle of the night. The nurse on duty walked in to find Brittany visibly upset and ranting as she cradled her sleeping daughter in the narrow hospital bed. First she claimed that her daughter's lips were turning blue. The nurse noted that the child was a bit pale but otherwise looked fine. Then Brittany said, frantically, that her fever wouldn't come down. The nurse noticed that she had four blankets piled on Alyssa and told her to take them off of her.

Brittany raised her voice and swore at the staff, demanding that Alyssa's blood get tested. Alarmed, the nurse encouraged Brittany to take a walk in the hallway to calm down, as she didn't want her

* Because the parent controls this aspect of hospital treatment, nurses and doctors have no ability to force a mother to let a victim eat. Medical professionals' only recourse is to report the mother to CPS.

to scare Alyssa, who'd been awakened by the commotion. Brittany bellowed at her daughter, "Baby, are you scared?" Alyssa shook her head, seemingly cowed. Brittany turned her ire back on the nurse, yelling, "I've fought hard not to lose her and I'm not going to lose her now!" As the nurse attempted to soothe Brittany, the phlebotomist came to take Alyssa's bloodwork. As the little glass vials filled with her daughter's blood, Brittany immediately quieted. By the time the blood was sent off to be tested, she was laughing and joking with staff.

But the results of that blood test were as alarming as they were baffling. The tests showed that Alyssa had multiple polymicrobial blood infections, with one that included three different organisms (staph, *E. coli*, and viridans strep). When the nurse came in the next morning to tell Brittany that her daughter had a possibly life-threatening blood infection, her reaction was downright bizarre. She was talking on the phone and wouldn't hang up. "What are the numbers?" Brittany asked blandly; when the nurse told her, she repeated the values to whoever was on the other end of the line.

"Do you have any questions?" the nurse asked, confused.

Brittany ignored her. After a beat, she turned to the nurse and said, "You can leave now, I'm on the phone."

Later that day Brittany called for a nurse, again complaining that Alyssa's lips were turning blue. "Her lips have been purple all day," Brittany wailed, "and nobody seems to think so! I am her mother and I know something is wrong. She could be going septic or she could have aspirated something into her lungs and no one is listening to me!"

Alyssa's oxygen levels were normal, but as the nurse was checking them, she saw that there were multicolored marks on her hands and face. "Has she been painting?" she asked, utterly baffled.

"She wouldn't put paint in her mouth," Brittany spat out. But a closer look revealed a bluish color on Alyssa's teeth: a scenario any parent of a toddler with art supplies would recognize.

Brittany also continued to insist that Alyssa had a fever. When they rechecked her temperature and got a reading of 99.8, slightly above normal, Brittany's reaction was bizarre. "Yeah! She has a temperature," she exclaimed. Once again, she piled blankets up to Alyssa's neck, which the nurse asked Brittany to remove.

For all of Brittany's erratic behavior, Alyssa's blood infection was very real and very concerning, so the doctors scrambled to get to the bottom of it. There were several possible explanations for the particular combination of organisms that had shown up in Alyssa's bloodstream. An untreated urinary tract infection was one; another was severe food poisoning—but Alyssa had neither condition.

There was a third possibility that registered now: she'd been intentionally poisoned.

As concerns about Brittany mounted, Alyssa was moved to a room with video surveillance. She was told there was an issue with the plumbing in her current room; indeed, it was nothing out of the ordinary to move a patient during a prolonged hospital stay.

On the evening of August 26, the new nurse on duty went in to introduce herself to Brittany. Brittany trained her steely gaze on the nurse and pointed straight at the camera in the ceiling and asked the nurse, "What is that?"

The nurse had been working there for fifteen years and no one had ever asked her such a question.

"Is it a camera?" Brittany asked, beginning to cry. "I would never hurt my child!"

The nurse tried to reassure her that no one said she had. And they hadn't, at least not to Brittany's face. But the bizarre series of events over the course of this hospital stay were merely the tipping point in a long cascade of incidents of suspected abuse. Those several days that Alyssa spent in the ER would change the course of her and her mother's lives. But the mystery of what really happened there would take years to uncover.

BORN IN TEXAS in 1983 and mostly raised outside Chicago, Brittany Phillips had a troubled upbringing. Her father, Joshua, worked in the accounting department at Radio Shack and her mother, Melinda, was a bank manager. The two had a tumultuous marriage and divorced when Brittany was only five; Brittany would later describe herself as having almost no relationship with her father, who died when he was fifty-nine. Brittany, whose childhood had been rough, suffered from mental health issues. The youngest of four children, she was known in her family for doing destructive and dramatic things for attention. "I love my sister," her older sister Melissa would later tell Mike about Brittany, "but the reality is she has mental problems and has for many years. She was a nutcase."

While Hope Ybarra had appeared happy and outgoing in her early years, and clearly had a loving upbringing, everything about Brittany's story struck a sharp contrast. No one seemed to have a single good thing to say about her. There is no record of any Munchausen behavior in Brittany's case, but everyone who knew her growing up described her as troubled and unstable. Family members recounted her numerous suicide attempts. Whether she really meant to end her life, only Brittany would know, but her family interpreted these incidents as attempts to create drama and seek attention. The troubled teenager's behavior took a toll on her family, which wasn't especially equipped to deal with her.

Family members didn't think Brittany's attempts were in earnest: she would take pills, for instance, and then immediately call her mother or grandmother, asking them to call an ambulance. "Everything Brittany has ever done was for attention," Melissa said in her interview with Mike. "I don't know how else to describe it." Each time someone else in the family became the center of attention, Melissa recalled, it would lead to a dramatic episode with Brittany. She was, at several points, taken into inpatient care at a mental health clinic in Champaign, Illinois, and was ultimately diagnosed with borderline personality disorder (BPD), a complex condition that can lead to intense emotional swings and a debilitating fear of rejection and abandonment, as well as suicidal ideation and threats of self-harm. According to Dr. Marc Feldman, BPD is extremely common in MBP offenders, adding yet another layer of complexity to these cases.

Brittany graduated high school in 2002 and worked occasional fast-food jobs and for a time as a certified nursing assistant, which requires a several-weeks course and involves mostly administrative and low-level patient care tasks. In her late twenties, Brittany became pregnant as the result of a short-lived relationship with Lucas, an old high school friend. The two weren't close, and Lucas was out of the picture by the time Alyssa was born.

In late February 2008, months in advance of her May due date, Brittany went to Provena Hospital in Urbana, Illinois. She arrived in a panic and told the staff there that she hadn't felt the baby move in several days. Alyssa Phillips was delivered via emergency C-section at twenty-nine weeks, weighing only 2.52 pounds. Though the odds of survival for babies born at twenty-nine weeks are high if they receive good care, they can struggle with a litany of issues due to their low weight and underdeveloped organs and nervous system. Alyssa was airlifted to a hospital in Peoria where she remained in the NICU for eight weeks. By the time Alyssa was released from the hospital eight weeks later in April, she was gaining weight and doing well.

Before moving to Illinois as a kid, Brittany, her siblings, and their mother, Melinda, had lived in the Fort Worth area, near members of their extended family. Melinda was still living there in

2008; now in her sixties, she was struggling with numerous health problems including COPD (chronic obstructive pulmonary disease), arthritis, and diabetes. Melinda was a hard woman, and she and Brittany had always had a complicated relationship. Nevertheless, in November 2008 when Brittany's stepdad passed away, Brittany took Alyssa and moved back to Fort Worth from Illinois to care for her mom.

After they moved to Texas, Brittany's hospital visits with Alyssa became more frequent. In April 2009, Brittany began bringing Alyssa to the Early Childhood Intervention (ECI) center in south central Fort Worth, claiming that her daughter wouldn't eat. But the specialists there observed Alyssa eating as much as her mother would allow her to, and even scrambling up onto Brittany's lap to get the food out of her hands. Still, by her second birthday, Alyssa had been to the hospital or pediatrician's office approximately seventy-five times, often admitted for several days at a time for various treatments and procedures. This was in addition to her frequent visits to the ECI. Taking care of any young child can feel like a full-time job, but this was especially true for Alyssa. Her care consumed Brittany's days.

Being in a new town was isolating, and on top of that, Brittany was a first-time mom with a constantly ill child and an ailing parent to take care of. So Brittany would look online to make connections and build a community for herself in Fort Worth. During her pregnancy, she'd joined a group on WhatToExpect.com, for mothers with babies due in May 2008—Alyssa's original due date—where Brittany discovered a cluster of moms who lived locally.

One mom from the group, Lisa, met Brittany for the first time at a local Chick-fil-A just outside Fort Worth. The moment the two women and their toddlers were settled in with their chicken sandwiches and french fries, Brittany launched into Alyssa's litany of health issues. After being born so early, Brittany said, Alyssa had all kinds of developmental delays. At two she was small for her age, and was having trouble gaining weight because she struggled with swallowing both solid foods and liquids. Brittany told Lisa she had to put thickener in anything her daughter had to drink so that she wouldn't aspirate (get liquid in her lungs). Lisa watched as Brittany stopped Alyssa from eating after she had had only a few small bites of food. Brittany explained that if she ate any more, "She'll just either gag on it or spit it out." Lisa hadn't noticed the toddler having any trouble swallowing. But Brittany was her mom; she knew her child best.

Lisa saw Brittany several more times with some of the other new moms from the group as they continued to try to get together in real life. New motherhood can be an overwhelming and lonely time, and many women on the forum were looking for connection and community. But every time she saw her, Lisa noticed that all Brittany could talk about were Alyssa's and her and Melinda's health problems and how hard it was caring for both her daughter and mother. Lisa thought Brittany seemed lonely and overwhelmed. Brittany told the other moms that she was taking Alyssa to the ER on a weekly basis, which struck Lisa as odd. She felt for Brittany, but she found her off-putting. Lisa also noticed how short-tempered Brittany was with Alyssa; she seemed to resent how much care her daughter required and referred to her frequently as a "brat," even though every time Lisa saw the little girl, she seemed cheerful and well behaved.

Even though Brittany seemed a bit off to Lisa, she still wanted to help her out, even offering to babysit Alyssa. Brittany constantly emphasized how much trouble Alyssa had with eating, how she would choke on food or spit it up. It made Lisa a bit nervous to be in charge of her care. So it seemed curious that when Alyssa was with Lisa, she ate every bite of the Gerber Graduates tray Brittany had left for her.

Lisa had a growing sense of unease about Brittany, but an incident in June 2009 put her over the top. Brittany called Lisa in a panic, screaming, "I don't know how, but Alyssa cut herself. There's blood everywhere!" Brittany pleaded with her to come with them to the ER, saying she couldn't bear to go alone. Lisa was at home with her one-year-old and by then pregnant with her second child; she was reluctant to go. She and Brittany weren't especially close friends and she lived forty-five minutes away; if it was a true emergency, it didn't make any sense to come all that way to get her. But Brittany persisted, offering to come and pick Lisa up. Lisa relented. When Brittany arrived at her house, it was not the gruesome scene she'd described. There were merely some tiny spots of blood on Alyssa's face and shirt. "It's her finger," Brittany explained, holding forth Alyssa's tiny hand and squeezing her finger to show that blood was coming out.

Lisa relaxed; this was just a little cut, Brittany was overreacting. To calm her friend, Lisa told her that her own niece recently got a cut on her finger and even though it initially looked bad, she got sent home from the ER with a Band-Aid. But Brittany wouldn't be dissuaded. Once at the ER, Lisa watched uncomfortably as Brittany squeezed Alyssa's finger to show it was bleeding. Sure enough, they were sent home with a Band-Aid.

The incident unsettled Lisa, who kept her distance from Brittany going forward. Without further context for what she was seeing, Lisa didn't necessarily think Alyssa was being abused; she mostly thought Brittany caused too much drama, and had little to offer in the way of reciprocal friendship.

Brittany was adept at finding people who were bighearted enough to try to help her despite their own misgivings, but she burned through them just as fast. Brittany didn't have the charisma or the warmth of someone like Hope Ybarra. She seemed socially clueless at best and like a bully at worst. But many people want to give a single mom with a sick child the benefit of the doubt, an instinct that Brittany preyed upon.

HEATHER HARRIS, ANOTHER friend from the new moms' group—
which had by then migrated over to Facebook—hung in long
after the others distanced themselves. A former nurse and now mother
of five, Heather had a reassuring, resonant voice and kind manner.
Heather had also joined the moms' group for support, hoping to
trade sleep secrets and learn from some of the other, more seasoned
moms. When she first met Brittany she seemed nice enough, though
a bit immature and clearly stressed by juggling the care of Alyssa and
Melinda. Heather remembers Brittany opening up right away about
her tough childhood and confessing that her mother wasn't exactly
the nurturing type. In Heather's eyes, Brittany was an overwhelmed
first-time mom who wasn't getting the support she needed.

"She did ask for a lot of advice," Heather said, but this wasn't
especially notable. "I did that with my first child, so I didn't think
anything of it. It's just . . . she needed a little bit more help than
normal." Brittany seemed to gravitate toward Heather because of
her nursing background, and would frequently call her for opinions
on Alyssa's myriad health issues. In fact, Heather could scarcely
remember talking to Brittany about anything else.

Anyone who has spent any time in a new moms' group knows
oversharing is the norm: being an overtired, hormonal, vulnerable
mess comes with the territory. As Heather put it: "You're a new
mother and secluded and lonely. You meet somebody in the same
boat and then you definitely verbal vomit."

Heather had communicated with Brittany for over a year online
before they ever met in person. When they did, a very different picture emerged. Brittany had no patience with her daughter, who was
not even two years old. "She was really rough with her, and I mean
physically rough: grabbing her. She called her names constantly:
she'd call her a brat, tell her she was spoiled and yell at her." Heather

tried to intervene, telling Brittany to take a break and cool off if she found herself getting angry, or to let Alyssa come stay the night at her house if she needed time away. Heather didn't approve of the way Brittany handled things with Alyssa, but all the same, she sympathized with getting frustrated and overwhelmed, just as any mom could. She tried to grant Brittany some grace.

"I felt that if she had some better idea of what to do, she would be better," Heather said. She got the sense that Brittany hadn't exactly gotten the best modeling from her own parents, and Heather wanted to believe she just needed a helping hand. But in addition to the physical roughness, there was the fact that Alyssa always seemed hungry, though Brittany claimed she would choke if she ate certain foods and that she had a whole host of allergies. "She was always hungry, but Brit wouldn't let her eat." At get-togethers with the other moms, when the kids would be snacking freely, Heather would notice Alyssa trying to sneak food. "If she got ahold of food, Brittany would yell at her and smack it out of her hand." Just as she'd told Lisa, Brittany said her daughter couldn't drink anything without a thickening solution in it or she would aspirate. Yet Brittany never seemed to remember the thickener, so Alyssa wasn't allowed any fluids. It was bizarre to be at once so vigilant and so careless about her daughter's health.

Heather didn't consider Brittany a close friend, but she worried about her and Alyssa, so she always tried to make herself available when Brittany called. Though they'd only met a handful of times, Brittany would call Heather whenever she was in the hospital with Alyssa. "The phone calls weren't necessarily about Alyssa," Heather said. "They were about her, how she had to deal with it, and she didn't want to have to do this and how it was impacting her and how she didn't have support. There wasn't a lot of talk about her daughter. It was *Oh, my daughter's in the hospital.* And now it's me, me, me type of thing, which seemed a little bit alarming."

One call from Brittany unsettled Heather for weeks. "She'd been at the hospital for multiple days and every time that they tried to discharge Alyssa, her blood sugar would drop. And I remembered that Melinda was diabetic. So I wondered if Brittany had access to insulin." Heather knew that Brittany had worked as a certified nursing assistant, a position that would give her just enough medical knowledge to be potentially dangerous. Heather was worried enough to call the charge nurse at Cook's to express concerns. She remembered that the nurse took the information but nothing seemed to happen as a result.

Heather also noticed Brittany's odd one-upmanship in their Facebook group. If someone else posted about their child being sick or having an accident, Brittany would immediately jump into the comments section and say that Alyssa had some more extreme health crisis or accident. Brittany seemed to always need her situation to be worse.

In March 2007, Heather shared a post with the group about her own mom, who was sick and had recently been hospitalized. Heather asked the group for their thoughts and prayers. Shortly after, Heather received a panicked phone call from Brittany saying that Melinda was having a cardiac event. Heather remembers it was late in the evening, and she took the call while she was in bed beside her husband. "She called frantic," Heather said, "and she said that her mother was dying. She was giving CPR and said the ambulance was on the way and she needed help." Heather, hearing then-two-year-old Alyssa wailing in the background, offered to come get Alyssa and bring her to her house while Brittany helped her mom. Overhearing her, Heather's husband implored her not to go out, given how late it was. But seeing how worried she was, he quickly agreed that they should get the baby out of there. Brittany refused her offer, saying she wanted to keep Alyssa near her. Heather found the whole call bizarre. "If something was happening to my mother, I wouldn't be picking up the phone to call somebody I barely knew." Then Brittany said something that sent a chill down Heather's spine: her brothers didn't like her, and if her mother died, they would blame her. Eventually Brittany was forced to hang up on Heather once she'd arrived at the hospital, so that she could speak to the doctors.

Melinda died that night.

Even though she'd ostensibly moved to Fort Worth to be near her, Brittany wasn't especially close with her mother and she seemed resentful about the burden of caring for Melinda, whose health had only deteriorated since Brittany had arrived. Melinda still smoked despite being on oxygen, and she had a litany of diagnoses including rheumatoid arthritis, diabetes, COPD, kidney failure, and a bleeding ulcer. The extended Phillips family was extremely concerned about Brittany moving to Fort Worth to "look after" her mother. Some recalled visiting the house and finding it in a state of squalor. Melinda would call her other children, telling them that her toilet was overflowing but that Brittany was refusing to come home from the hospital—where she perpetually was with Alyssa—to help.

Because Melinda had stubbornly refused to go into a nursing home, her eldest son and his wife had been planning to relocate from Illinois to Texas, and to pay for a home health aide to come in and replace Brittany. But they would turn out to be too late: Melinda died a week before their scheduled move.

No autopsy was performed on Melinda, but everyone in Brittany's life seemed to have an uneasy feeling about her death.

MEANWHILE, THIS LATE-NIGHT phone call was a turning point for Heather. Her husband had been worried about her friendship with Brittany, and the phone call he'd overheard solidified his concerns. He knew how openhearted his wife was and he suspected that

Brittany was taking advantage of her kindness. Heather had been trying to give Brittany grace, but what happened next exhausted both her credulity and her sympathy.

Heather hosted a get-together with the moms in the group, and when Brittany and Alyssa arrived, she noticed right away that the little girl had a bruise on her cheek. When Heather asked what happened, Brittany replied nonchalantly that she'd hit her. Unnerved, Heather made sure to take lots of photos at the event, determined to get clear shots of the mark on Alyssa's face, in order to document the incident. When everyone else left, Heather confronted Brittany, who had no explanation other than that Alyssa "was being a brat." Alarmed, Heather told Brittany that this wasn't appropriate parenting and that she needed to find other ways of disciplining her child. But Heather got the sense that her words weren't resonating for Brittany. Maybe she didn't see anything wrong with clocking her two-year-old across the face. "She didn't seem remorseful. She just seemed like, *This is normal. This is how you raise a kid.*"

Heather finally called CPS and reported the incident. Brittany was furious when CPS disclosed to her that Heather had called in the report. "It totally changed the dynamic that we had," Heather said. "She still called me, but there wasn't that openness anymore. And anytime she did get visited—because, apparently, I wasn't the only one calling CPS—she would then blame me for it." Heather continued to maintain an open line of communication out of concern for Alyssa, but she also worried that CPS wasn't doing enough. "They said they went and knocked on her door and everything seemed fine and that was it."

Heather felt uncomfortable about needing to call CPS, and doubly so knowing that it hadn't seemed to help anything. Little did she know that by the time Alyssa was separated from Brittany, her CPS file would be thicker than the Bible itself.

11

Fooling No One

Though Child Protective Services was by no means perfect, in his years working crimes against children, Mike had developed a deep respect for CPS workers. By and large they were hardworking, and often came into the job with lofty ideals that too quickly got torched by long hours, abysmal pay, staggering caseloads, and the overall stress and trauma of the horrors they witnessed. Those who stuck it out were made of steel.

CPS workers—a mostly young, female workforce—often got thrown under the bus for decisions made above their heads. The job of CPS was to look after the well-being of a child, and to help families that needed support, not simply to punish abusers or rip children away from their parents: in fact, they were given the mandate to keep families together whenever it was safe to do so. Mike knew that while they might loom large in the public imagination as terrifying—what parent didn't blanch at the idea of a call from CPS?—they were essentially powerless without intervention from the justice system. They could investigate and come to a conclusion about abuse, but they didn't make custody or dependency decisions—those happened in family and juvenile court.

Of all the systems that need to be working properly in order to hold MBP perpetrators accountable, none is more integral than CPS. They are the first line of defense when it comes to protecting children from abuse, the first to take in reports of abuse from medical professionals, schoolteachers, family members, and anyone else with concerns. Unfortunately, in Texas, just like in almost every other state in the United States (other than Arizona and Arkansas), CPS has no policies that deal directly with medical child abuse, and investigators often haven't even heard of it.

But the agency is nonetheless crucial. Criminal investigations are all too rare in medical child abuse cases, so CPS may often be the only government body involved. Not every case was going to hit Mike's desk, and even those that did would still have to deal with myriad custody and placement issues before he could make an arrest. In shelter care and dependency hearings—the proceedings that determine who looks after a child while an investigation is ongoing—Mike might be asked to testify, but he is limited in what he can say. And if those court decisions go sideways, as they often do, his work can end up being for naught.

LAURA WAYBOURN HAD once been one of those wide-eyed young CPS workers, and it was on a late-night shift at the office when she'd first met her future husband, Bill. Her coworker and friend, Kim Garrison, was often there with her, burning the midnight oil typing up reports and trying to make deadlines. The police offices were right across the hallway. Laura and Kim had a friend who worked dispatch for the police, and whenever they were feeling loopy from too many hours in front of computer screens, they'd pop over to visit her. One night, the chief of police, Bill Waybourn, was there, too. Laura was struck by Bill: six feet four, with a thick moustache and impeccable manners. Her dispatch friend introduced them by saying that Laura was *really* interested in handgun safety and that she ought to take Bill's class. Laura didn't give a damn about handguns, but she was definitely interested in Bill. The two started dating soon after and eventually married. And Laura did indeed learn her way around a handgun.

The CPS investigator job had been Laura's first out of college. She'd had her first interaction with CPS as a young teenager working for an in-home daycare when the agency had been called about the parents of one of her charges. Though the incident didn't amount to anything, she knew she'd found her calling: to help children in distress. And while she worked for CPS for only a short time, Laura remained a beacon for kids in need. She and Bill would go on to adopt eight children together, beginning with a Russian teenager whom Bill learned about in church.

In December 2002, Laura was home taking care of their eldest grandchild—the baby of one of Bill's sons from his previous marriage—and Bill was sitting in the pews of the Fort Worth campus of the Christ Chapel Bible megachurch, where he and Laura were devoted members of the congregation. Their Sunday services drew hundreds of attendees, with thousands more watching online. The service had the production value of rock concerts, with dramatic lighting effects, charismatic pastors delivering passionate sermons, and soul-shaking musical performances. This particular Sunday, the pastor told them about a church-sponsored group of fifteen Russian orphans, all of whom, save a fourteen-year-old boy, had found families from the church to take them in. The pastor, standing behind a lectern as his image was projected on a huge screen behind him, explained that in Russia, you age out of the system at sixteen, at which point you're on your own. Bill felt moved. "I was sitting there hearing this story and I believe the Holy Spirit was just laying it on us," Bill said. "And I remember going in and telling Laura, I think we need to go to Russia and adopt this boy. She probably thought

I was drinking communion wine." In April 2003, they traveled the six thousand miles to Russia and returned home with a son. When they discovered their son's friend from the orphanage and his two brothers were also up for adoption, Laura called Bill at work. "Are we going to Russia?" he asked.

They were. But before they could even make the trek, an old friend of Bill's called. Her daughter was pregnant and not in a good place, and she wanted Bill to speak with her. "We went to lunch with her," Laura recalled, "and we had a family in mind that could possibly adopt the baby if she chose to do that." Laura remembered that the young woman was ambivalent, both about giving the baby up for adoption and the prospect of parenting the child—stuck in an excruciating middle. Something happened during this meeting that surprised them both: the one outcome the girl felt good about was Laura and Bill taking the baby themselves. She told Laura to be at the hospital the next morning, as she was scheduled for a C-section. Three weeks later, they finished up the adoption paperwork for the baby and went to bring their three sons home from Russia, while Laura's mom stayed with her precious new grandbaby. There are not many families that could take on adopting so many children—especially in such a short period of time—but Bill and Laura counted themselves lucky to have an extensive support system, through both their church community and a large, close family on both sides. It was a stressful but beautiful time as their family grew overnight.

BRITTANY PHILLIPS WAS a distant relative of Bill and Laura's: Bill's sister-in-law, Judith, was Brittany's great-aunt. Judith and Bruce, Bill's eldest brother, had a big house that was the go-to spot for family gatherings, and Bill remembers first meeting Brittany and Alyssa in 2009 at one such event. He and Laura immediately

noticed that Brittany never stopped chattering about Alyssa's medical issues. "She was extremely obsessed with Alyssa and her small
size. She would talk about it to anybody that would listen and just
obsessively go over symptoms and hospitalizations and procedures.
Anybody around her would have been sort of jarred by it," Laura
recalled. But Brittany's descriptions of her daughter didn't match
what Laura saw when she was with Alyssa. "She was an entirely
different little girl. She was active and lively and she could eat. That
was the biggest thing—there was always talk of her being so little
because she can't eat and then she's sitting there eating at the table."

Not long after this first meeting, Brittany complained to Laura
about her latest entanglement with CPS and how they weren't helping her find housing. When she mentioned that Alyssa's delayed
growth and development was one of the things CPS was investigating, Laura's interest was piqued. She asked Brittany if they'd used
the term "failure to thrive."

"Oh yeah," Brittany replied, "but it's not the kind that I did."

The comment sent a chill through Laura. After that, Brittany
started to avoid her.

WHEN BRITTANY PHILLIPS moved back to Fort Worth in 2009, Bill
was working as the chief of public safety in Dalworthington Gar-
dens, a small suburb in Tarrant County where the couple lived with
their now five children. His niece, Faith Preston, a petite, bright-
eyed mom of five, was Brittany's cousin. The two had been close
before the Phillips family moved to Illinois, but when Brittany and
Alyssa returned to Texas, the cousins hadn't seen each other since
childhood. "I didn't really have a one-on-one relationship with her.
When she would come over and see my mom, I would visit with
her," Faith said. She admitted that she found her prodigal cousin
"strange." From the moment they reconnected, their conversations

were utterly dominated by Alyssa's medical issues. "She had some problems because of being born premature. And every time I saw her, there was a new issue: her allergies, she wasn't able to swallow, she had stomach problems, she needed to wear braces on her feet because she walked on her toes. It was just always something. And the entire conversation would be about Alyssa and her medical needs."

Laura remembered when her niece, Faith, confided that she had concerns about Brittany's behavior. "She had heard of Munchausen by proxy," Laura said, "and she knew that I had worked at Child Protective Services. She asked me if I thought that Brittany was exhibiting those signs and I said, absolutely. . . . I absolutely suspected it. But I didn't have anything solid to go on." As Laura knew from her time in CPS, investigators looked for medical neglect,* not medical abuse. And while neglecting a child for necessary medical care was an easy-to-spot red flag, a parent who was *always* taking their child to the doctor may not seem suspect. It was no secret that previous CPS investigations into Brittany's behavior had gone nowhere, so Laura prayed that Alyssa's doctors would catch on and intervene. Meanwhile, Laura tried to confront Brittany about the discrepancies in her claims about Alyssa's health issues. Brittany said that Alyssa needed leg braces, for example, but Laura watched as she ran around without them. If her daughter needed them, shouldn't she be wearing them?

Faith Preston was especially disturbed by Brittany's questionable claims about Alyssa's food issues. "We were having Easter dinner," Faith recalled. "Alyssa was walking around to the tables where everybody was eating and she just wanted food. You could tell she

---

* In cases where a child has an underlying medical condition, medical abuse and medical neglect can often exist simultaneously. It is also worth noting that charges of "medical neglect" disproportionately affect poor families that may not have access to adequate medical care.

was really tiny and she was hungry and she just was trying to get everybody to feed her. So I just finally picked her up in my lap and started feeding her because it was obvious to me that she was starving." Faith remembers multiple instances of Brittany flat-out denying Alyssa food: "She would always carry around coconut water with her. And that's what she would put in her cup. Like that's what she was basically giving her to shut her up and get her to not be hungry, I guess."

Unlike with Hope, there was no carefully crafted facade of a loving mother doing her best: Brittany's abuse was in plain sight, observable by all who interacted with her. But no one knew what to do. It seemed impossible to prove that Alyssa didn't have these medical issues—and after all, why weren't the doctors doing something? But even if people in Brittany's life suspected she was mistreating Alyssa, they had no idea what she was truly capable of. And the darkness in Brittany would shock them all.

12

"Unable to Determine"

On September 2, 2011, a week into Brittany and Alyssa's fateful final hospital stay, two CPS workers arrived in Alyssa's room— accompanied by security—to inform Brittany of an emergency order to remove Alyssa from her care. There would be a court hearing the following day. Brittany screamed at the workers that they couldn't take her baby, that she'd done nothing to hurt her. One of the workers tried to hand Brittany her business card, but she threw it to the floor in a rage, and continued to rant until she was escorted from the room.

Despite the chaos swirling around Alyssa, when CPS worker Brooke Bennett went with Kim Garrison—Laura's former coworker, who was now Cook's CPS liaison—to see the toddler, she was surprisingly cheerful. She was munching on a graham cracker and proclaimed, "I'm jumping today! But my mommy said I couldn't." They asked what she meant, but she was immediately distracted by something else—as three-year-olds often are—and wouldn't answer their question.

Susan Rial, the CPS supervisor who oversaw the investigation, was already a seasoned pro by the time she got a call from Kim about

Alyssa Phillips. Having made a career shift in her forties from financial services, Susan started in social work with a focus on crimes against children. An abuse survivor herself, Susan was passionate about working with both victims and offenders. Working with the Children's Advocacy Center in Tarrant County, she'd seen the worst of the worst: from child deaths to sex crimes to things that she could only file under "bizarre." She'd even worked with Mike before, on the Ohio MBP case where she'd helped facilitate the emergency removal of the child and then testified in family court to support separation.

When the Brittany Phillips case hit Susan's desk in 2011, she discovered a long history of reports to CPS, including no fewer than four previous reports of medical child abuse, all of which had been closed after little investigation and no further referrals to law enforcement. Only one report had been pursued, after Alyssa had been bitten by Melinda's dog: this one cited "reason to believe" that neglectful supervision had occurred. Susan explained to me that it's pretty common for someone to be "RTB'd," in CPS parlance, but still have no further action take place, especially for something like neglectful supervision. The family might be offered support services, but it would be up to them whether or not they took them.

Another report had been filed after a January 2010 emergency room visit at Carle Foundation Hospital in Urbana, Illinois, where Brittany had taken Alyssa while visiting family in the area. Alyssa had somehow gotten a clonidine pill (used to treat hypertension) while no one was watching her. Brittany had posted on Facebook about the incident, claiming that she'd discovered Alyssa "unresponsive" following the accidental overdose. One of Brittany's Facebook friends noticed that she had originally posted that she'd found Alyssa unconscious at 1:45 p.m. on January 7. But she posted again at 2:50 p.m.—a full hour later—that she was going to call 911. After confronting Brittany in the comments section of the post about the time lapse, the friend reported her to CPS. Others chimed in on the Facebook post and expressed concern, while some jumped to Brittany's defense, saying that she was a great mom and that the important thing was that Alyssa was getting the help she needed.

During this visit to Carle Hospital, Brittany also reported that Alyssa had cystic fibrosis. But compared to Hope's ruse of Sophia having terminal CF, this claim appears to have been a less committed endeavor. In reality, Alyssa had been given a sweat test the previous year at Children's Medical Center in Dallas and she'd tested negative.

Another report came from an inpatient feeding program at Our Children's House at Baylor in Dallas, where Alyssa was admitted for much of April 2010. During that hospital stay, she thrived and gained weight. But the staff documented numerous alarming moments with Brittany: Alyssa would consistently eat well when Brittany wasn't in the room, but not when she was present. Brittany threatened to leave the program at one point following an argument with the staff, and several staffers witnessed Brittany strike Alyssa on the hands and mouth on several occasions.

Throughout the latter half of 2010, Brittany was reported to CPS five times, four with suspicions from four different institutions of medical child abuse, and once from her friend Heather Harris. These were all rolled into one very cursory CPS investigation, and all were given the disposition—or determinations—of "unable to determine." Though the intake was forwarded to the Dallas PD in early 2011, no criminal investigation appears to have been initiated.

LOOKING AT BRITTANY'S voluminous CPS record, it's difficult to understand how no one intervened sooner, but the process is slow and bureaucratic. In Texas, Susan Rial explained to me, a CPS investigation typically lasts for thirty days and can result in one of three possible determinations by the investigator. The first is "ruled out"——meaning the investigator feels assured that abuse didn't occur. On the other end of the spectrum is "reason to believe," which means a preponderance of the evidence points to the abuse having occurred. And between these two designations lies the vast gray area of "unable to determine"—meaning the investigator cannot rule out abuse but also cannot produce a preponderance of evidence that abuse has taken place. "'Unable to determine' is a real catchall," as Susan put it. This is the no-man's-land that Alyssa was stuck in.

But that all changed in September 2011. CPS liaison Kim Garrison called Mike Weber immediately after Alyssa's removal. It was less than a year after he'd put Hope Ybarra away, and Mike had investigated several other medical child abuse cases in the interim. Mike and Kim had investigated a second offender, Kristin Shreve, who'd ultimately been convicted on charges of injury to a child for an unnecessary feeding-tube placement.

Mike had become accustomed to working with assistant district attorneys on witness interviews and putting cases together for trial, learning a lot along the way. In his previous work as a police detective, Mike had often been baffled by the outcomes of cases that went to trial, but now he had a front-row seat to how the justice system worked—or, too often, didn't. There were so many factors at play once a case was before a judge and jury: everything from how likable the attorney was to what kind of mood the jury members were in on any given day could affect the final verdict. Mike had seen firsthand the bias toward mothers in the courtroom; he knew the bar his investigative work had to reach for these cases, and it was high. Motherhood could evoke a powerful sympathy in people, irrespective of the details of a case. As the one detective willing to take these abuse cases on, he had his work cut out for him.

Mike had settled into a peaceful life in Granbury and had spent a happy summer roaring around on his jet ski, taking in sunsets on his pontoon boat with friends, or just contemplating life as he looked out over the still water of the lake, the lights of the other waterfront homes glittering in the distance. The grisly nature of his work wore on him sometimes, and some days Mike felt very far indeed from the happy-go-lucky police academy graduate he'd once been. He found solace in live music, letting the sounds of local acts like Red Clay Strays, Grady Spencer & the Work, and William Clark Green carry him away while he sipped a cold beer. Concerts were cheaper than therapy.

But Mike's interest was piqued by the Brittany Phillips case: it was the fifth case in a row where he'd seen a child with a feeding tube they likely didn't need. That was a straight shot to injury to a child if he could prove it, and he was beginning to understand the MO. He hadn't set out to become an expert on medical child abuse, and it certainly wasn't anything so grandiose as a "calling." But Mike understood now how difficult these cases were. Child abuse investigations were never easy, but medical child abuse cases required educating CPS and family courts in real time, alongside complex investigations that took months, if not years. This timeline was far lengthier than most physical or sexual abuse cases. The paperwork was titanic—with tens of thousands of pages of medical records alone—and the details were confusing, full of rabbit holes and dead ends. Mike had already committed to taking on these cases, which no one else wanted, and he'd learned what was required of him as a detective to make them stick. But now he had to make others throughout the system care, too.

After syncing up with Kim Garrison, Mike dove into the affidavits from the doctors who had treated Alyssa during her most recent ER stay, supporting her removal from her mother. Dr. Matthias, who'd been the attending pediatrician, provided one of the more damning affidavits Mike had ever seen. He laid out the case for

Alyssa's removal in stark terms, noting first the bizarre and concerning blood infection with no apparent cause. He also mentioned the previous CPS report from Alyssa's onetime primary care provider, Dr. Hasan, and the fact that Brittany had not taken Alyssa back to see Dr. Hasan since that visit. And again, there were the eating issues no one else observed.

Finally, Dr. Matthias pointed out that nearly every specialist and nurse who'd seen Alyssa had made note of Brittany's exaggeration of her daughter's health problems. "Mom's view of the child's symptoms and problems seem not to mirror what is seen by the staff." Nearly all of the nurses who'd treated Alyssa also reported "unusual maternal behavior" and noted that she was not cooperative with suggestions on how to help her daughter, and that her interactions with Alyssa were "inappropriate and not helpful to child's well-being." He summarized the relationship between mother and daughter this way: "The mother's history and observations about her child seem to portray a child that is much sicker than what health professionals observe. These fabrications lead to unnecessary medical tests which could be harmful to the child and are consistent with Munchausen by proxy." Dr. Matthias ended his affidavit with a resounding judgment: "I strongly believe that if this mother is continued to be allowed to care for her child that the child may be at risk for abuse and possibly death."

IT IS ALWAYS difficult to anticipate how cooperative a suspect's friends and family might be in an investigation. Mike had seen plenty of spouses, friends, and family members rally around abusers even when the evidence against them was strong. Hope Ybarra's friends and family had been deep in shock as the truth about her cancer hoax and lies about Sophia's health unfolded. The revelations around Hope were like a meteor hitting her community—a group of people who'd been living within the false reality she'd created for almost a decade. As Mike started talking to the people in Brittany's life, it became clear that she wasn't at all like Hope: nobody believed she was a good parent. They just didn't know what to do about it.

Hope had used her intelligence to play on people's emotions with surgical precision, but Brittany was a blunt force instrument. But as different as the two appeared, Mike saw in both women the same malignant need to deceive and harm their children in order to get their needs met. And both needed to be stopped. As Mike dug into the records, he also saw strikingly similar patterns in their behaviors: the premature births, the doctor shopping, the mysterious and lengthy lists of symptoms, the feeding tubes. In every case Mike had seen by this point, there'd been a feeding tube.

As Mike and CPS investigator Brooke made their way through the notes, it seemed clear that Alyssa was being starved by her mother under the guise of medical issues—but such a claim would be very hard to prove. And even if they *could* prove it, the most Brittany would be charged with would be endangering a child, a low-grade felony unless Alyssa was so emaciated as to be near death. Still, Mike knew Alyssa had received a G tube that had subsequently been removed—which meant Brittany had subjected her daughter to at least one unnecessary surgical procedure, which would allow him to charge her with injury to a child. As with Hope, this charge had the potential to lead to real jail time and, crucially, Alyssa's permanent removal. There were plenty of disturbing things Brittany had done as a parent, but Mike became hyperfocused on this element of the case: the feeding tube was the devil he knew.

THE FICTION OF Alyssa's eating issues became evident immediately: within a day of being removed from Brittany's care, she was showing significant improvement. She was cheerfully chatting with staff, eating chicken nuggets and french fries with no complications, and running around without leg braces. The CPS workers made sure to have someone by Alyssa's side 24-7, and everyone who sat with her noted how well she was doing—and that she seemed to know an exceptional amount about medical devices and tests for a three-year-old, but was otherwise behind developmentally. She could only name a couple of colors and numbers, and could not name, when asked, a single friend.

Her caretakers during this time also remarked on how little the separation from Brittany seemed to affect her. "Alyssa was one of the least bothered of kids I've worked with when her mother was taken away," Susan said. "I just can't help but feel that she was really cognizant that it wasn't right."

Alyssa remained in the hospital for six days after she was removed from Brittany's care, and even in this short time, she began to blossom. Susan recalls a worker trying to take her to the playroom and Alyssa insisting that she couldn't walk because she didn't have her leg braces. The worker waited patiently and, after a moment, Alyssa tested out her legs and was soon running along the hallway to the playroom. By time she left the hospital, both the port in her chest and the gastric tube in her stomach had been removed.

As CPS prepared for Alyssa to be discharged from the hospital, the search for an appropriate placement began in earnest. CPS looked into Alyssa's father, Lucas, but it immediately became clear that he'd had very little to do with his young daughter and would not be a good option. His relationship with Brittany had been tumultuous and he was a stranger to Alyssa. They set out to look for the next best option: another family member who might be able to take Alyssa in.

Brittany's cousin, Faith Preston, was relieved when she heard that Alyssa had been separated from her mother. Faith had been trying to keep Brittany as close as possible, hoping to help Alyssa in any way she could. Brittany originally asked Faith's mother if she would volunteer to CPS as a placement for Alyssa during the separation, but Judith was older and didn't want to be put in the middle of such a tough situation, especially since she was convinced Alyssa was legitimately medically fragile. Brittany then asked Faith to take Alyssa, but given that she already had five children at home, that seemed impossible. But Faith had an idea.

In late September 2011, Laura Waybourn learned that Alyssa had been removed from Brittany. She was overcome with relief. "I just remember thinking, *Finally, finally she's been rescued.*" The big ask came next: Would the Waybourns be willing to serve as a placement for Alyssa?

Bill Waybourn was on a trip with his brother Bruce when Laura called him. By this point, the Waybourns' four older adopted children were out of the house, so they had only one at home. "We're driving out of West Texas and Laura had come to the conclusion that Alyssa needed to be with us," Bill recalled. "And now she needed to convince me. The drive back from West Texas began to get a little bit longer, cuz I saw where this was going," he said, chuckling. They'd taken turns over the years convincing one another to go forward with adoptions, and Bill knew how determined his wife could be. He also knew that Laura was uniquely qualified to parent a child coming from such tough circumstances. "With both her CPS background and her biblical counseling background, Laura was in a perfect spot to be the mother of this child. She's a lot smarter than me," he said admiringly, "and she hit all the logical and emotional nails on the head, and by the time I got back to Tarrant County, I knew I was gonna be a new dad."

Faith set out to convince Brittany that the pair—whom she didn't know that well, despite their distant family connection— would be a great fit for Alyssa during the separation. Under Mike's guidance, Faith kept lines of communication with Brittany open, asking her to reiterate all of Alyssa's alleged medical issues via text so that she could communicate them to Laura. Even if everyone around Brittany believed she was exaggerating Alyssa's health conditions, no one knew what was real and what wasn't by that point. Indeed, a common misconception about MBP cases is that the existence of *any* legitimate health concern rules out MBP. Many victims of medical child abuse *do* have some health issues, even if they've resulted from the parent's abuse or from being born premature, as so many victims are. Faith didn't know it at the time, but these texts would come to be an integral part of Mike Weber's investigation, providing a contemporaneous record of Brittany's claims about Alyssa's health that could be held up alongside the facts in her medical record.

Meanwhile, Brittany made no secret of the fact that she was being investigated by CPS. To Susan's eyes, this was just another opportunity for Brittany to play the victim. "She was texting everyone she ever knew. It was on Facebook. She was texting relatives, wherever they lived, whatever state they lived in. She just craved that attention, however she could get it," Susan Rial remembers.

Under Susan's supervision, the CPS investigator began working her way through the long list of collateral contacts Brittany had provided them. No one had anything positive to share about Brittany's parenting. A few relatives even mentioned the term "Munchausen by proxy."

Meanwhile, Susan remembers that Brittany seemed to have no reaction to the news of Alyssa's quickly improving health, which was its own red flag. Any loving parent would be elated at the news of a sick child's health taking a turn for the better, but it's different for MBP offenders. "When they're separated from their child and they have some kind of improvement, they never show any happiness. They either don't believe it—they're gonna argue about it—or nothing," Susan said. Thinking about the sheer relief I feel when one of my kids gets over a minor cold, or when a skinned knee turns out not to be an urgent-care-worthy event, I can see exactly how dissonant this reaction would be.

Alyssa's miraculous turnaround was a key piece of evidence. A period of complete separation is crucial in medical child abuse investigations: if the key factor is the mother, then taking only the mother out of the picture will demonstrate that. The trouble, as Mike had seen with Hope, is that separation isn't always easy to come by, because family and juvenile court judges—the people who made these decisions—were usually unfamiliar with medical child abuse and had trouble understanding why a doctor would ever perform a surgery or a procedure that wasn't medically required. But in this case, the affidavits by Dr. Matthias and Dr. Jamye Coffman, as well as Brittany's lengthy CPS history, worked against her. There was also the unfortunate and unjust fact that Brittany was at a disadvantage because she couldn't afford the best lawyer in town at the first sign of trouble. Mike knew that there were two different justice systems in this country: one for the haves—those with money or status—and one for the have-nots. It was a sad reality he'd long since accepted.

Alyssa was safe as long as the separation order was in place, but Mike knew that they had a long road ahead of them before Brittany would face justice. And Mike knew the clock was ticking: every day Alyssa was away from Brittany she got stronger, yet there was still every chance she'd end up right back where she'd been—in a home where she was slowly being starved. It would take everything they had to get her out.

13

The Turn

Over Labor Day weekend in 2011, Bill and Laura put themselves forward for a home study—the first step in becoming guardians for Alyssa. In the meantime, Alyssa was placed with a foster mother who had a young child her age and who had a background as a nurse practitioner. Jessica kept detailed logs of Alyssa's behavior and activity during this period. She observed a sweet, happy child who ate voraciously. In fact, Alyssa seemed obsessed with food and it dominated even her imaginary play. Alyssa's reaction when Jessica would show her family pictures each night before bed was also striking. "I don't need my mommy anymore," Alyssa said one time. On another occasion she said, "I'm not sick anymore," while looking at a picture of her and Brittany.

As I'm writing this book, my own daughter is the age Alyssa was during this period. My mom friends and I bemoan how difficult it is to be away from our kids for even a few days, as it will reliably turn their world upside down: my husband and I nixed the idea of video calls when I'm traveling as it proved impossible to hang up without causing a complete meltdown. For my friends who are single moms—as Brittany Phillips was—these brief separations are even more dramatic. To say Alyssa's reaction to being separated from her mother was unusual is an understatement.

Alyssa was well-behaved, until she was taken to the doctor for a checkup. She started screaming, "I'm not sick! I don't need a doctor or a hospital." This was a common refrain for the little girl.

One day, Brittany sent some additional toys and family pictures with the CPS worker to give to Alyssa—a standard practice at the time, but one that proves particularly dangerous in cases of medical child abuse. Jessica noted that after looking at one family photo, Alyssa started jumping up and down saying, "I can jump now!" When Jessica looked more closely at the picture, she saw that Alyssa was wearing leg braces in it. "I don't need those special things," Alyssa explained, pointing to the photo. "I'm not sick anymore."

Brittany's care package also contained a bag that was so heavily doused with perfume that Jessica had to roll the window down when she was driving back with it. Once home, she put it in the garage to air out. Brittany had also sent along a DVD of the Disney movie *Tangled*—a take on Rapunzel that features a witch who keeps her daughter locked away from the world in a tower, controlling her every move. When Jessica overheard the song "Mother Knows Best," she felt a shiver go up her spine listening to the lyrics about how Mom is the only one you can trust. (Thankfully, my own daughter prefers *Brave* and *Moana* to *Tangled*, a movie I'm now deeply unnerved by.) The perfumed backpack made sense to Jessica once she learned that one of the fifteen daily medications that Alyssa had previously been prescribed was for asthma, which she did not actually suffer from. The strong scent, Jessica believed, had been intended to induce an allergic reaction in her daughter, a means to "prove" that Alyssa had symptoms even when Brittany wasn't around.

By the end of September, Bill and Laura had jumped through all the necessary hoops to take temporary custody of Alyssa and welcome her into their home. The child seemed overjoyed to be with the Waybourns and their son. "She had always been very happy and playful, but she just seemed to latch on to us very quickly," Laura told me, smiling as she remembered her first days with Alyssa. The Waybourns also immediately noticed that Alyssa was anxious about food being available: "If you fed her and then took away her plate, she would absolutely lose her mind. And so we learned that we needed to leave food out for her all the time, even if it was just goldfish crackers, cuz she was so, so small, we'd have to leave 'em down low so she could reach 'em. If you had any kind of food in your hand, she was just gonna come and try to eat it." Laura also noticed that Alyssa's imaginary play was always medical. They took her to the Alliance for Children to work with therapists there. "She had a therapy doll, and within a few months she had graduated from taking her baby to get shots and surgeries and such to actually taking care of her baby. And that was a beautiful thing to see."

During this period, Brittany still had regular visitation privileges, and it was a struggle. Alyssa often didn't want to go and there were always meltdowns after. Her lack of attachment to Brittany seemed shocking, especially in light of how affectionate Alyssa was with everyone else. Laura remembered having to work with Alyssa on boundaries after she climbed into the lap of an older male stranger in the doctor's office waiting room. Alyssa seemed as starved for affection as she was for actual food.

Brittany wasn't supposed to be able to send anything home with Alyssa from their visits, but the constant changeover in CPS workers supervising these sessions meant that the rules weren't always adhered to. Alyssa got a mysterious rash after Brittany gave her gifts to bring home, and both Bill and Laura were convinced the two events were related. "There was something in the toys," Bill said. "We don't know what. Those visitations were bizarre."

Her attempts to create symptoms in Alyssa showed Mike that

while Brittany might not be book smart, she was plenty cunning. He became adamant with the courts that visitation be prohibited, as it was during investigations into child sex abuse. With his long history working crimes against children, Mike could see the many parallels between medical abuse and child sex abuse in a way others couldn't. At their root was a compulsion to abuse that overrode any fear of consequences; both types of offenders were also deeply manipulative and, in both scenarios, the victim usually felt a deep attachment to their abuser. Of course, no court in Texas would let an alleged sex abuser have visitation with a victim. But the courts still had trouble seeing mothers of "sick" children for what they were: a potentially deadly threat.

Despite the upheaval, Alyssa was quickly bonding with the Waybourns. During this time, the Waybourns adopted a sixth child—another young victim who'd been separated from his parents after an abusive head trauma case—and Alyssa told them she wanted to become a permanent part of their family, like her little brother now was. But the investigation was ongoing and Brittany showed no sign of wanting to give up her claim on Alyssa—which meant the little girl's fate still hung in the balance. She could easily end up back in her mother's clutches.

As ALYSSA WAS regaining her health, Mike was going full steam ahead in his investigation. He and CPS investigator Brooke were tasked with reviewing and organizing the massive amounts of information contained in both Alyssa's medical records and Brittany's Facebook posts. They built out a spreadsheet that would be searchable by date: in one column were doctor visits and their diagnoses and outcomes, in the other were Mom's claims about what was happening with Alyssa's health at the time. Often, they did not even remotely match up.

For example, May 28, 2009: Brittany reported to Dr. Hasan that she'd taken Alyssa to the ER at Children's Medical Center in Dallas for a fever of 102. The ER records show no such visit happened. Ten days earlier, on May 18, 2009, Brittany had reported to Early Childhood Intervention that Alyssa had a positive sleep test for apnea. The medical record, however, showed that the test, which had been performed four days earlier, had come back normal.

There were dozens upon dozens of these discrepancies in the record and, crucially, Brittany's claims always leaned in one direction: making Alyssa seem sicker than she was. Mike knew that any medical child abuse case was going to rely on circumstantial evidence, so in order to build a strong case, they needed to illustrate strong patterns, to show the overwhelming number of lies Brittany had told. He and Brooke were tasked with putting together a jigsaw puzzle with twenty thousand pieces, and they needed every single piece.

Despite the mountains of evidence—including the corroboration of seemingly every person she had ever met—that Brittany appeared to be starving her child, Mike still needed to make her behavior fit with a specific criminal charge. By June 2012, they had two things they were able to charge her with: the slap bruise that Heather Harris had photographed in August 2010 and the placement of the feeding tube, which Mike now had ample evidence to prove was an unnecessary surgery. Brittany was arrested on both counts. She posted bail and was soon back home in her apartment in North Tarrant County awaiting trial. What she got up to during that time was anyone's guess; she worked a fast-food job for a time but was mostly not employed.

Because the feeding tube had been placed in Dallas County rather than Tarrant, the more serious charge was not under Mike's jurisdiction, so he was forced to pass it on to the Dallas County's DA's Office and hope for the best. Mike knew that the Dallas County ADA who took the charge was very diligent and would do what she could, but he feared that the Dallas judge wouldn't be able to wrap his head around the case, and that Brittany was likely to get off with probation. She might even regain custody of Alyssa.

But a conversation Mike had with Brittany's sister Melissa several months earlier would end up changing everything. Melissa told Mike that she'd been at Brittany's house several days before Thanksgiving in 2009 and had noticed a stack of printed pages next to the computer with lists of illnesses and their symptoms. She told Mike that her initial thought when she read through them was that these papers were evidence of Brittany's research on how to make Alyssa look sick. She said it nonchalantly, but it was a striking statement coming from Brittany's own sister—one of the few people who still seemed attached to her. Mike cross-checked the Facebook records he'd collected from Brittany and, sure enough, in November 2009, she'd posted that Alyssa had swine flu (the pandemic du jour that year). When he checked this against the medical records, of course, Alyssa did *not* actually have swine flu.

Brittany had told a multitude of such lies, but the tip-off from Melissa about her computer gave Mike probable cause to search Brittany's residence and confiscate her computer to prove that the Facebook records he had were actually Brittany's—and, more important, he had a hunch about something else. Mike knew that Brittany had brought Alyssa into the GI clinic in June 2011—a few months before she'd been removed from Brittany's custody—and that her G tube had been working during that visit. But two weeks later, Brittany had brought Alyssa to Cook Children's for a chest X-ray. The medical records of this visit showed Alyssa having an NG tube inserted—a tube that goes through a child's nose down to the stomach to deliver nutrients—in addition to her existing G tube. It would be extremely unusual for a child to have both types of feeding tubes, especially if the G tube was working.

But it didn't seem so mysterious from Mike's vantage point:

Mike knew from the Facebook records he'd received that Brittany was about to go on a trip back home to Illinois and would be visiting with family and friends. An NG tube was much more visible than a G tube, meaning it would prompt more questions about Alyssa's health: more concern, more sympathy. Mike looked at the medical records, which had been collected from multiple area hospitals in Tarrant and Dallas Counties. There was no record of the NG tube being placed. Mike did a Google search to see if one could buy an NG tube online, and sure enough, you could. His theory was that Brittany had purchased the NG tube online and put it in herself—meaning she'd fed the tube through her daughter's nose down into her stomach. Confiscating the computer would allow Mike to see Brittany's search history and determine if this theory held water. Mike sent them both to the department's computer forensic lab, which, frustratingly, was very backed up at the time.

There was another big holdup, which was getting the complete records of Brittany's innumerable Facebooks posts. Mike had requested records from all three years of Alyssa's life, but Facebook wasn't as adept at collecting records in those days. Mike's tactic had always been to wait until he had as much evidence as possible with which to confront an offender, but the delay getting computer evidence had cost him: by the time he had it in hand, Brittany had lawyered up and he wouldn't get a thing out of her. He'd have to hope that there was evidence damning enough to not need any admissions from Brittany herself.

About a year and a half into the investigation, he got the break he'd been waiting for. The forensic analysis of Brittany's computer had taken ages. Mike knew trials got pushed out and justice delayed (or never served) because of purely bureaucratic issues like this all the time, but it didn't make the holdup any less frustrating. Finally, Mike received a call from forensic investigator Raymond Bilson in December 2013 that changed everything.

Raymond asked Mike if some search terms he'd discovered meant anything to him, rattling off a horrifying list: "poop in feeding tube," "pee in veins," "pee in blood," "pee in IV," "poop in IV line," and "poop in picc line." Mike was stunned, and his mind went immediately to the mysterious polymicrobial blood infection that Alyssa had gotten during her final hospital stay. He asked Raymond when she'd searched these terms. August 26, 2011—precisely when Alyssa had been at Cook's with the infection.

Raymond told Mike he'd found something else. On that same date, Brittany's search history showed that she had perused an online true crime forum called Dreamin' Demon, where she'd landed on a post about Emily McDonald of Austin. The twenty-three-year-old mom had been criminally charged after she was found putting feces in her three-year-old daughter's IV line. She'd been caught by the hospital's video surveillance. Suddenly, the bizarre moment when Brittany had pointed at the camera in her room and loudly declared that she would never hurt her child made sense.

Mike told Raymond he'd be right over, and he hotfooted it across the street to the lab. As he and Raymond dug deeper into his findings, they discovered that Brittany had opened the article and then, two minutes later, googled the damning set of search terms, crafting a plan to make Alyssa sick. The lab was also able to trace the location of where Brittany had been doing this grim research project: it took them back to the Cook Children's Wi-Fi. She'd literally been sitting at Alyssa's bedside.

Mike kicked himself for glossing over the blood infection as a dead end. In his twenty-nine-year career as a police officer, he'd never come across anything like this. It reminded him to heed the advice he was always giving rookie detectives: follow the evidence, because if you don't look, you don't know.

Mike went back to interview the staff who'd cared for Alyssa during that fateful August hospitalization. Dr. Matthias—who'd provided Mike with that damning original affidavit supporting Alyssa's removal—had also consulted with Dr. Arnaud, an infectious disease specialist, about the highly unusual polymicrobial blood infection that Alyssa had developed while she was at Cook's. Dr. Arnaud told Mike that he believed Brittany had caused the infection and that if the doctors hadn't intervened, it could have led to heart failure, meningitis, stroke, organ abscesses, and even death. But without the computer records, there would have been no way to show that Brittany had caused the infection, even if the suspicion was there. Now, however . . .

Mike checked in with Dr. Shannon from the Cook's care team and asked: If someone had put a harmful substance in Alyssa's feeding tube, how long would an infection take to show up? She told him about twenty-four to forty-eight hours. It was thirty-six hours after her Google searches that Brittany had started demanding—with no reason other than Alyssa's slight fever—that they test her blood: she'd thrown a fit, yelling and berating the staff.

The original prosecutor on the case, Eric Nickols, was a good friend of Mike's. The two had worked together many times and even played on the same rec basketball league team. Mike knew Eric would trust him when he said this case had teeth, but the story was, frankly, bizarre. Mike asked him to come meet with Dr. Arnaud, the infectious disease specialist, and told his basketball buddy to keep an open mind.

Even with an overall picture as damning as Brittany's, Mike knew a good defense attorney could chip away at it, squeeze in just enough doubt to turn jurors. But this was their best chance to make it land and keep Alyssa safe.

Mike knew not to ask a doctor if something was possible—doctors weren't black-and-white thinkers: they worked with a constantly evolving science where a great many things were *possible*. Instead, he asked Dr. Arnaud if he'd ever seen anything like the particular polymicrobial mix that was discovered in Alyssa's blood during his fourteen-year career. Dr. Arnaud said never, not once. Mike said: "Put on a black hat for a minute. If someone was going to induce this, how would they get those three pathogens into a child?" Dr. Arnaud told him that it would make the most sense that Mom had taken feces from Alyssa's diaper and put it in the IV line or feeding tube.

The same thing the Austin mother on Dreamin' Demon had been caught doing.

As they walked away from the meeting, Mike saw the wheels turning for Eric as he absorbed the doctor's words. He told Mike he was convinced and asked him to wrap his investigation up so that they could arrest Brittany on the more serious charge of poisoning her daughter.

On March 7, 2014—a full two and a half years after Alyssa's removal—a second arrest warrant was obtained for Brittany, for inducing a blood infection in her daughter.

Faced with an arrest warrant, Hope Ybarra had taken a plea. But Brittany made no such concessions, and instead pleaded not guilty. She was going to fight.

14

The Trial

Dawn Ferguson had been with the DA's Office for eight years but was new to the crimes-against-children unit when she took on the Brittany Phillips case. (Mike's friend Eric had, unfortunately, left the DA's Office to do defense work before the case went to trial.) This was Dawn's first experience with Munchausen by proxy, so Mike worked on getting Dawn up to speed. By then, Mike had built a friendly working relationship with psychiatrist and author Dr. Marc Feldman, indisputably one of the world's top minds on the subject. He handed Dawn a copy of Dr. Feldman's book and told her he'd put her in touch with Dr. Feldman when she finished reading (which, to her immense credit, she did). Mike knew how crucial it was that Dawn *really* got it. She would be tasked with making a judge and jury—who would likely have never even heard of Munchausen by proxy—understand this complex and horrifying form of abuse. She'd need to be a quick study.

Initially, it was hard for Dawn to wrap her mind around, especially with two young kids of her own at home. How could any mother do this to their own children? It felt viscerally wrong, but the facts of the Phillips case were so stark and so shocking that they spoke for themselves—and all the evidence pointed directly to Brittany.

Between the medical complexities of the case, and the fact that she'd be presenting a type of offender that the jury had likely never encountered before, Dawn's prep for the case was intense. As a prosecutor, Dawn could normally prep for a case in a few weeks. But Brittany's case took almost six months. There were tens of thousands of pages of medical records, and Dawn spent hours with the various doctors who'd treated Alyssa as they walked her through the files. Meanwhile, Brittany wasn't budging on taking a plea deal. A court battle loomed.

The first step was jury selection: the pool begins with about sixty people and the prosecution and the defense each gets ten strikes.* Dawn knew this was a crucial part of the process.

Mike had a specific idea of whom he wanted on that jury. Through pretrial filings, they could see that Brittany intended to emphasize that she was a poor, inexperienced single mother overwhelmed by the hand she was dealt. Mike's ideal jury would be made up of working moms with several kids, who would not be impressed by the idea that someone with no job and one child would mistreat her simply because of "overwhelm." Mike thought that fellow mothers were the most likely to see through Brittany's facade. There was a form of benevolent sexism that Mike had seen play out numerous times when it came to female offenders of any stripe: men were less willing to believe that women were capable of harm, especially to their own kids. Besides which, he also knew that since moms were far more likely to be taking their kids to the pediatrician than dads,

---

* Neither side has to explain their reasoning for a strike, though they're not allowed to discriminate on the basis of sex, ethnicity, or race. If the other side suspects someone is striking jurors in a discriminatory way, they can issue what's called a "Batson challenge," but this happens very rarely, as it constitutes a very serious charge.

they would have a better grasp on how easy it would be to pull this kind of deception off.

In the end, they lucked out: the jury comprised ten women and two men.

The prosecution's strategy was to keep things as simple as possible. Dawn knew that if they threw doctor after doctor on the stand, the jurors would lose track of who said what. So they narrowed it down to a handful of specialists from the various places that Brittany had taken Alyssa, each of whom held especially compelling pieces of the puzzle. They walked the jury through the many treatments, including surgeries, that Alyssa had undergone to correct her alleged feeding issues, and then shared the piles of evidence that these feeding issues were a fiction. Dawn advised the doctors to speak as plainly as possible when testifying, as though they were talking to a lay patient, not a colleague. Dawn was pleasantly surprised at how the jury appeared to be taking it all in.

One of the doctors who testified was Dr. Prasad of Children's Medical Center in Dallas, who'd originally placed Alyssa's G tube. She explained to the jury how easy it was for a parent to fabricate feeding issues, given that a child's food intake is determined almost exclusively from the report of a parent. Doctors couldn't do their jobs if they didn't trust what their patients and caretakers were telling them. Dr. Prasad had a notable moment of humility in her testimony, admitting that she'd been duped and would never have put in the feeding tube if she'd known then what she knew now.

The prosecution didn't get into the mental illness aspects of Brittany's behavior. Given that it wouldn't reduce her culpability, Dawn concluded it would create yet another point of confusion in the jury. What mattered was that Brittany had systematically starved and poisoned her daughter. It didn't matter *why*.

Dawn knew the defense would try to wedge enough uncertainty into the prosecution's story to make a jury unsure that Brittany was culpable. The prosecution's obligation was to prove Brittany's guilt beyond a reasonable doubt; if there were any holes in the evidence, the defense would immediately exploit them. Indeed, the defense argued that it was *possible* someone else had typed those searches into Brittany's computer and, furthermore, the prosecution didn't know *exactly* how she'd gotten the feces into the tube, or whom the feces belonged to. Was it her own? Was it Alyssa's? Without video evidence there was room for speculation, and speculation could lead to that all-important factor for the defense: doubt. Alyssa's case could be the one in a million medical mystery; how could they possibly be sure? The defense also attempted to argue that Brittany didn't even read the blog post on the offender in Austin, claiming she'd only had it open for two minutes before she started googling "poop in feeding tube," and so on, so she wouldn't have had time to fully absorb the impact of the article.

Just as the prosecution tried to keep the facts of the case simple and concise in their direct examinations, the defense did the exact opposite. They went hard cross-examining the medical profession-als the DA brought to the stand, asking some variation of "Why did you do the surgery if you didn't think it was necessary?" before following up with dozens of technical questions. Dawn could see the jury starting to glaze over: exactly what the defense was hoping for.

But Dawn felt like they had the truth, and the evidence, on their side. She was especially impressed with the testimony of Dr. Jamye Coffman, the head of Cook's care team, and their closer on the medical side. Dr. Coffman was the perfect person to walk the jury through the case at a macro level. With her approachable, big-sister energy, she brought it all down to earth.

Mike didn't hear most of the trial because the defense had in-voked what's known in Texas as "the rule," meaning that no one who is testifying in a case can be present for any other testimony—only theirs and the closing arguments. Mike spent most of the fourteen-day trial pacing a hole in his office carpet as he waited for news.

Mike's testimony focused on Brittany's pattern of behavior, which they'd established throughout the course of the investigation. Raymond would present the compelling findings of the search into Brittany's computer. The defense didn't offer their own medical or forensic experts; instead, their strategy appeared to be to present Brittany as incapable of having pulled off such a deceit. She'd lost a significant amount of weight throughout the course of the investigation; in the courtroom, she looked hollow-eyed, with greasy hair pulled back in a low ponytail. Mike thought she was pretending to look lost. Mike knew brute force was Brittany's tool of choice, but it wouldn't work in this setting; so instead, he thought, she was playing dumb.

The defense also argued that the blood sample that showed Alyssa's infections had been somehow contaminated. Mike was relieved that the prosecution had on the witness list one of the nurses who was in the room at the time of the blood test. During a pretrial hearing, the defense protested that the witness was worthless if they didn't have the phlebotomist who actually drew the blood testify, claiming that Alyssa could have put the poop in the feeding tube or central line herself.

Laura Waybourn was dismayed when Mike asked that Alyssa—then seven—testify against Brittany; to make matters worse, because Laura and Bill were also testifying, the little girl would have to go in without them. Luckily, Alyssa's adored first-grade teacher volunteered to take her in, so Alyssa would be able to hold the hand of someone who loved her. By that point, Alyssa had been living with the Waybourns for years.* After one particularly awful

---

* Brittany's parental rights were terminated before the criminal trial. If she had fought termination, she would have been forced to testify in civil court, as there

visit with Brittany, the Waybourns told CPS they weren't bringing Alyssa to see her anymore; fortunately, CPS didn't push the issue and Brittany—who'd stopped attending her mandated counseling sessions—didn't either. Alyssa continued to thrive with the Waybourns: all of her "illnesses" had disappeared and she was a happy, healthy little girl who considered Bill and Laura—whom she had now lived with longer than she'd lived with Brittany—to be her real family.

Laura waited anxiously outside the courtroom door for Alyssa to emerge. "And then the most beautiful thing happened," Laura recounted. "Alyssa didn't realize that Brittany was there. Brittany had lost a lot of weight between the last time that Alyssa saw her and that day. I believe that was God intervening on her behalf. She came out and she didn't even realize that Brittany was in there. And that was so nice." Laura remembers learning of the particularly horrific details of what was found on Brittany's computer and being elated because she'd felt that it would be the nail in Brittany's coffin, that Alyssa would be safe now. For years, Brittany had been torturing Alyssa in plain sight and getting away with it, but surely *this* they couldn't ignore.

Once the testimonies had wrapped up and the closing arguments had been made, there was nothing left to do but wait for the jury to give their verdict. The trial had gone on for two weeks, unusually long by Texas standards. The jury was huddled in their cramped room deliberating at the orange-brick criminal court building on the banks of the Trinity River. Everyone was on edge as the jury met for two full days. The jurors eventually sent a note out saying that they were deadlocked, 10–2. The judge told them to continue deliberating. The following day, they sent out a note saying they

---

is no self-incrimination protection in civil court. Mike believes that if she were compelled to testify, there is every chance she would have incriminated herself.

were still deadlocked: this time, 11–1. Neither side knew which way they were leaning, but the majority had managed to pull at least one holdout over. The other one, it appeared, was hopeless. On day three, they sent out a final note.

The jury was hung.

The judge declared a mistrial.

DAWN FERGUSON WAS beside herself. A hung jury was basically a win for the defense: "not guilty" verdicts were rare because if the state was going to take something to trial, it was usually because they knew they could win.

In Texas, if a jury so chooses, they can speak to anyone involved in the trial after their verdict is given. Both Mike and Dawn talked to the jury and discovered that eleven of the jurors had been convinced that Brittany was guilty. In the original split, it had been the ten women versus the two men on the jury, but one male juror had been convinced by a female juror who worked as an IT professional and was able to dismantle any doubt he had about the Internet searches being Brittany's.

The lone holdout was a white male dentist in his midsixties. Mike watched him in the corner of the room, his arms crossed over his chest. The dentist sat back, not saying much, while the rest of the jurors were forthcoming and even thanked Mike for his work on the case. Mike heard the dentist say, quietly, "She's not smart enough to do this." Brittany had never actually testified, but her deer-in-the-headlights act had worked on at least one person: the man had been fooled into thinking she wasn't clever enough to be a criminal.

Dawn thought maybe the dentist believed he knew the medical field better than his fellow jurors, to say nothing of the many doctors who'd testified and provided affidavits about Brittany's abuse.

Maybe he just thought women in general weren't that smart. Dawn knew that jurors walk in with preconceived notions, and sometimes it doesn't matter what the evidence shows—they're sticking to their beliefs.

Laura Waybourn was devastated by the news of the hung jury. She'd been in full mama bear mode for years and probably knew the ins and outs of the case better than the prosecutors themselves. It seemed so clear that Brittany was guilty. How could the jury have been fooled?

Now THE DA's Office had a decision to make. They could either dismiss the case and let Brittany go free, or retry the case, devoting untold resources to a second trial and taking a chance on a whole new set of twelve citizens, and who knew how they'd react? But they'd been *so* close. Just one juror away.

As Dawn drove home from court that day, she felt like it might have been easier to just lose and have the closure of a not guilty verdict; as it was, they were all in purgatory. Dawn and her colleagues had been working the case for half a year, and now they were faced with the prospect of doing it all over again with no guarantee of a more favorable outcome.

But not long after, Dawn came into work to find an email from the defense attorney, and it felt like the sun breaking through the clouds: Brittany wanted to plea. With someone as unpredictable as Brittany, Dawn knew they had to act fast. Of course, she'd rather have a guilty verdict, but they didn't want her to be on probation. Brittany was dangerous, and she was young; there was every possibility she could have more children. Dawn could only guess at what had led to the change of heart. Maybe the defense attorney—whom a family member of Brittany's had paid to represent her—quoted her an astronomical fee to represent her in a second trial. The state had almost gotten her once; perhaps it felt too risky to try her luck again. Dawn offered the defense ten years. They settled on five.

Mike felt her sentence was too light, just as he'd felt Hope's sentence for twice as much time had also been too light. These were both women who could have easily killed their children. And, furthermore, they posed a very real threat to anyone else they got close to. Prison time wasn't only about punishment: it was supposed to help keep the community safe, and it was hard for Mike to think of two people who belonged behind bars more than Hope and Brittany. But jail time was better than nothing. Brittany went on to serve every day of her sentence before being released on November 17, 2020.*

And what mattered most was that Alyssa was now safe, and with a loving family. Laura was relieved that Brittany was behind bars. "Mike is a hero and I don't care what he says," Laura says, chuckling, knowing full well that Mike would object to the distinction. "He's a hero. And without him this case would have not ended the way that it did."

Indeed, if Mike had been any less dogged about following every possible lead, he never would have discovered the computer evidence that eventually led to a more serious charge and jail time for Brittany. If CPS hadn't been so thorough, the Waybourns might not have been able to terminate Brittany's parental rights (which still involved a costly court battle). If the doctors hadn't been so vigilant, Alyssa might not have survived at all. And if the Waybourns had not been so determined to bring her into their family, Alyssa may have ended up right back in the custody of Brittany, someone who posed a mortal threat to her.

---

* Brittany also pled guilty for the feeding-tube insertion in Dallas. As part of the deal, she received the same five-year sentence from Dallas County that was to be served concurrent with the five-year sentence in Tarrant County.

This case is as happy of an ending as you'll see in a medical child abuse scenario: an entire community rallied around Alyssa Phillips in order to give her the happy, healthy life she was meant for. It's what every child deserves.

If only it was what every child got.

15

Reason to Believe

In 2011, while my family life was splintering over the first investigation into my sister, Alyssa Waybourn's life was starting anew. From the moment of her removal in 2011, she was on a trajectory toward a happier childhood. Alyssa's destiny as part of the Waybourn family was the life that God (if you're the Waybourns) or the universe (if you're a semispiritual agnostic like me) had meant for her to have. I met Alyssa Waybourn—then fourteen—on a trip to Fort Worth in 2022 when I was about six months pregnant with my second child. The moment she walked in, the whole room seemed to fill with sunshine: Alyssa is petite and cheerful with a luminous smile and a big laugh. She told me about her life now—she'd been homeschooled since Covid started, but was involved in all kinds of activities like basketball (she plays wing or box) and choir, where she sings mostly soprano but fills in with the alto section as needed. She's also very artistic and loves to write and draw. Later that afternoon, she was heading to her first day of work at Cicis Pizza, her brand-new after-school gig. Alyssa is one of eight children in the Waybourn family: six boys and two girls. You can tell she's a tough cookie. "I like to boss my brothers around," she told me. She's testified twice before the Texas legislature in an effort to get tougher laws enacted around medical child abuse, on a bill that bears her name. So far, the legislation hasn't passed, but no one is giving up on it.

Even though she was very young when she was removed from Brittany's care, she's still haunted by memories of that time. "I try to push them away," she said. "Sometimes I would just be like asking God, why did he do this to me? Why did he pick me? And sometimes I would think I'm the only one that ever went through it. . . . And I just hope that no one else has to go through it. It's just tremendously terrible."

Her words echo what every other survivor or family member has told me they felt, what I've felt myself at times: *I thought I was the only one.* Alyssa tells me she always tries to reach out when she's feeling alone. "I would not try to isolate myself because that's one bad thing that can happen. Like you could feel all alone. Like no one understands you," she said.

Alyssa's mom, Laura, came with her to the interview. It was immediately evident how close the two are. It's the kind of bond I hope to have with my own daughter when she hits her teenage years: they smiled and teased each other, and I was impressed by Laura's ability to sit back and let Alyssa say her piece without interjecting, even as she recounted some of the most harrowing parts of her past. Laura never once interrupted Alyssa or corrected her, only offering clarifications or additions when asked. I could see the emotion on Laura's face as Alyssa talked: how painful some of these things still are to hear, but also how proud she is of her daughter.

Alyssa does remember testifying against Brittany, how her parents weren't allowed to go in with her, and that she didn't recognize Brittany while she was on the stand. She remembered feeling really proud of herself after. "I was like, wait, I did that?" she recalled. "Wow. I'm amazing."

Mike told me that, counter to the fears many parents and new-bie prosecutors have, he's actually seen many child abuse victims really benefit from taking the stand: they often feel a tremendous sense of pride after doing so. It should never be pushed on a child who doesn't feel safe, but Mike believes it can be an important part of the healing process.

Alyssa told me she didn't really have much desire to talk to Brittany again, especially if she was only going to continue to lie. Laura reminded her that she actually confronted Brittany during a visit when she was about five. Alyssa had asked Brittany directly why she'd hurt her, and she'd been angry when Brittany had denied everything.

Alyssa nodded. "That sounds like me," she said.

When I asked Alyssa what advice she might have for her fellow survivors, she was adamant that no survivor should feel the need to maintain a relationship with the person who hurt them. "I don't have to owe anything to Brittany," she declared. I could see Laura welling up with pride when she said this. "If someone does something bad to you, then you shouldn't be held accountable for their actions," Alyssa continued. "You shouldn't live with regret. You shouldn't do anything to put yourself on hold or any of that, because you didn't do anything wrong."

Indeed, Alyssa was remarkably clear on the point of Brittany's culpability. "Whenever I was little, this thought came into my head, What if she had a mental illness or any of that? And I'm like, no, that's not right. Even if she had a mental illness, she shouldn't be doing it to her child. . . . We know that she had a rough family, but even if you have trauma as a kid, it's not like I'm gonna go and do the same thing to my children. I mean, I'm not. Because that's not the kind of person I am. . . . She might have had trauma as a kid. I had trauma as a kid. But that still doesn't make it right."

Everything about Alyssa makes me feel hopeful: her strength of spirit is evident, as is the love she has for her parents and vice versa. But as well as she's doing, there's no denying that she will carry the physical and emotional scars of her abuse for the rest of her life. She's tiny for her age, under five feet, a result of being starved as a baby and toddler. And, because no one can ever keep their opinions about a girl's body to themselves, people comment on it: how young she looks, how tiny she is. It's not what any young woman coming of age wants to hear.

The blood infection Alyssa contracted during the hospital stay provided the dramatic evidence that put Brittany away. But barely. And while that incident was notable, it was also one of many similarly traumatic incidents. The truth is, Brittany was no mastermind: everyone around her knew something was wrong. For one thing, she'd been starving her daughter in plain sight—a trait that's unfortunately common with medical child abuse. Yet if it had been "just" that, the prosecution might not have had a case.

I met with Laura and Bill Waybourn separately during that trip to Fort Worth, and they both told me how proud they are of Alyssa. "She is one tough cookie," Laura said of her teenage daughter. "That girl is small, but mighty; I cannot wait to see what she ends up doing. She is smart and compassionate in a way that I don't know that I've ever seen from a kid. She's a teenage girl, too," Laura added, "and it's hard to deal with hormones and such, as all girls know"—indeed, I can still viscerally remember how awful it was to be fourteen—"but she's handling it with grace and she is a beautiful, beautiful person."

Bill told me how proud he is of Alyssa and how she sings him his favorite songs, like "Fly Me to the Moon" by Frank Sinatra. He told me he can't wait to see what lies ahead for her. "Whoever she grows up to be is going to be magnificent," he said, imagining her as a future champion for children and, undoubtedly, a strong woman. He tears up when he tells me about shopping with Alyssa for a card for Laura the previous Mother's Day. She chose something for Laura that referenced the day she was born. "She just forgot that Laura isn't her birth mother. Isn't that beautiful?"

I MADE SEVERAL attempts to track Brittany down for an interview. I couldn't find any contact information for her: unlike Hope, no one had kept in touch after her release from prison. Laura—who had tried over the years to keep a watchful eye on Brittany's whereabouts—sent me a link to a Facebook account that had popped up with Brittany's name. As I went to message her, I stopped short: The profile picture was an old one. In it, Brittany was reclining on a lawn with a three-year-old Alyssa next to her. Wearing leg braces.

I had mixed feelings about talking to Brittany. I was in the middle of my second pregnancy, which seemed like particularly accursed timing. I'd spent my first pregnancy spelunking through my worst memories of my own family's experiences to draw on for my novel; now, in my second pregnancy, I was back diving deep into the same horrific subject matter—only this time, I was asking strangers to reflect on *their* worst traumas as well. It was also true that Brittany felt neither compelling nor familiar to me in the way that Hope had. But I still wanted to hear what she had to say, and I was curious if she would express any remorse. I sent her a Facebook message and never heard back.

I halfheartedly tried some other sources before I got a text from Mike letting me know that I was too late: Brittany was dead. In early April 2022, Brittany Phillips died in an apparent overdose. The news was more sobering than tragic. After all, I had no reason to believe that Brittany had changed during her time in prison, and at thirty-eight, she was still young enough to have more children.

Mostly, I thought: *What a sad end to a sad life.* I confess that there was also relief in the news, too: Brittany would never be able to hurt anyone again, and for Alyssa, it meant she could fade forever into the background, and become a distant memory. Perhaps now Alyssa would be able to forget her. That, too, was a beautiful thing.

PART 3

THE
UNRAVELING

16

After the Fall

During spring 2013, Mike was still waiting for the forensic results from Brittany's computer when he got a call from Kim Garrison, the CPS liaison from Cook Children's, about yet another case. A woman called Mary Welch was suspected of medically abusing her ten-year-old son.

Mike was beginning to understand that the phenomenon of medical child abuse was much more common than anyone in his office—or anywhere else—wanted to believe. He'd spent half of the previous year investigating Elisabeth Hunnicut, a mother who'd had an intracranial pressure monitor needlessly placed in her son's head; much like Brittany Phillips, she had also been starving her son. Every case was the strangest thing Mike had ever seen, until he saw another one just like it.

Despite its challenges, working at the DA's Office was a dream job for Mike: he was surrounded by other people who took their work in criminal justice as seriously as he did. The majority of his work was second line, so Mike spent most of his days assisting attorneys with trial prep, joining them as they tracked down leads, even shepherding witnesses from the airport to the courthouse—anything that was going to help strengthen their case. Sure, Mike ran across the occasional arrogant attorney who was just trying to climb the career ladder, but, by and large, his colleagues were smart people who were invested in their cases and cared about doing the right thing. He'd been in and around the legal community in Fort Worth long enough now to know how insular it could be. All the attorneys knew one another, whether they were working prosecution or defense, as did the judges, who'd all started off as attorneys. With just under a million people, Fort Worth was a big city in one sense, but it was also a small town: most people had grown up there, and roots ran deep.

Mike knew that not all attorneys working child abuse cases had respect for the other professions they worked alongside—some could be shockingly dismissive about the opinions of detectives and social workers, whom the community relied on to keep children safe. Criminal justice had its petty hierarchies like everywhere else: life was nothing if not a high school cafeteria. But Mike was still reporting to Alana Minton, whom he adored, and the leadership at the top was solid, too. No one worried they'd be fired if they lost a tough case. The pursuit of justice mattered more than the scoreboard. Mike always rolled his eyes when he heard an attorney boasting that they'd never lost a case, thinking, *You must never have tried a hard one.*

The day-to-day of investigating child abuse was taxing, but Mike was fueled by a sense of purpose. As a younger man, Mike had imagined that he would have children of his own one day, but at forty-nine, that image was in his rearview: God just had other plans for him. Besides, he wasn't sure he could have kept working crimes against children if he was going home to look at his own babies every day. He'd seen how the rigors of the job burned out countless other colleagues who were parents. Even though Mike resisted any florid descriptions of himself as a hero, he slept well at night knowing he was helping kids, knowing that there were children who might not be here if it were not for him. He knew not everyone got to find meaning in their work, and felt lucky that he did.

That spring, Mike had even gotten pulled into the investigation of Geronimo Aguilar, a high-profile megachurch pastor suspected of molesting two sisters, ages thirteen and eleven. The file had sat untouched on a Fort Worth PD detective's desk for seven years by the time Mike took it on. In addition to his specialized work on medical child abuse, he was becoming Fort Worth's patron saint of forgotten cases.

Mike couldn't imagine leaving the DA's Office, and planned on spending the rest of his career there. He put in extra hours when needed but generally was off by four thirty, and spent long Texas evenings by the lake in Granbury with his then girlfriend. But everything was about to change.

KIM GARRISON HAD been invaluable in protecting the kids of Tarrant County, and Mike trusted her. So when he saw a call from her cell come in, he dropped what he was doing to answer. Mike sat at his desk in the DA's Office as Kim gave Mike the same rundown she'd received from Dr. Coffman about yet another bizarre and complicated case. Mike now recognized the pattern: the child's alleged health issues were numerous and dizzying. But the brain surgery element really perked Mike's ears. The child had had a ventriculoperitoneal shunt placed in his skull to drain excess fluid that was allegedly building up on his brain—it was similar to Elisabeth's claims that her baby suffered from hydrocephalus, but this mother was claiming that her child had an even more rare form of the disease, almost never seen in people under the age of sixty-five. To make matters worse, Kim told him, the mother had been taking her child to not only several hospitals in Texas but also a facility in

Minnesota for treatment. Mike groaned. This case was going to be extra-complicated if it crossed state lines, but as always, he was up for a challenge.

ON SEPTEMBER 19, 2008, retired FBI agent Rodney Russell threw a surprise thirtieth birthday party for his wife, Connie, at their beautiful five-bedroom brick house in the upscale town of Keller, Texas. Two dozen friends congregated for a lively adult pajama party. Some of the guests, like their newly divorced friend Mary Welch, brought their kids along to play with the Russells' own small children. Mary's five-year-old son, Gabriel, had always seemed like a sweet boy, but several of the parents complained that night that he was being overly rowdy and even aggressive with the other kids. At one point, he tried to jump the family's back fence—a big problem, as there was a pond on the other side. After sunset, the kids were herded inside and sent to play upstairs while the adults continued socializing downstairs.

Rodney took on the task of checking in on the kids regularly so that his wife could relax and enjoy her party. Not long after sundown, Rodney went out to the foyer, where a large staircase curved up to the second story, creating a small balcony fifteen feet over the hard tile on the floor below. He was met with a heart-stopping sight: Rodney's four-year-old daughter was standing over Gabriel, who lay on his back, eyes rolling back in his head. He was moving slightly but not crying. Rodney's daughter told him Gabriel had fallen from the railing above. Later, other children who'd witnessed the fall said that Gabriel was pretending to ride a horse on the banister when he'd tipped over the edge.

Moments later, Gabriel's mother, Mary, appeared behind Rodney and knelt beside Gabriel, telling Rodney to call 911. A crowd of guests gathered behind her, the news rippling like a shock wave through the party, and Rodney looked up to find that someone was already on the phone with emergency services. They handed the phone to Mary.

The wail of ambulance sirens could be heard shortly after and, soon, EMTs rushed into the house. The medics made a plan to transfer Gabriel to nearby Cook Children's. But Mary was insistent: she wanted Gabriel sent to Children's Medical Center of Dallas instead, ten miles farther away. Mary claimed Dallas had a superior trauma center and, furthermore, she insisted that Gabriel needed to be care-flighted to Dallas by helicopter, arguing with medics on scene who said it was safe for him to travel in the ambulance. Mary was forceful and, because she was the mother of a child with a potentially serious injury, they complied and called in a medevac.

The EMTs checked Gabriel's vitals as they waited for the helicopter to arrive. Soon, the grass on the front lawn was being flattened by the winds of the incoming medevac helicopter. Mary and Gabriel flew away into the night.

Back in the house, a shaken-up Connie phoned Gabriel's father, Doug Welch. Doug was also a friend, but since the divorce, he and Mary had been socializing separately. Connie offered to keep their younger daughter, Madison, who was also at the party, overnight so Doug could go see Gabriel. Doug gratefully accepted, and got in his car immediately to make the harrowing forty-minute drive to Children's in Dallas.

Over the next few days, several friends of the Welches would visit Gabriel in the hospital, where he was being treated for a small skull fracture. He had two black eyes and a bandage on his head, but he was alert during his four-day stay. Mary slept over at the hospital with Gabriel while Doug drove back and forth each day to be by his son's side. There were some immediate concerns over dehydration from vomiting—a common side effect of concussions—but by the time Gabriel was released to his parents' care, his prognosis was good. He was expected to resume all normal activities once he recovered.

Though they were divorced, Doug and Mary Welch shared custody of their two children and generally got along well. At the hospital, the two discussed a plan for taking care of Gabriel, and decided that Mary and the kids would move into Doug's house temporarily while their son was recovering so that Doug could help out. When Gabriel was discharged, the two set off in separate cars—Mary riding with her parents and Gabriel—with the intention of meeting up at Doug's house.

DOUG HAD PREPARED the house to accommodate his son and ex-wife, and a group of the kids and parents from Gabriel's tight-knit private school had even come to decorate: there was a big "Welcome Home Gabriel!" banner waiting outside, with signatures from all the teachers and kids from the school.

To this day, Doug has no idea what transpired on that car ride, but by the time they reached his house, everything had changed. Suddenly, Mary was adamant that she didn't want to stay with Doug after all. Mary's parents, too, were suddenly inexplicably icy with Doug. He'd always had a good relationship with her father, Philip; the two had even considered going into business together at one point. Doug had admittedly always found Mary's mother, Rose, a bit odd and dramatic, but they'd all been on good terms until this moment. Suddenly, Philip was holding Gabriel in his arms and Rose was putting herself between them as though Doug might try to abscond with his son. Before Doug could wrap his head around what was happening, he was watching them drive away with Gabriel.

Stunned and exhausted, Doug collapsed in a chair at his kitchen table and cried. Mary had always been overprotective with the kids, especially with Gabriel, and he knew she was upset about the fall, but she'd never tried to get between him and his children like this. Though it would be a long time before he was able to face it head-on, a lingering gut feeling about Mary was beginning to assert itself within Doug: he was starting to feel afraid.

17

When Mary Met Doug

Doug Welch met his fourth wife, Mary, when she attended an open house that he was hosting. It was the turn of the millennium and Doug was the owner of a thriving real estate company. The pretty, blond thirty-year-old with a sunny smile and an outgoing demeanor caught Doug's eye immediately, and he was thrilled when he found out that his sister-in-law, Pamela, knew her. Pamela played Cupid, setting them up to go to a party hosted by a local Realtor that Doug was pals with.

Doug's younger years had been somewhat tumultuous. Throughout his twenties and thirties, he'd been married three times and been through myriad personal dramas. When he was twenty-nine, a neighborhood teenager who was friendly with Doug's step-daughter had accused Doug of molesting her. Doug was shocked by the charge and—at his lawyer's suggestion—sat for a polygraph test, which he passed. The charges were soon dropped, and he never heard anything further about it.* At the time he met Mary—he

---

* At the time of the arrest, Doug and his family had already moved to a different part of town for his work, and his stepdaughter had lost touch with the neighbor.

was then forty-four, thrice divorced, and already a father of three kids—this strange incident was Doug's only brush with the law outside of a speeding ticket or two.

He hit it off with Mary immediately. She was charming and intelligent, instantly likable. She'd grown up in Alvarado and was the oldest of three children: two girls and one boy. Mary was a strong woman who'd survived two bouts of cancer: melanoma and breast cancer. But by the time she met Doug, she appeared to gleam with good health. She'd also been married twice before, and she told Doug she'd worked as a nurse in a NICU. Doug remembered her going off to work in scrubs each day: he loved how maternal she seemed. Even if Doug hadn't had the best luck with marriage, he adored his three kids. After dating for several years, the two tied the knot, hoping that the fourth time would be the charm.

Doug's business was booming and he bought them a beautiful, five-thousand-square-foot house in Argyle, a cozy suburb north of Fort Worth. Once married, Doug noticed that his exuberant wife tended to exaggerate. She'd left her old job and started working for Doug's real estate company as an assistant, but she would often tell people she was a co-owner. It irked him a bit—he'd put in years of hard work to buy the company—but he chalked it up to a self-esteem issue. If Mary wanted to sound a little more important at the office than she was, well, that was understandable. He wanted her to feel good about herself, and everyone fudged things a little now and then.

Doug was naturally positive and hardworking. Born in an Indiana farming community, Doug had worked since he was eleven and moved to Fort Worth after the factory that both he and his parents before him had been employed by shut down. He'd worked his way up from selling automotive trailers to becoming a successful Realtor.

Before long, he and Mary started their own family, and Doug

was thrilled to be a dad to a fourth child. Gabriel Welch was born about a month premature in 2002 and ended up in the NICU—as fate would have it, the very same NICU where Mary had once claimed to be a pediatric nurse. But it became clear very fast that Mary had never been an employee there, instead working as a volunteer, taking shifts holding premature babies. When Doug confronted Mary on the discrepancy, she blew it off. "I don't think I ever said I was a nurse here," she told him. "I just said I worked here." Doug was certain she'd said she was a nurse; hadn't he seen her wearing scrubs to work? But with the stress of having a new baby—and a preemie, at that—it didn't feel worth bickering over.

After two weeks, Gabriel was released from the hospital and the new family of three went home to Argyle. Mary seemed perpetually anxious, despite reassurances that Gabriel was completely fine. She kept a constant vigil over her son, and when he was big enough to be moved to his own room, Mary went right along with him. Doug tried to be patient—it was normal for a first-time mom to be nervous, especially with a premature baby. In his early years, Gabriel had minor issues: a tonsillectomy, and some visits to the hospital for diarrhea and reflux. Doug, the more experienced parent, tried to reassure Mary that their son was fine; he hoped things would eventually go back to normal. One of Doug's older children suffered from a rare condition called neurofibromatosis—a disease that causes tumors on the brain, spinal cord, and nerves—and he'd always been very involved in her care. Maybe because of that, he had an easier time keeping Gabriel's more minor issues in perspective.

It wasn't until their daughter Madison was born in 2006 and Mary continued her fixation on Gabriel that Doug began to really worry. He was a busy dad to five kids, working full-time, and suddenly he was the primary caregiver for their new baby girl, while Mary remained hyperfocused on Gabriel. The months went by in a blur of real estate and parenting responsibilities.

According to Doug, things began to splinter between him and Mary in 2007, when Doug made the shattering discovery that Mary had been having an affair with her ex-husband. One afternoon at their house in Crowley—the second home that they'd lived in together—he'd stumbled upon explicit email exchanges between the two of them on the computer Doug and Mary shared. In a particularly heartbreaking missive, Mary recounted how she'd been with her ex the morning before coming to meet an unsuspecting Doug for lunch, even wearing a sweater her ex had given her. Doug was angry but tried hard to save their marriage. Mary, however, didn't seem so invested in staying together; before long, it came to light that the affair with her ex-husband had been just one of several indiscretions. In late 2007, the two officially separated.

Despite the circumstances, Doug and Mary remained amicable as they negotiated the terms of their divorce and custody agreement. Mary hired a lawyer and presented Doug with a custody plan that seemed fair to him. Mary assured Doug she would never try to keep him out of his children's lives; she knew what a devoted father he was. Having been through three of them already, Doug knew how financially devastating divorce could be, and was loath to hire an attorney to run up the bill when he and Mary weren't even disagreeing. It was a decision he would later regret.

A little less than a year after they separated, Gabriel suffered his dramatic fall from the banister during the party. At the end of that year, Mary moved in with her boyfriend, Chad, whom she'd started seeing while he was still married to his ex-wife, Misty—Mary's onetime best friend.

If Mary was fixated on Gabriel's health before the fall, afterward it became an obsession. Over the next five years, Gabriel would spend more of his life in the hospital than out of it. The main concern was Gabriel's brain, which was first operated on in November 2011. Gabriel had received a diagnosis of normal pressure hydrocephalus—exceedingly rare in children—where fluid builds up on the brain. This was purportedly a result of his skull fracture, and he had a shunt put in to drain the fluid and relieve the pressure on his brain.

Mary's whole life became about Gabriel's health: she would tell anyone who would listen about her son's many ailments, ranging from complications of his brain condition, to gastrointestinal distress, asthma and lung problems, trouble walking (for which he was sometimes wheelchair-bound and at other times used leg braces), issues with his vision that required special glasses, epilepsy, and a laundry list of behavioral issues including ADHD and autism. By the time he was ten years old, Gabriel was taking more than fifteen medications each day.

Doug didn't know what to think about Gabriel's health troubles. Every time he was with his son—weekends, mostly; less often than he would have liked since Mary had primary custody—he seemed like a healthy little boy. But Mary insisted that their son's medical issues were complex, and that Doug just didn't get it. Mary had long since quit working outside the home. Her full-time job now was going to doctors' appointments with Gabriel, so Doug figured she must be right about all these complications, about his invisible frailty. After all, Mary wasn't writing the prescriptions for Gabriel, she wasn't performing the surgeries. The doctors must know what they were doing.

Then, in May 2013, Doug got a call that changed his life. An investigator from CPS wanted to talk to him about Mary.

18

Jane Justin

During this time, Gabriel was a student at the Jane Justin School. Named after the philanthropist and wife of former mayor and owner of the Justin Boot Company, John Justin, this school for special needs children is housed in a nondescript, tan, one-story building on the south side of downtown Fort Worth. The school is affiliated with Cook Children's and has a dedicated and medically knowledgeable staff, with a very low student-teacher ratio.

Mike would later learn the details of Gabriel's time there during his police investigation. Mary first brought Gabriel in for an assessment at the Jane Justin School in July 2010, when he was seven years old. It had been two years since the fall and the subsequent alleged complications had transformed Gabriel from a healthy, rambunctious five-year-old into a special needs child, at least according to his mother. Mary wanted to move him from his small private school, Holy Cross, which was located in Burleson, just south of Fort Worth, to an environment where he could get additional help.

During their initial visit with the medical director at the school, Dr. Aiello, Gabriel appeared to have a well-developed social repertoire, despite being behind academically due to how much school he'd missed for his innumerable doctor visits. Dr. Aiello listened as Mary—who was warm and exceedingly polite throughout their two hours together—laid out Gabriel's long, complex medical history, explaining that he'd been born premature and that this had led to frequent behavioral and medical issues. She said he'd been diagnosed with ADHD as a toddler, and that things had taken a horrible turn when he'd fallen from the second-story banister during the party at age five: the fall had also led to a spike in his ADHD symptoms, lack of impulse control, and difficulty following directions, she said. She also noted on her application that Gabriel suffered from autism* and sensory processing disorder.

When a spot opened in December 2010, Gabriel was accepted and immediately enrolled. Mary quickly became an active member of the school's community, a frequent volunteer at school events, and active in the parent-teacher organization. Dr. Aiello noticed that Mary seemed to consider herself something of an expert in parenting a special needs child, and he frequently overheard her doling out medical advice to fellow parents at the school. In the early days, Mary was well-liked around Jane Justin, as she was consistently pleasant and gracious with the staff and the other parents. Despite her good nature, Dr. Aiello heard from Mary much more frequently than other parents, even though many of the children at the school were far more severely disabled than Gabriel. Mary wanted to speak to Dr. Aiello constantly about Gabriel's medical issues and his behavioral problems at home. She also had a habit of rehashing these concerns ad nauseam with Gabriel's teachers during pick-up and drop-off, monopolizing their time. Dr. Aiello recalled frequently seeing Mary in conference with one teacher, Tiffany, in

---

* Mary sometimes reported Gabriel as having autism and sometimes as having Asperger's syndrome. There is no evidence that he has either diagnosis.

the hallway long after her classes had started, leaving Tiffany's assistant teacher to manage the entire class on her own.

Not long after Gabriel began his time at Jane Justin, Dr. Aiello also met his father, Doug Welch. He remembered Doug explaining that though he and Mary were divorced, they got along and managed well as co-parents. He did not share Mary's concerns about Gabriel's behavior, but Doug himself attributed this to the differences in home environments and schedules. Doug mostly had Gabriel and Madison on weekends and knew he was a more relaxed parent, overall, than Mary. Madison was healthy and bright, an adorable little blond-haired four-year-old, but her mother's constant focus on her brother's needs left her yearning for attention. Doug noticed that she would report everything back to her mother, as though she was her delegate, and she constantly referred to Gabriel as her "special needs brother." But Madison always seemed happy when she was at her dad's house, and there was no major discord between the two households from Doug's point of view.

Gabriel's teacher, Tiffany,[1] had a very different impression of the relationship between Mary and Doug. Not long after Gabriel started at the school, Mary pulled Tiffany aside to tell her that Doug was not allowed to pick Gabriel up unless she gave specific permission in advance. Mary intimated that there was a heated, ongoing custody battle between the two of them, though in truth, no such thing was happening. One day Gabriel was bemoaning the fact that his mother had forced him to cancel a fishing trip he had planned with his father. "Mom says I can't go fishing with Dad because he doesn't take good care of me," he told Tiffany, "but it's not true."

Gabriel's academic progress at Jane Justin stalled because he was out so much. Dr. Aiello began to notice a consistent pattern with Gabriel's absences: Mary would tell the school of some ailment Gabriel was suffering from—a range of unrelated symptoms from reflux to headaches to seizures and blurry vision—and ask them to keep an eye out. The school would subsequently *not* observe any issue, and report this back to Mary. Mary would then nonetheless take him to the doctor for whatever the supposed problem was, pulling Gabriel out of school. Gabriel would then take additional days off to rest and recover. He'd return to school with the problem supposedly fixed, only to have Mary report a relapse or a whole new issue a few days later, beginning the cycle all over again.

Tiffany noticed this pattern, too. Mary told Tiffany that Gabriel suffered from "debilitating" headaches and asked her to give him medication if he complained about his pain. Gabriel told Tiffany that "everything gave him a headache," but he didn't seem to Tiffany as though he was ever in any pain, something Tiffany was finely attuned to in her work with special needs children. In September 2011, Mary told Tiffany that a swallow study had been performed and that Gabriel's vocal cords were collapsing. This was allegedly another consequence of his fall, but Tiffany never noticed any sign of Gabriel wheezing or gasping for air. Mary nonetheless pulled him out that month to address the supposed problem.

As the incidents piled up, Dr. Aiello and Tiffany began to wonder how it was possible for so many medical interventions to go wrong.

Tiffany remembered that Mary had told her that Gabriel had a brain bleed and that she'd taken him all the way to Gillette Children's Hospital in Minnesota—where there was a renowned specialist in Gabriel's rare condition—to have the shunt placed. As a result, Gabriel was out of school from late November 2011 to the second week of January 2012. Mary seemed oddly proud of Gabriel's new brain shunt upon their return, telling Tiffany it was one of only a few of its kind done on pediatric patients: "You can google him," she told the teacher. Mary told Dr. Aiello that Gabriel was now a national case study and that the medical field had learned so much from him. She said she hoped the Texas doctors would take notes from the superior expertise of Gabriel's Minnesota doctors.

One January day, not long after Gabriel had returned to her classroom, Tiffany noticed that Gabriel had clear fluid seeping out of the incision on his head. His shunt was leaking. This led to yet another long absence; when he returned in March, he was in a wheelchair and wearing leg braces, though Tiffany noticed he functioned perfectly well without them while he was in school.

In late 2012, Mary told Tiffany that Gabriel had been diagnosed with esophageal varices and would be returning to Gillette Hospital in Minnesota for a Nissen fundoplication—the same surgical procedure that four of the children in Mike's previous cases had received, where a sphincter is created at the bottom of the esophagus—and to have a gastric feeding tube placed. Upon his return, Mary was very worried about Gabriel's lunchtime, concerned about him throwing up or the tube becoming dislodged. She suggested that she or Gabriel's grandmother come each day to help him eat in private. After that, Mary or her mother was there every day sitting with Gabriel at lunch, cutting his food up into small pieces. Jillian, the assistant teacher who oversaw lunch, noted that Gabriel ate normal foods—pizza, burritos, apples, and so on—without any trouble, and wasn't actually taking any feeding via his G tube.

For Tiffany, things came to a head when Gabriel told her that he'd be out of school the following day because a home health nurse was coming for a home visit, to evaluate the family's benefits. Gabriel told his teacher, "Some people from the state are coming to my house tomorrow. Mom said I have to act sick, because people don't believe her that I have a brain injury." Tiffany was deeply alarmed.

For Dr. Aiello, the suspicions had been slowly coalescing. Then, in July 2013, he attended a Cook Children's grand rounds that focused on Munchausen by proxy and medical child abuse. The presenters were child abuse pediatrician Jamye Coffman and Detective Mike Weber. As he listened to them explain the typical characteristics of a caregiver with MBP and the types of illnesses they might claim their child was suffering from, all of Gabriel's strange incidents and failed medical interventions finally added up. Dr. Aiello assembled an expert panel at the school that included social workers, Gabriel's teachers, the school psychologist, and other professionals to put together a complete chronology of Gabriel's time at Jane Justin and their interactions with Mary. Once their ducks were in a row, they filed a report with CPS.

19

Turning Doug

At the heart of the Mary Welch case was the shunt in Gabriel's brain for the rare condition—normal pressure hydrocephalus—he'd allegedly developed after his fall.

After Tiffany had noticed the fluid seeping from Gabriel's head in January 2013, Mary took him to Cook Children's. According to interviews with the doctors during the official investigation into Mary, the two neurosurgeons treating Gabriel were immediately alarmed; Mary had already been told by Cook's that Gabriel didn't need a brain shunt. She'd then gone to Minnesota to have one placed there, though the doctors weren't sure how she'd done it. It was always possible they'd missed something, so they did a test. They clamped off the leak and kept watch. If Gabriel *really* suffered from normal pressure hydrocephalus, his symptoms—trouble with balance, confusion, loss of bladder control—would quickly return. But they saw nothing. Dr. Davies, the surgeon in charge of his case, continued to test Gabriel thoroughly, then removed the brain shunt. Mary was livid and berated the doctors.

Both doctors attempted to reach the neurologist at Gillette Hospital in Minnesota to see why the shunt had been placed at all, but despite leaving several messages, they never heard back. In fact, it appeared from the records Mike collected during his investigation that these two hospitals where Gabriel had received extensive, overlapping treatment had never been in touch with each other. Shortly after, Mary took Gabriel straight back to Gillette to have the shunt put back in.

ON MAY 22, Doug came in to meet with CPS. He was on edge.

"Am I being investigated?" Doug asked, before they began. The young Johnson County CPS worker assured him that he wasn't, that he was only there to be interviewed as a parent. It was cold comfort.

The investigator explained they'd noticed discrepancies between Mary's reports to doctors about Gabriel's health and Doug's own reports. None of the things—the seizures, the headaches, the GI symptoms—that Mary listed as regular symptoms seemed to happen to Gabriel when he was with Doug. The investigator wondered what Doug made of it all.

Doug's head was spinning. He told the investigator that their experiences were just different. Mary looked at her son through the lens of an overprotective mother; as Gabriel's dad, Doug felt like he had to teach him to be tough and to feel capable. The investigator asked Doug if he felt Mary had ever crossed the line and insisted on unnecessary procedures.

"No," he said adamantly, "she's his mother." Doug figured that Mary had been right that the doctors at Cook's had dropped the ball on the brain shunt, and he was grateful that the doctors at Gillette had performed what he assumed was a necessary procedure. He repeated Mary's refrain that the Minnesota doctors had technology and expertise superior to those in Texas.

The investigator reminded Doug that she wasn't accusing anyone of anything, but she had to ask the hard questions. She began to try to explain the nuances of Munchausen by proxy.

Doug felt a bolt of horror and cut her off. Doug told her that Mary had only ever done what she needed to help Gabriel, and that they were aligned in wanting the best for their son.

Later that day Doug got a call from Mary's attorney. He was trying to see where Doug stood, and Doug assured him they were on the same side. He knew Mary would never hurt her son.

Mary was just anxious, Doug told himself, and Gabriel would be fine. At his house, Gabriel was always in good spirits: he and his sister would take off with Doug on their bikes, tearing around the nearby dirt-bike tracks. Being a little out of shape at the time, Doug sustained some minor injuries of his own trying to keep up with them a few times, but the kids loved it.

Doug's life was in its own state of flux: like so many others, he'd gotten out of the real estate business after the housing market crashed in 2008 and was now selling cars. Doug had also met a lovely woman, Jo, through family in the Midwest, and they'd been dating long-distance. He was hoping the *fifth* time might be the charm for him.

Doug was doing well in the car business. Scrappy and likable, he was always willing to go above and beyond for his clients. One afternoon, he took a long drive out to a Dallas suburb to deliver a Ford F-150 Raptor to a retired nurse called Betty, who'd purchased it for her son. Betty invited Doug in and they chatted while he walked her through the paperwork. They got on the subject of whom they knew in common, and it turned out that Betty was a distant cousin of Mary's. Her eyes got wide when Doug mentioned she was his ex-wife. Betty said she'd heard through the family grapevine about the CPS investigation. Doug was caught off guard; he hadn't expected to be discussing this with a stranger. "Yeah," he told Betty, "but I don't buy it. It'll all get worked out."

But Betty shook her head vehemently. "No, Doug. You need to get custody of those kids. Something's wrong there; the whole family knows it."

Doug was shaken and called his girlfriend, Jo, as soon as he got home. He'd hoped maybe Jo would reassure him, but he was mistaken. Even after meeting the kids only via Skype, Jo was extremely suspicious about Mary's claims that Gabriel had autism, among other things. She'd had a bad feeling for a while now; she'd just been unsure how to bring it up with Doug.

The pieces began to fall into place for Doug. After all, he knew firsthand how deceptive Mary could be, considering, it was deception that had ended their marriage. But was she really capable of lying about *this*? And why would she do such a thing? She'd always seemed so protective of Gabriel. Why would she want to hurt him?

But the unsettling conversation with Betty shook something loose in Doug, and over the next few months, he requested some of his son's medical records to have a look himself. One of the files from Children's Medical Center in Dallas stopped him cold. Gabriel had been tested for autism and the test had come back negative. But Mary still claimed that Gabriel was autistic, that the test had been positive. He called to ask Mary to share Gabriel's records from the Minnesota hospital, but she refused, telling him he wouldn't understand them. Since Mary had always been in charge of Gabriel's medical care, Doug didn't even realize he could simply request the records himself.

Initially, Doug had taken Mary's side because he'd had no real awareness of Munchausen by proxy. Now he went down a rabbit hole of Internet research, much of which sounded terrifyingly familiar as he read about other cases involving preemie births, GI issues, neurological conditions, and lengthy lists of ailments that never seemed to add up. He thought of all the times Mary had shut him down during doctors' appointments if he ever dared disagree with her. It had never been like that with Doug's other ex-wife, with whom he shared a disabled child. It made no sense: Doug had always been right there championing Gabriel, even fundraising for a private plane to bring him to and from one of these Minnesota appointments.

But at some point, he now realized, Mary had just stopped telling him about the appointments. Doug thought back to one of Gabriel's appointments that he'd planned to attend in Minnesota, in August—right before the CPS report arrived from the Jane Justin School. At the last minute, Mary had forbidden him to come. He was also worried that his son seemed to be acquiring a vast medical vocabulary, reporting to Doug all the names for the conditions he supposedly suffered from. Doug found it inappropriate to talk so candidly about all of this with a ten-year-old. Furthermore, Doug would often observe Gabriel exhibiting symptoms only after hearing Mary go on and on about them.

Had she been making it all up?

FROM THE GET-GO, the Mary Welch case had some serious jurisdictional issues. Mike had been assigned the criminal investigation because the Texas surgeries in question had happened at Cook's in Tarrant County. Originally, Mary was believed to be living in next-door Johnson County, so the CPS investigation had begun there. But when it was discovered that Mary was living with her boyfriend, Chad, in Tarrant County, the CPS case was also moved there: Mike was relieved because it meant Brooke Bennett would be handling it, so he and Dr. Coffman would not be tasked with giving Medical Child Abuse 101 to some green young investigator one county over. Knowledge about how to navigate is handed off like a baton to whichever investigator—if any—actually knew how to work one. It never seemed to occur to anyone that they just needed more batons. Nonetheless, Mike was happy to have Brooke on this tricky case with him. He knew the two systems needed to work together, and that any of these systems were only as good as the people in them. Brooke was the same CPS investigator who'd sat at Alyssa's bedside after she was separated from Brittany: she and Mike had developed a great deal of trust.

On September 5, 2013, Doug came in to meet with Brooke and Mike Weber at the welcoming redbrick building that then housed Arlington's Alliance for Children. Meeting the stout, friendly Doug, Mike was relieved that he seemed more worried than defensive. Doug spoke slowly and deliberately, his accent a mix of midwestern and the Texan from where he'd lived more than half his life. Mike could see where a laid-back guy like Doug might get bulldozed by someone like Mary. Mike knew that as much as these perpetrators might seem to differ, they had one thing in common: at their core, they were bullies.

This time, when Mike and Brooke walked Doug through what MBP looked like, he listened intently, the horror of the situation coming clear. This was exactly what his ex-wife was doing to their son.

Doug gave Mike the medical records he'd gotten ahold of for Gabriel, complete with the notes about the inaccuracies he'd unearthed. Paging through the records, Mike found one instance especially glaring. There was a Baylor Hospital visit about two months after Gabriel's fall. Mary reported that when he'd fallen from the banister during the birthday party, Gabriel had suffered a grand mal epileptic seizure that lasted three minutes. Mary said he'd turned blue and stopped breathing, that she'd administered three rescue breaths before EMTs had arrived. According to her, he'd then been in a coma for more than ten hours. Mike had already read multiple accounts of the fall—to which there had been many witnesses— and this simply wasn't what happened.

Mary, it would turn out, had told some version of this same story—that Gabriel had fallen right at her feet, that she'd given him CPR, and that he'd been in a coma following the accident—to many people, both medical professionals and other family members and friends. The truth was that Gabriel never lost consciousness after the fall, and Mary had not even been in the room when it had happened—as Rodney Russell, the former FBI agent whose house the incident had taken place at, confirmed. Nor had Mary administered CPR, which wouldn't have been necessary.

Gabriel's fall had been plenty dramatic, so why had Mary felt the need to embellish it further? First, Mike needed to know more about Mary. And he was about to learn that her lies weren't confined to her son's health—they'd permeated every part of her life.

20

"Nurse" Mary

As Mike got busy reaching out to Mary's friends, the picture of who she was started to become clear. Mary had always been extremely social and well liked, consistently boasting a large circle of friends. But whether those friends stuck around was another story. In recent years, Mary's social circle had largely been parents at the Jane Justin School in particular. Mike started with this group.

Erin first met Mary at a parent-teacher organization function for Jane Justin four years earlier, where Mary immediately shared Gabriel's harrowing story of falling from the banister, which she'd described as a "near-death" event. The assembled parents got the version where Gabriel had fallen at Mary's feet and she'd heroically performed CPR on him before the paramedics took over. She told them he'd been helicoptered to the hospital where he was in a coma, and then required many months of intensive care and therapy at Dallas Children's. Mary credited her nursing training with helping her save Gabriel's life, and presented herself as the ultimate self-sacrificing mother, saying she'd had to quit her job to manage Gabriel's complex, ongoing care. She feared for Gabriel's future, she confessed to Erin, and believed he'd probably never be able to read, or drive a car. She explained that she'd moved Gabriel to Jane Justin because regular schooling had been a disaster, leading him to have such an intense meltdown that he was admitted to the psych ward for a time.

Over the next few years, Erin and Mary grew close, frequently having deep conversations over dinner about their children and their fears for them. Mary was always there to provide encouragement and a sympathetic ear, and the two bonded over their shared history as NICU nurses, talking about how rewarding the experience of taking care of fragile newborns had been. Erin felt for Mary and admired her resilience, especially when Mary opened up about her own health troubles: her bout with breast cancer, lupus, infertility struggles, and heart problems. She told Erin about a botched hysterectomy that had led to such dramatic blood loss that she'd nearly died.

Erin knew what a toll being the parent of a special needs child could take on you, and was awed by Mary's vigilance and persistence in tracking down specialist after specialist to get answers about Gabriel's myriad problems. The ups and downs never seemed to wear on her.

Once, when Mary and Gabriel had a Minnesota doctor's appointment coming up, Erin rallied some of the other parents in the Jane Justin PTO to donate snacks, toys, and gift cards to make the long car journey more comfortable—Mary said Gabriel could not travel by air because of his shunt.

Erin visited Mary and Gabriel at Cook's after his shunt became infected and Dr. Davies had ordered it removed in January 2013. Mary wasn't her usual self during this visit, and she seemed extremely agitated to Erin. Mary claimed that the Cook's doctors didn't understand Gabriel's complicated condition and weren't doing what they needed to do to help him. But when Erin looked over, Gabriel was busy playing a game on an iPad and seemed perfectly content.

In the beginning, their children's health issues had been a point of bonding, but as time passed, Mary's fixation on it started to wear on Erin. There was something else, too: though Mary offered endless and vivid descriptions of Gabriel's supposed symptoms, in all the time they spent with one another, Erin never actually witnessed any. Gabriel always seemed like a normal, energetic boy to her. Yet he would constantly disappear from school for days or weeks at a time due to his alleged illnesses.

Erin was also becoming concerned that Mary's younger daughter, Madison, was being neglected. Erin frequently picked Madison up from school for Mary, sometimes even keeping her over the weekend. She thought the little girl seemed attention-starved, with so much of her mother's focus directed toward Gabriel. Erin noticed that Madison had also begun to imitate Mary in the caretaker role and was beginning to complain of her own stomach issues.

In May 2013 Mary called Erin, distraught, to tell her that she was being investigated by CPS. Mary blamed the investigation on Dr. Davies, the neurosurgeon from Cook's. Mary thought he was holding a grudge against her for ignoring his advice to not replace Gabriel's brain shunt. She mentioned that they suspected her of Munchausen by proxy.

Erin, horrified, assured her that the evidence would exonerate her. It all had to be there in the records, right?

CARRIE HAD A very similar experience with Mary. She had two children at Jane Justin and became fast friends with Mary when Gabriel joined the school. In the version Mary told her of Gabriel's fall, he'd been *pushed* off the banister by another child, had fallen at Mary's feet, and had gone on to spend a month—rather than three days—in the hospital. Mary also told Carrie about his litany of other health issues, but, like all of Mary's other friends, Carrie never witnessed these symptoms firsthand. The most extreme thing

Carrie ever observed was Gabriel getting red in the face when he was running around—just like her own son did; they were both big boys. But Mary would make Gabriel stop playing to do special breathing exercises whenever this happened. It seemed a bit much.

Carrie also had a younger child who was Madison's age, and the two families spent a lot of time together. Madison was allowed to come for sleepovers at Carrie's, but never Gabriel. Mary said Gabriel had to be on an oxygen monitor at night, and it would be too much of a burden to ask another parent to watch it. She explained Gabriel's diagnosis of normal pressure hydrocephalus to Carrie and said that he was one of only two children in the country who suffered from the condition. Mary told her about the special shunt she'd had placed in Minnesota because the Cook's doctors refused to learn the lifesaving procedure.

Carrie was one of very few to accompany Mary to Minnesota in early 2013—a fact that would come into play later—when she brought her own son, as well as Madison, to visit Mary and Gabriel as he recovered from the fundoplication and feeding-tube surgery.

Mary's history as a NICU nurse resonated with Carrie because of her own heartbreaking loss of twin girls born three months early, who died at one week old. Mary seemed to know a lot about preemie twins, and they discussed the details of what had happened to Carrie. She remembered Mary telling her she'd seen both outcomes at six months: babies who made it and babies who passed.

Mary told Carrie so many complicated medical things about Gabriel that she started taking notes so that she could keep up when Mary talked. At one point, Carrie remarked to her husband that the details seemed to change a lot.

"She's probably just overloaded with so many things going on," he told Carrie.

"I just don't see how this many bad things could happen to one person," Carrie replied.

Carrie eventually got worn out by the never-ending drama of Mary's life. Mary told her she'd been married four times* by then, all of them rich men. Her new relationship with Chad—the husband of Mary's former best friend—seemed toxic to Carrie, and she became uncomfortable with her kids being around the couple. She backed off the friendship and began seeing Mary only for the occasional girls' night out and lunch.

When the CPS investigation began in May 2013, Mary asked if Carrie would serve as a character witness for her. Just one little thing, Mary added: Could she be sure to tell CPS what a huge improvement she'd seen in Gabriel after the brain shunt surgery he'd had in Minnesota? After all, Carrie had visited them in the hospital. "Don't elaborate," Mary said, "just keep it simple." Mary also told her not to mention to CPS that she'd been a nurse, since this was a red flag for being an MBP perpetrator.†

The request to lie—especially with the mention of MBP—made Carrie so uncomfortable that she didn't return CPS's call. It was not until Mike Weber reached out to her that she realized how serious things were—and that most of what she thought she knew about Mary had been a lie.

HEIDI KNEW MARY before Gabriel joined Jane Justin, when their kids were at Holy Cross. Heidi had, of course, also heard about the big accident and received a constant deluge of details about

---

* How many times Mary has been married is one of many difficult-to-confirm details about her past. During the writing of this book, she appears to have gotten remarried. Again.
† Before the Internet era, almost all known cases of Munchausen by proxy involved perpetrators with a medical background. In today's era, anyone with an Internet connection can access the relevant information, as evidenced by the Brittany Phillips case.

Gabriel's health. Heidi remembered numerous occasions when Gabriel was in the hospital and Mary would tearfully tell her that he "might not make it." Mary complained to Heidi about Doug not providing the same obsessive care that she did when Gabriel was with him. "I got the sense that he was fine when he was with Doug, but when she had him, he was constantly at the hospital," Heidi told Mike. "He always seemed like a normal little boy to me. It just seemed like if he was really that sick, you'd see *some* evidence of it, you know?" Heidi volunteered at the school frequently, and she observed a happy, social, energetic kid when she saw Gabriel running around the lunchroom.

Mary was frequently bemoaning her financial troubles, claiming that she'd had to quit her nursing to look after Gabriel. She also told Heidi about her skin cancer, saying that she'd undergone chemo and had a large patch of skin removed from her thigh. The drama eventually turned Heidi off. She also suspected that Mary had a nasty side, after watching her be nice to someone's face only to trash them the moment they walked away. Heidi figured she'd get the same treatment if she hung around.

But of all the dramatic friend fallouts that Mike would later hear detailed in his interviews with those who knew her, nothing beat her bust-up with Misty—another parent from Holy Cross—who'd once considered Mary Welch her best friend. Mary had even called her from the helicopter the night of Gabriel's accident, when he was being care-flighted from Fort Worth to Dallas. Misty had visited Gabriel in the hospital the day after his accident, and though he had two black eyes, she remembers being relieved to see him awake, and recalled that he was his normal, smiling, happy self.

Misty was so close with Mary that she went to some of Gabriel's doctors' appointments to provide moral support. "It seemed to me that she'd make things out to be worse than what they were. There were always things I wondered about," Misty told Mike when he called her. She recalled Mary switching doctors frequently and getting very angry if she felt a doctor wasn't doing what she wanted. Misty remembers Mary saying that Gabriel wasn't eating and that she insisted on coming to school with special bowls to get him to eat. But whenever Mary and Misty went out to eat with their kids, Gabriel wolfed down food like any other little boy. She remembered feeling like Mary was invested in seeming like a supermom. And far from appearing to have trouble keeping food down, Gabriel was heavier than Misty's son, who was the same age. He just didn't look sick.

As with Erin, Misty and Mary bonded over the fact that they'd both been nurses in the NICU before their kids were born. Everyone at school thought Mary was still a nurse, Misty told Mike, and she even had some people convinced that she used to run the hospital where she worked. She told Misty that she'd fallen behind on her CEs (continuing education credits that nurses are required to take to keep their license up-to-date), which was why she was currently working as a receptionist at an eldercare facility. But then she would tell Misty a story about intubating a patient who was coding. This rattled Misty, who reminded Mary that she could get in a lot of trouble for doing something like that if she wasn't licensed. "They're old people," Mary told her dismissively. "They don't care."

There was one incident that stuck out in Misty's memory as being especially bizarre. Misty invited Mary and her kids to join them at her brother's lake house. Mary told Misty that Gabriel "did not do stairs" because of balance issues from his head injury, and that her parents were even remodeling their house so that Gabriel could have a bedroom on the ground floor. There were lots of stairs at the lake house, and Misty was especially concerned about a steep set of steps that led down to the pool. But once they arrived, Mary barely noticed the stairs, and was happily drinking beers by the pool while Gabriel ran around with the other kids—including tearing up and down the steep steps. Misty was a nervous wreck all weekend fearing something might happen to him, yet his own mother was suddenly oblivious.

Mary and Misty's friendship exploded spectacularly when Misty's eight-year-old daughter revealed that Mary and her father—Misty's then husband, Chad—were having an affair. Her daughter didn't like Mary and was worried that she would become her new mom. "I know I'm the enemy because of everything that happened," Misty told Mike.

After their friendship crumbled, Misty began to question all the things about Mary that didn't add up. She saw her former best friend in a new light—and though their relationship was over, Misty still heard *plenty* about Mary. "She'd supposedly been getting treatment for skin cancer one day, but then someone sent me a picture of her on the boat Chad and I owned. You know, out in the sun."

Things were spiraling between the two former friends. Nonetheless, Misty didn't seem eager to trash Mary as a parent. When Mike spoke to her, she simply seemed relieved that they were looking into things. "I know she loves her kids," she told Mike. "She's just sick. She doesn't understand what she's doing."

Mike didn't correct her. By then, he understood that this was a comforting misconception.

Mary's alleged professional credentials weren't just another of her exaggerations or a troubling fabrication: They'd also given her additional credibility with her son's medical team. Several doctors would go on to admit to Mike that the professional consideration they gave Mary allowed her to be more involved in decision-making. As in any other profession, people trusted their own.

But when Mike looked into her work history, it did not take long to discover that Mary was not—and had never been—a nurse in the NICU or anywhere else. Before Gabriel was born, she had worked as a receptionist and patient care tech at Harris Hospital NICU, and when Mike spoke with her onetime coworkers there, they didn't paint a rosy picture of Mary. Multiple coworkers relayed that she had the habit of saying she'd finished some task when she hadn't. They also recalled her bragging about having been a pharmacist and saying she left because it was too high stress, which is why she'd instead taken a job as a patient care tech. Needless to say, this struck everyone as a very odd career move: PCT work wasn't necessarily less stressful, and it paid one-third as much. Nonetheless, everyone bought it because Mary was charming and confident, utterly convincing. Coworkers confirmed that there was no way anyone could confuse the role of a nurse with that of a patient tech: patient techs are not allowed to interact with patients without the supervision of a registered nurse, and they don't do anything more involved than check temperatures and change diapers.

Mike could also find no evidence that Mary was ever treated for breast cancer, skin cancer, or a heart condition. His attempts to follow up with Mary's physicians led him to either clean bills of health or, in one instance, a wild goose chase for a doctor who didn't even exist. Mary's lies about her own health and career history were just like Hope's: once Mike began to pull at the thread, they unraveled completely.

Mary was the sixth offender Mike had investigated. Like Hope, she was charming and smart, adept at manipulating people in her life into thinking she was a good parent. But underneath, she was as much of a bully as Brittany, and she had the trail of broken friendships, scorned colleagues, and ex-husbands to prove it. Mary had plenty of superficial charm, but scratch the surface and it was pure chaos.

21

A Tangled Web

In any child abuse case, Mike knew family court would be intertwined with the criminal investigation, but in medical child abuse, it was especially complex. He had a long history of working crimes against children by this point, and in physical or sexual abuse cases, everyone involved seemed to appreciate the seriousness of the risk of leaving a child in the home. But it was a crapshoot with medical child abuse, and it didn't help that these investigations took three times as long as other abuse cases to investigate—meaning family court was likely to make lasting decisions before all the evidence was compiled.

Brooke, who was helming the investigation on the CPS side, was excellent and Mike trusted her. Her investigative efforts would be represented in family court by Jake Wilkinson, an attorney in a unit of the DA's Office assigned to handle things like visitation, custody, and placement—all of which had to be sorted out while the investigation was ongoing. Mike didn't know Wilkinson well: he worked in a different building, and cops and lawyers didn't mingle unless they had a reason to. But the Texas Tech graduate seemed smart and capable and had won several awards from Texas CASA, an organization that represents the interests of children in court.

In early December 2013, Brooke met with Wilkinson and laid out the evidence for removal. No one takes the idea of separating a child from their parent lightly, and in order to get an emergency removal from a judge before an investigation is complete, as happened in the Brittany Phillips case, CPS needs to make a strong case that a child is in imminent danger.

But according to CPS records, that is not what Wilkinson did. Instead, he made the fateful suggestion that Doug Welch hire his own attorney and file an emergency motion with family court to gain custody of his two children, using Dr. Coffman's affidavit outlining Mary's abuse as supporting evidence as well as testimony from Mike and Brooke about their investigations. This meant that Doug was the one asking for his children to be removed, rather than the state.

Initially, the strategy appeared to have worked: Doug was given custody of Gabriel and Madison, and a custodial restraining order was put in place until the next hearing, which was scheduled for February of the following year. Mike didn't reveal much in his testimony, only that his investigation was ongoing. But his involvement on its own was no small thing. From the stand, he got his first good look at Mary Welch in person. It wasn't encouraging: he suspected Mary of depraved behavior, but to see her in person, she just looked like a pretty mom next door. Thankfully, the judge took Dr. Coffman's affidavit seriously and granted Doug's motion.

Two days later, Gabriel Welch and his younger sister—who was just coming home from a Disney cruise with her aunt—were removed from Mary, and brought to live with Doug. Within days of being separated from his mother, Gabriel's health saw an incredible turnaround. Under his father's care, the routinely hospitalized ten-year-old was revealed to be a healthy, robust child.

Though he'd never fully believed that Gabriel was as sick as Mary seemed to think he was, Doug was nonetheless vigilant about ensuring that Gabriel received any medical help he legitimately needed. Mike also knew this was a delicate transition period, because Gabriel needed to be weaned off of his many medications under a doctor's supervision. He also knew that the more doctors who saw Gabriel's "miraculous" return to health, the better for the case.

The lightning-fast turnaround in Gabriel's health reaffirmed Doug's suspicions that Mary was the sole cause of his impairments. Suddenly, everything looked different. He recalled a particularly bad morning several years back: Doug had been driving Gabriel to school and his son had appeared unusually dazed; his eyes were glassy and his head bobbed as he fought to stay awake. What had at the time looked like symptoms of his alleged brain injury now appeared far more likely to be the side effects of his being on so many unnecessary medications. As he came off his extensive list of medications, it was as though the light inside Gabriel was turned back on to full wattage.

Doug enrolled Gabriel in the fifth grade at the local elementary school and even signed him up for baseball. Doug, devoted to helping his son recover, took several weeks off of work to help him adjust to his new life. They played catch with each other, and as Gabriel regained his strength, his former boyish rambunctiousness began to reveal itself as athletic prowess.

By the beginning of 2014, Mike had spoken to many people who'd known Mary. But as had been his strategy with Hope, he didn't want to talk to Mary herself until he'd made his way through the mind-boggling amount of paperwork on the case, collecting as much evidence as possible with which to confront her. Unlike Hope's or Brittany's, Mary's family supported her and had money

to burn, and she was lawyered up to the teeth on the civil side by
this point. Still, if you could get someone to talk, it was always
worth a shot. Mike had been able to intercept Hope and got her to
speak with him on the spot, but he wouldn't have serendipity on
his side with this case. He knew if he asked Mary to meet in person,
she'd call her lawyer, who would advise her not to say a word. He
could swing by her house, but a six-foot-four police officer with a
gun in his holster on your doorstep tends to read as intimidating,
and Mike was going for the opposite—if Mary didn't fear him, she
might try her luck lying to him. So in early January 2014, Mike
simply picked up the phone and called Mary Welch.

As always, Mike presented himself as a confused cop who simply couldn't make heads or tails of the medical records and needed
Mary's help to walk him through her son's complicated health history. Mike had come face-to-face with her only in that early family
court hearing in Johnson County, where he'd been subpoenaed,
but he knew that she likely already considered him the enemy. Sure
enough, Mary told Mike that she shouldn't talk to him without her
lawyer. Mike reassured her that that was absolutely her right, but
that he was just trying to get to the bottom of things. Mary became
tearful. "I'm a mother who loves my son," she told Mike, her voice
breaking with emotion, "and I haven't seen him in a month! He
has medical needs and there are people controlling him that don't
even know what they are. Dad is after a custody battle," she said.
She went on a furious rant about Doug: he was conniving and
vindictive and hadn't been involved in his children's lives up to that
point. But now that he'd moved in with a new girlfriend who could
watch the kids, he wanted them back. "My children don't even
know her!" Mary wailed. "And I'm sorry, sir, but you don't give two
shits about me."

Mike reiterated that getting to the truth was his only aim and asked for her help in understanding what he was looking at. "I'm just a cop," he told her. "I don't understand medical records."

Mary murmured her agreement. "It's taken me a long time to understand what half these doctors are telling me. The truth will come out," she added cryptically, "and you don't have a case."

Then, she was back to Doug. She claimed that Gabriel had been on a good trajectory with his health precisely *because* of her efforts, but he was now in danger of backsliding without her. "Now he's falling apart again," she said. In reality, nothing could have been further from the truth: Mike knew Gabriel had been thriving since he'd been separated from Mary. "He [Gabriel] doesn't have what he needs. There are witnesses telling me he's dragging his feet. Dr. Coffman evidently didn't read the medical reports. She would know if she talked to those Minnesota doctors why they gave him those braces anyway," Mary continued. When Mike pressed her on *who* had witnessed him dragging his feet, she demurred. "I'm not as clever and conniving as Doug," Mary said.

Mike pivoted and asked Mary if she'd ever told anyone that she was a nurse.

She paused and explained that she'd been trained as a certified nursing assistant* and that some people might have *misinterpreted* this. She also admitted that she might not have corrected them when that happened. Mike asked her if she'd told any doctors she was a nurse. "Oh, hell no!" Mary replied, as though shocked at the suggestion.

And what about telling people she had cancer? Mike pressed.

Mary explained that *she'd* been told that she had a cancerous

---

* One of Mary's coworkers referred to her as a "tech"—which Mike took to mean patient care tech—a job that requires slightly more training than that of a certified nursing assistant. Since Mary reported she was a CNA, that is what we're using in this instance.

lump in her breast and had taken a chemo drug for it. She'd then sought a second opinion that found it to be benign. She claimed it was a doctor "Robert Smith" who'd given her the original diagnosis. When Mike asked which hospital he was with, Mary became defensive. "You can find him. Look him up! I know what you're doing." Mike did look him up, but no doctor by this name appeared to exist in the greater Fort Worth area. Regardless, Mary maintained that she "didn't recall" ever telling anyone else she had cancer.

Throughout the call, Mary was by turns guarded and weepy, one moment reiterating that she shouldn't talk to Mike without her lawyer, the next moment making an emotional appeal to him that she was just a mom who loved her son and was overwhelmed by the complexity of his situation. She insisted that the doctors in Minnesota knew best. "Read the medical records," she said. "If you read the ones from Gillette, from the day I arrived there, it will make perfect sense! Those are so easy to understand. I have been at the same place for two years with his team at Gillette. I don't do anything without consulting them and they call the shots. Because they know what's going on with him. I do exactly what they tell me to do." Mike had seen the records, but the hospital's attorney was stonewalling him, and he had been unable to speak to Dr. Rahman, Gabriel's physician there, for further explanation.

Mike asked Mary about the incident that had started this downward spiral: the now infamous fall. Just as Mike had been hoping, Mary told the fantastical version of the night's events that she'd repeated to so many others. She claimed that Gabriel fell from the banister while she was standing there below. "I heard a little girl say, 'Gabriel, get down from there,'" Mary said, choking up at the memory. "I had my back to him when he fell. I turned and I couldn't catch him." She said he was unconscious after he fell. "They called an ambulance but it was so bad, they called care flight and we went to Children's." In reality, of course, Mary hadn't been in the room when Gabriel was discovered, and he hadn't been unconscious. Moreover, it had been Mary who'd insisted on having him airlifted to Dallas, not the other way around.

Mary continued, saying that Gabriel had become a nightmare after the fall: "When we left, I had an out-of-control child who didn't know who I was! I didn't know what to do. The hospital said 'Go home, he'll be okay,'" she recalled, sounding exasperated. She claimed that when she brought Gabriel to see his pulmonologist several weeks later, Dr. Sorkin had been horrified that they'd released Gabriel and insisted he go straight into a rehab facility. Mary had previously told her friend Carrie—in a recorded phone call, with Mike listening in—that Dr. Sorkin had even sent a "scathing" letter to Dr. Price, the doctor from Dallas Children's who'd initially treated Gabriel. "We fell through the cracks when we left there," Mary said woefully.

As to why it looked like they were doctor shopping, Mary could explain. "It looks like we've been to all these hospitals, but these doctors all have different offices and where you get the appointment is where you go. That Dr. Coffman should know that." Her voice was venomous at the mention of Dr. Coffman.

Mike had managed to keep Mary on the phone for a half hour, but at last—perhaps intuiting that she would be unable to manipulate Mike with her tearful accounts—Mary said she really did need to hang up and, polite as ever, ended the call. "I'm fighting for my kids and I'm fighting for myself," she said firmly.

Dr. Sorkin was the pulmonologist who'd treated Gabriel for asthma-related issues since he was nine years old. He was one of many doctors Mike had spoken to about the case, and his affidavit told a very different story from what Mary had reported. Dr. Sorkin explained that Mary *had* told him that she was a nurse, and that yes, he remembered the follow-up visit that Mary had spoken to Mike about. Though he had indeed recommended therapy at Baylor, he'd done so because of the lies Mary had told about Gabriel's fall. She'd claimed that Gabriel had suffered a three-minute-long seizure following the incident and had been in a thirteen-hour coma at Dallas Children's. She said he bled from his ears two weeks after the incident and had been acting out and having trouble focusing. As far as the "scathing letter" to Dr. Price, Dr. Sorkin had recently been asked by Mary's lawyers to send them a copy of the document. He had been baffled by the request, as no such letter existed. He called Dr. Price to consult with her, but he had never been critical of her care of Gabriel.

Dr. Sorkin saw Gabriel and Mary many times over the years, and as with so many of Gabriel's other doctors, the reports Mary provided were so multitudinous they were hard to track: she'd alleged issues with Gabriel's breathing, his sleep, his vocal cords, his swallow function, his behavior, his eyesight. It went on and on. As to what Dr. Sorkin actually observed: Gabriel had some behavioral issues, but these could have just as easily been a result of taking Advair—prescribed for the alleged asthma—a drug known to cause aggression, agitation, and mood swings in children.

In June 2011, Mary brought Gabriel in to see Dr. Sorkin, telling him she believed he'd suffered a series of "small strokes." An MRI and MRA were performed, and no damage was found other than that sustained during his fall. A neurologist affirmed that there was no evidence of stroke.

In September 2011, at a follow-up visit with Dr. Sorkin, Mary reported Gabriel was having difficulty swallowing and was catching his breath. Dr. Sorkin referred Gabriel for a swallow study that produced perfectly normal results. Mary would go on to claim to other doctors in Minnesota that the test had revealed vocal cord dysfunction, premature vocal cord closure, and dysphagia. The result of this false claim was two additional unnecessary surgeries for Gabriel: a G-tube placement, and a Nissen fundoplication.

Dr. Sorkin had initially been concerned about Gabriel's brain injury, but over time he became much more concerned about Munchausen by proxy. He didn't feel Gabriel had vocal cord dysfunction or required a fundoplication, as Mary suggested; he didn't feel Gabriel needed oxygen; he'd never even heard of normal pressure hydrocephalus—the rare brain condition Mary insisted he'd been diagnosed with, though there was no record of it in his chart—occurring in a child. The overall picture of Gabriel's symptoms just didn't make any clinical sense.

Meanwhile, Dr. Price—the alleged recipient of the "scathing letter," and the physician who treated Gabriel after his fall—gave a sworn affidavit that Gabriel's time in the hospital was unremarkable. She confirmed that he had never been in a coma, was never transferred to the ICU, and was kept for four days mostly out of concern that he might become dehydrated because of vomiting, a common side effect of concussions. Upon discharge, Dr. Price said, Gabriel's long-term prognosis was excellent and he was expected to resume all normal functions after an initial recovery period. Dr. Price said some head injuries, rarely, *can* lead to post-traumatic hydrocephalus, though not the kind Mary alleged Gabriel had—and in fact, a follow-up MRI at Dallas Children's showed no evidence of either condition.

DURING THIS PERIOD of the investigation, Mike followed up with Mary's immediate family members, who were coalescing around Mary as some of her sole supporters. First, he spoke to her sister, Brandy. Mary and Brandy also had a brother, who never returned Mike's phone call.

First, Mike asked Brandy about Mary's alleged skin and breast cancer diagnoses. Brandy recalled that Mary had "a cyst or something" on her breast and that a doctor had "carved skin cancer" out of her leg, which left Mary with a visible scar. (In reality, the doctor

Brandy mentioned had never treated Mary for skin cancer or any-thing else.)

Brandy seemed exceptionally naive about her sister. When Mike told Brandy that Mary had presented Gabriel to doctors with a false medical history, she leapt to her sister's defense. "I can tell you a million times over that Mary *loves* her children. Beyond any-thing." She kept reiterating what an amazing advocate Mary had been for her son: the heroic mom who would go to any lengths to make sure Gabriel got the care he needed. Brandy seemed genu-inely confused as to why Doug had gotten custody of the kids, and when Mike explained medical child abuse to her, she had clearly never heard of it. She tried to rationalize Mary's behavior. "Every child is different with a brain injury," she told Mike. "Doctors have different opinions!" This was true enough, but most parents didn't lie to their children's doctors.

Brandy had repeated Mary's line that *only* the Minnesota doctors were capable of properly treating Gabriel. When Mike explained that Gabriel's medical issues had swiftly and wholly resolved after being separated from Mary, Brandy asked who'd determined this: "Was it here or up north?" Brandy explained that while she and her own son had had good experiences with many of the same Texas doctors that Mary had been so aggrieved by, every kid was differ-ent. "The Minnesota doctors won't let him fall through the cracks because of their medical egos," Brandy said.

Brandy seemed loath to accept that medical child abuse was even a possibility for her nephew. When Mike explained that doc-tors *do*, in fact, get fooled into doing unnecessary surgeries and pro-cedures, she exclaimed, "I can't believe that!" Brandy was perhaps a bit oblivious in her support of Mary, but what Mike encountered when he spoke to Mary's mother, Rose, was of another order alto-gether.

Rose started off the call sounding guarded, wondering aloud if she needed her lawyer on with her. "I don't feel good talking to you. Everything I've said has been ignored or twisted," she told Mike. Rose started off the conversation saying that she wouldn't talk to Mike—whom she clearly viewed as the enemy—but then continued to speak. She said it was all Doug, and that he'd managed to pull everyone else into a conspiracy to achieve his ends of getting sole custody of his children. "She's a good mother and Dad is on a rampage," Rose said to Mike. Rose was going to be tough to convince, but Mike had to try to make her see the light: Mary's parents were footing her considerable legal bills, and Rose was clearly the decision-maker in the family. Mike tried to explain that the CPS report had not originated with Doug, but she was unmoved.

Mike had seen this kind of scapegoating before in abuse cases when custody was in play: accusations that the investigation was caused by a vindictive father, or some other rogue family member with a vendetta against the mother. However, Mike knew that for a case to make it all the way to his desk, it needed to involve medical professionals themselves being concerned because there had been *evidence* of abuse, not simply a suspicion.

Mike explained to Rose that Gabriel had been just fine since being removed from Mary—a miraculous turnaround from the fragile boy he'd been portrayed as. "You're saying he's been removed from all medication? Is that what Dad is telling you?" Rose said. Mike explained that Gabriel's improved health had also been confirmed by his doctors and his school. Rose was incredulous: "As of when? That's not what they told the attorneys!" She became combative, saying, "Those aren't even his doctors!"

"But do you understand that Gabriel is fine now?" Mike pressed.

"Gabriel was fine when he was taken! There wasn't anything wrong with Gabriel when he was taken," Rose said, despite the fact that at the time of his removal, he was prescribed more than a dozen daily medications.

Mike asked Rose to confirm what she'd observed following Gabriel's big accident.

"Was he in a coma at the hospital?" Mike asked.

"Yes," Rose said emphatically.

"For how long?"

"You need to check the hospital records," she spat back.

"Well, what did Mary tell you about Gabriel being in a coma?"

"I was there," Rose said indignantly. Mike already knew there would be no convincing Rose that her daughter was guilty, but with that statement, he realized she was also willing to lie for Mary. He knew he needed to keep her on the call and let her talk, to discredit herself on the record. To make herself useless as a witness to the defense.

Mike asked again how long Gabriel had been in a coma; Rose again told him to check the records.

"You realize that nowhere in the hospital records does it say he was in a coma?" Mike continued.

"Are you sure?" she asked.

"Absolutely."

"Oh, I see," she said, "I see. Well, it sounds like someone is covering up something at Cook's."

"Well, number one, it wasn't at Cook's, ma'am, it was at Children's Medical Center Dallas," Mike said. Her mistake was telling: the two hospitals were a forty-minute drive from one another. How likely was it that she'd mixed them up if she was really there?

"Well, wherever it was, someone is covering it up. I was there that night. He was *out*," she insisted.

"No one who was at the hospital says that," Mike said.

"I think you're lying to me!" Rose said. "Nobody was saying he was ever unconscious at the hospital, is that what you're telling me?"

"Correct."

"I'm not talking to you anymore," she said. "You're very much misled." Rose insisted that she'd seen Gabriel unconscious after the accident and that he'd remained that way until the following morning.

"So you're saying the hospital records are lying?"

"They very well could be," Rose said.

Mike pivoted and asked when she'd last seen Gabriel. "Two days before he was taken, when he was *kidnapped* from Walmart," she said, referencing another wild tale from Mary—that Doug had snatched Gabriel away from her under false pretenses while they were shopping at Walmart.

Mike tried to debunk this story, telling her that he'd spoken to the process server, but Rose dug her heels in. "I don't know how you're getting all this information."

"I'm trying to enlighten you about what's been going on with your grandson," Mike said. "Mary has been lying to you." Whatever slim hope Mike had had of turning Rose around was now extinguished.

Rose doubled down about a cover-up and a conspiracy. "This just sounds like Doug," she said, exasperated. "He's just Mr. Drama Queen."

Mike switched tactics, asking if Mary had ever had cancer.

There was a pregnant pause. "I'm not going to answer that," Rose said, before claiming that she didn't remember. Finally, she concluded, "She's had several surgeries. I've been there."

Mike tried to get her to specify *where* these alleged surgeries had occurred.

"I'm not telling you anything! You're using it to build a case. Y'all are just letting Doug run amok. All I hear is Doug coming out of your mouth and some friends that don't know her very well. You get them on the stand! We'll see what happens."

Mike explained that every place Mary claimed to have been treated for her alleged cancers had no records at all for her. "So if you do know a place that she's been treated—" he began.

"Oh, don't play this game with me!" Rose spat. "This sounds so tricky. I'm not telling you where! You go get off your butt and do your work. I'm not giving you any information to use against her."

As Mike enumerated the many people in Mary's life who had reported her lies, Rose seemed to have an answer for each one of them. Her Aunt Julie? "She's a drunk. She hates Mary! Whatever she says is crap." The friends Mike had talked to? "Her archenemies for years! All girls have 'em." As for the reports from Dr. Coffman, she was colluding with CPS and Doug. "She's their go-to gal. All she does is rest on what the dad says."

When Mike explained that Dr. Coffman had spoken to Dr. Rahman—the much-lauded Minnesota doctor—and that he'd told her he'd done the procedures on Gabriel solely based on Mary's reports, without doing his own tests, Rose was incredulous.

"No brain surgeon is going to do brain surgery on a kid based on what the mother said. You are off the chart on that one. If Dr. Coffman says that, she's a bozo."

Unfortunately, Rose wasn't alone in this misconception. But Mike knew from his many conversations with Dr. Coffman and other doctors that no physician could diagnose a child in the fifteen minutes they were in the office with them *without* reporting from the parent: it was especially true with very young children, but even teenagers were often not the most faithful reporters of their own symptoms. Pediatric doctors relied utterly on the parents—a sacred contract that most caretakers would never dream of breaching.

Mike tried to enlighten Rose: "Ma'am, doctors do surgeries all the time based on the parent's report."

Rose stayed on the call, but she refused to tell Mike much else. "You're going to use it against Mary," she said. "Y'all are wanting this. Y'all don't even understand his injury, and neither does his father."

"Who does understand his injuries?" Mike asked.

"His doctors!" Again with the notion that the Minnesota doctors could clear all of this up. "You can call me a hostile witness," Rose said, "because I think y'all are on a witch hunt. There's a lot to learn about his injury and y'all are just trying to twist shit."

"I don't twist anything, ma'am."

"You're looking for facts—" Rose said.

"That's correct."

"Facts to bury her with," she continued.

"If the facts bury her, they bury her; if they clear her, they clear her. That's how facts work!" Mike said, growing exasperated.

"You should have been an attorney," Rose said in a tone that made it clear this wasn't a compliment. "You can take facts . . . and put them in a line and make it look different."

It was clear that there was no evidence that Rose could be confronted with that would cause her to doubt Mary's word. Anyone could understand how hard it must be for a mother to imagine that their daughter could hurt her own children. Any explanation—that it was all the ex-husband's doing, that her enemies were colluding against her, that CPS and the doctors and the police had formed some sort of bizarre conspiracy to take her down—must have felt preferable to what the evidence was pointing to: that Mary had knowingly subjected Gabriel to unnecessary treatments and procedures, including brain surgery.

But for those close to Mary, that unwillingness to face the awful truth would come at a very high price.

IN FEBRUARY 2014, when it was discovered that Mary was no longer at her old address and had moved in with Chad, the CPS case was transferred to Tarrant County, where a follow-up hearing was held in family court.

Mary Welch had been under a no-contact order with her children

since the previous December. Mike knew from experience that visitation could interfere with the investigation and put the child in
danger: he'd seen Brittany attempt to induce symptoms in Alyssa,
and he'd heard of numerous other cases where perpetrators tried
similar methods to "prove" that their child was truly ill.

Family court associate judge James Mumford* presided over the
hearing where both Mary and Doug were present with their lawyers. Things had obviously curdled between the once friendly exes:
they avoided eye contact. As Mike took the witness stand to testify,
he spied Mary at the defense table looking prim. When the judge
asked the bailiff to find Mary's attorney, Mary interjected, "Judge,
they're just out in the hallway. I'll go get them for you." She sounded
sweet as pie, every inch the teacher's pet. Mike watched, dismayed,
as her charms seemed to be taking hold of the judge: it occurred to
him how lovely and normal Mary must seem. Mike testified, once
again, reminding the court that this was an active investigation. Dr.
Coffman followed him, explaining that her medical record review
indicated that she'd discovered numerous instances of Munchausen
by proxy abuse. As she began to explain the terminology to the
court, the judge cut her off and said he knew what Munchausen
by proxy was. But another witness in court that day would later
tell Mike that from her vantage point on the witness stand, she'd
observed Judge Mumford google "Munchausen by proxy" from his
laptop on the bench.

Just as Mike feared, Mary got exactly what she wanted out of the
hearing: the right to have visitation with her children supervised
only by her mother, Rose. Mike knew Rose didn't believe that Mary
was any kind of threat to Gabriel, and was therefore unlikely to

---

* An associate judge is appointed by the elected judge in family court to help
with the court's caseload. Mumford would later become an elected family court
judge in Tarrant County.

keep a watchful eye on their interactions. Rose had already lied to Mike on Mary's behalf—claiming to have seen Gabriel in a coma—and he knew she couldn't be trusted.

Meanwhile, there'd been a big change in Mike's daily work life, as he'd lost ADA Alana Minton, who'd left to travel the world with her family. Mike and Alana had worked a half dozen of these cases by that point, but once he met her replacement, he was reassured. ADA Letty Martinez was a comely, dark-haired mom of two who understood her role as a prosecutor to be one of seeking justice, not just of winning cases. This was the ethos of the leadership at the time, and it made the Tarrant County DA's Office one of the most coveted workplaces in the state. In her midthirties, Letty was an experienced crimes-against-children prosecutor who, interestingly enough, had a daughter with a legitimate autism diagnosis who attended a special school. She was as good of a partner as Mike could hope for on a case like this. With the children now left vulnerable by the new family court order, Letty understood the urgency of wrapping the investigation up and charging Mary.

Though Doug had finally lawyered up at the behest of the CPS attorney, Wilkinson, Mike worried that his counsel was no match for Mary's team as the family court battle carried on. Mike could see that Doug's attorney was consistently outflanked by Mary's team. Mike also knew the Fort Worth legal community could be an insular one, and he felt Kenneth Newell, the amicus—a court-appointed attorney meant to represent the child's interests in court—seemed overly sympathetic to Mary's cause.

After Newell was appointed, he reached out to Mike.

Mike had dealt with innumerable amicus and ad litem attorneys in his years in crimes against children, and had by and large found them to be impartial, dedicated to protecting children. Mike arranged a meeting at his office with Newell and Dr. Coffman.

Mike and Dr. Coffman walked Newell through the medical

history and explained that Gabriel—a supposedly chronically and seriously ill child—had experienced a rapid recovery after being separated from Mary. Mike revealed that he'd discovered Mary Welch's other lies, including the fabricated cancer diagnoses and the alleged nursing background. But Newell cut him off. "I'm only interested in whether or not she lied to the doctors about Gabriel," he told them. Mike tried to explain that a pattern of deception was germane to the case, and that Gabriel's doctors had—by their own admission—allowed Mary special considerations because of her claimed history as a nurse. But Newell seemed deeply incredulous that Mary had done anything wrong, despite Dr. Coffman's clear and thorough explanations of the medical records.

Mike had the sinking feeling that Newell had made up his mind about the case before he'd walked through the door. It would be nice to believe that someone in Newell's position wouldn't be swayed by Mary's well-resourced family, his personal friendship with her attorney, or the fact that Mary was an attractive, persuasive woman. But to think these factors do not affect how things play out in the justice system would be naive: the system comprises human beings and all their biases. People's emotional beliefs easily outweigh any evidence they are presented with, especially when it comes to medical child abuse, a crime that challenges our deepest convictions about motherhood.

Eventually Mike lost his cool at Newell's intransigence, saying, "If this boy is returned to Mary Welch, he is at risk of serious harm or even death." Newell pursed his lips, unmoved. Mike's outburst seemed to only cement his idea that Mike was an overzealous investigator on a mission. It didn't seem to matter that Dr. Coffman—an experienced and extremely well-respected child abuse pediatrician—shared his concern. Mike feared Newell was acting as another lawyer for Mary, rather than for Gabriel.

In April, Assistant District Attorney Jake Wilkinson realized his mistake in pulling CPS from the family court proceedings and assigned one of his attorneys to petition the judge to allow CPS to re-enter the case. But just as this attorney was unpacking her files and preparing to present in court, the judge told her she didn't need to be there: this was no longer a CPS matter. Mike couldn't help but think Mary's attorneys had gotten to the judge. Doug was on his own. He and his lawyer had subpoenaed a half dozen key doctors as witnesses to explain the importance of not allowing visitation, but after two witnesses, the judge had heard enough. The doctors—including Dr. Sorkin—were left in the hallway, their opinions unheard. The judge denied the appeal. This meant Mary's visitation with Gabriel—done not by CPS but by her mother, Rose, a person who didn't believe Mary needed supervising—would stay in place. She'd be with Gabriel every other weekend and for an entire month in the summer.

22

Minnesota

Throughout the investigation, Mary claimed she'd been the victim of medical egos and neglectful doctors. She stuck to her guns that the *good* doctors of Gillette Hospital in Minnesota—to whom she'd gone through so much time and expense to shuttle Gabriel back and forth over the years—were the only ones who truly understood his rare condition. But the fact that these doctors were a thousand miles away, in another state, presented significant jurisdictional issues. Mike had begun to suspect that Mary had *decided* upon Gabriel's alleged rare diagnosis and then sought out the expert in Minnesota to confirm it, rather than making a genuine search for the truth.

In January 2014, Mike put in a call to the Ramsey County DA's Office in Saint Paul, Minnesota. Mike had needed to coordinate with an out-of-state DA's office once before for a medical child abuse case—that time in San Diego—and he hoped he'd get the same level of cooperation this time around. His first case in Ohio had also been across state lines, but he'd just passed that over to the Cleveland PD, erroneously assuming they'd handle it. Mike walked his Saint Paul contact, Cheryl Barber, through the case and received a curt reply: "What do you expect me to do, charge the doctors?" Mike was stunned. Barber was supposedly a seasoned prosecutor, but she clearly didn't have the slightest idea what she was dealing with. Before hanging up, she told Mike that he would need to report this to the Saint Paul Police Department.

So Mike put in a call to the supervisor of the crimes-against-children unit in Saint Paul, where Gillette Children's Hospital was located and where many of Gabriel's more invasive procedures had been performed. Mike told the supervisor this was a complicated case. "It needs someone open-minded and motivated." What he got was Detective Richard Dixon. Mike ran down the case facts with Dixon, and was relieved when the detective seemed eager to help.

From the outside, agencies like CPS and the police could seem faceless and immovable, but Mike knew that they were made of individuals. It was always a roll of the dice whether he'd get a detective motivated enough to dig into these extraordinarily complicated cases that came with tens of thousands of pages of medical records, or someone who'd just see a headache. And now that CPS was out of the picture, the criminal case was going to be the only way to keep Mary Welch away from her son.

BUT IN THE midst of his investigation, the ground beneath Mike's feet began to shift. On March 4, 2014, Sharen Wilson easily won the Republican nomination for district attorney of Tarrant County and became the DA-elect in the absence of Democratic opposition. The current DA, Joe Shannon—who'd taken over when his predecessor, Tim Curry, passed away in office—was retiring after just over one term. In his over thirty years at the helm of Tarrant County, Curry had established himself as the most stable DA in the state and made the office a sought-after workplace. Shannon, a Curry protégé, had maintained the same culture: hiring good people, training them properly, and letting them do their work. Curry's style involved patiently hearing out his prosecutors and then asking them what they thought was the right thing to do. Once they answered, Curry would usually say: "Well then, let's do that." And if the right thing meant bringing extra political heat? Curry protected his people.

But Mike had heard Sharen Wilson—previously a criminal district court judge—was a bully on the bench. He was unsettled at the idea of working for her, but he kept his head down, and carried on pursuing the biggest missing piece of the medical puzzle around Gabriel—interviewing the doctors from Gillette Hospital in Minnesota. Throughout the investigation, Mary's claim had been that she'd brought Gabriel north for treatment not because she was looking for doctors who would do what she wanted, but because the team at Gillette were the only people qualified to care for Gabriel. What would the doctors have to say about that?

In April 2014, Mike was finally able to get through the hospital's red tape and speak to Mary's much-lauded and relied-upon Dr. Rahman. This was in spite of the hospital's attorney, who had been nothing but a pain in Mike's ass. There was usually a shared understanding that a criminal investigation was a necessary exception to patient privacy laws—it's one of the reasons actually pursuing criminal charges is so crucial in medical child abuse cases. But in his first conversation with the hospital counsel, Dick Kaur, Mike was asked to produce a civil court order to interview Dr. Rahman, a bizarre request. The back-and-forth lasted months, and Mike could only surmise that the hospital feared a lawsuit.

Mike finally met with Dr. Rahman via conference call, with the hospital's attorney, Kaur, and Detective Dixon of the Saint Paul

PD also on the line. This conversation solidified Mike's long-held suspicion that there was no evidence that Gabriel had suffered from hydrocephalus, and that he had never needed a brain shunt. Dr. Rahman confirmed that he had not done an MRI or any other testing, nor had he reviewed any of the medical records from Cook's or Dallas Children's, where Gabriel had previously been treated for his injury. He'd relied instead on what Mary had told him: that Cook's had concerns about an MRI they'd performed, which, of course, they did not—Gabriel's MRI had shown no issues whatsoever. The brain shunt had been placed based solely on the history of Gabriel's health that Mary had provided and her reports of his symptoms. Mike suspected that this mess-up was the reason for the hospital attorney's caginess. Most of the many doctors who'd treated Gabriel had simply been doing their jobs by taking Mary's word for it. But Dr. Rahman went a step further. He wasn't making his decision based on imaging of his own or another hospital's—what's worse, he hadn't even returned the calls of Dr. Davies, the Cook's surgeon who'd removed Gabriel's shunt. Mike appreciated Dr. Rahman's honesty; he knew it was devastating for a physician to realize they'd been manipulated into harming a child.

Dr. Rahman recalled Mary saying she worked as a neonatal nurse, and that she'd played the part extremely convincingly. It had been her detailed reports of Gabriel's health alone that had led Dr. Rahman to diagnose the boy with normal pressure hydrocephalus. For context, Mike asked him how many cases of normal pressure hydrocephalus Dr. Rahman had ever seen in children in his career as a neurosurgeon. Dr. Rahman said that including Gabriel, he'd seen three. Mike immediately wondered about the other two cases— though he knew better than to express those doubts out loud. It was clear that Dr. Rahman had done the opposite of the old med school adage to "think horses not zebras when you hear hoofbeats."

Dr. Rahman's admission was huge, but there was still more to uncover in Minnesota. Dr. Spiva, also within the Gillette Hospital system, was a pediatric pulmonologist who'd seen Gabriel on a number of occasions for his alleged respiratory and reflux issues. Two affidavits written by Dr. Spiva, under a year apart, paint an enlightening picture of just how credible Mary had appeared. The first letter—which Mary had requested from Dr. Spiva, claiming it was for her custody case—described Mary as a perfectly normal mom of a medically complex child. Dr. Spiva wrote how complicated Gabriel's medical condition was: the traumatic brain injury that led to his hydrocephalus, the respiratory and reflux issues, and so on. He reported that Mary had "appropriately noticed" these symptoms over time and had "never seemed to overreact." He said the family had been compliant with reflux therapy and that pharmacy records didn't indicate overuse of medication. He reported that both Gabriel and Madison seemed like happy, independent children, and that Mary always seemed appropriate and calm with them.

Dr. Spiva's second affidavit, from May 2014, told an entirely different story. "Mary always presented a knowledgeable, caring, and compliant persona. She seemed a real advocate for her son and his medical issues." But then the letter took a turn. "I have come to learn that Mary was surprisingly dishonest about Gabriel's previous medical diagnoses." He went on to explain that he would never have recommended Gabriel for the procedures he had referred him for if he'd known that Mary had already received test results from other hospitals showing there was no need for them. "As I later discovered, Mary had a documented history of skilled deception and fabrication involving many clinicians in several hospital systems. I too was fooled," he admitted. He expressed regret at Gabriel's unnecessary suffering and praised the investigation, saying: "I applaud your thorough approach to Gabriel Welch's case, as it may have saved his life."

Dr. Spiva had referred Gabriel to pulmonologist Dr. Barton for another surgery in Minnesota: the Nissen fundoplication. In a sworn affidavit, Dr. Barton confirmed that this procedure had been performed on the basis of Mary's reporting of Gabriel's symptoms. Dr. Barton added that—given the information he now had—there was likely no need for the fundoplication or the feeding tube Gabriel had had placed. Furthermore, Mary had omitted a key piece of information: another pediatric gastroenterologist who'd seen Gabriel had *ruled out* reflux.

All in all, the conversations with the Minnesota doctors had been illuminating. Rather than providing the exoneration Mary had counted on, they offered yet more evidence of her intentional and far-reaching deception, and the pain she'd inflicted on Gabriel. But had Mike gotten these final puzzle pieces too late?

23

A Seismic Shift

Even though the evidence on the Texas side was strong, ADA Letty Martinez felt it would be better to have Mary charged in the state where the most serious surgeries—the brain shunt placement, the G-tube placement, and the Nissen fundoplication—took place. But Mike wasn't sure he could rely on Detective Dixon and, furthermore, he knew Minnesota's laws would be even more difficult to work with than those in Texas. Texas had something known as the "law of parties," which essentially stated that an offender could be charged for convincing an unwitting person to commit a crime, meaning Mary could be held as responsible for the harm she'd caused Gabriel as if she had been holding the scalpel herself. But Minnesota had no such law—and furthermore, Minnesota CPS would have no involvement with this case because Mary didn't live there.

Mike called Detective Dixon to discuss the case and what else he needed to move forward. Mike hoped for cooperation, but the conversation was utterly dissonant. Though Dixon had been in the same meeting as Mike, he claimed to have no recollection of Dr. Rahman saying he did the surgery based only on Mary's report of Gabriel's medical history—despite the fact that Dr. Rahman said so twice, in separate interviews with both Dr. Coffman and Mike, and that his statement was backed by the medical records and interviews with Dr. Davies and another neurosurgeon at Cook Children's Hospital. Mike had the sinking feeling that the Saint Paul detective was hearing what he wanted to hear—and looking for an excuse to let the case go.

"Saint Paul is full of liberals," Dixon complained. "They're soft on crime up here. I can't wait to retire and get out of here." Mike was appalled. What a sorry excuse. Personal politics aside, he knew no one on either side of the aisle who was keen on letting child predators get away with it. But instead of being invested in protecting the life of a child, Dixon waxed on about his retirement plans. Mike realized that he was on his own.

Even without Minnesota, Mike had a lot to work with, and he took it back to Letty. With the most crucial pieces in place—the doctors' accounts from both states, as well as a truckload of collateral interviews about Mary and Gabriel—Mike believed he had probable cause to arrest Mary Welch. It was far from a perfect case: because the surgeries had taken place in Minnesota, injury to a child wasn't on the table.

"The doctors have to be with us one hundred percent," Letty told Mike. He assured her they were. It would be an uphill battle, but Letty agreed that they had to try. She wasn't afraid of a tough court battle if she felt it was the right thing to do: sometimes you just had to chance it.

Letty authorized an arrest warrant for Mary Welch for "endangering a child" based on the unneeded drugs Gabriel had been taking. Judge Mollee Westfall signed the warrant and placed bond conditions of no contact on Mary for both Gabriel and his sister. Mary Welch was placed under arrest on May 28, 2014.

Mike called Doug to share the news, and even over the phone, his relief was palpable. At the time, Doug didn't especially want Mary thrown in jail—he knew how hard that would be on his kids—but he accepted that she was truly dangerous to them, and he wanted to make sure she could never be alone with them again. To Doug, the threat she posed was clear, and he felt sure a jury would see it, too.

Mary was bonded out by her parents immediately. The no-contact order that went into place with her arrest was a relief, but it was a stopgap measure, in effect for only ninety days—after which point custody would revert to the preexisting court order giving Mary full visitation. The underlying assumption was that family court would modify those terms once criminal charges were filed, but family court had proven to be an unreliable ally in this case.

Mike proceeded to write an extensively detailed and exhaustive arrest warrant affidavit on Mary Welch—including every damning piece of evidence from doctors, friends, and family members over the course of his thirteen-month investigation. He always tried to make these as complete as possible in the hope of getting through to anyone reading so they would understand the seriousness of the charge. Doug's attorney presented the warrant to family court, where it appeared to have been summarily ignored.

In July 2014, the amicus on the Welch case, Kenneth Newell, was replaced with Barry Barbour. Mike was hopeful this might mark a turn in the family court proceedings, but when he and Letty met with Barbour, it was clear he was equally credulous of Mary. Even after they explained the entire case to him, he didn't ask a single question. Mike thought: *Seriously? We've just told you about a mother who convinced doctors to—among other things—perform unnecessary brain surgery on her eight-year-old son, and you have no questions?*

In October 2014, Mary Welch's case went to a grand jury, which would be tasked with determining if there was enough evidence to warrant moving forward with a trial. By this point, Letty and Mike knew that prosecution in Saint Paul wasn't going to happen.

They couldn't use the surgeries in their case, since they'd occurred in Minnesota, but Mary had attempted one. They added the charge of "criminal attempt injury to a child—serious bodily injury" for Mary's efforts to get Gabriel's brain shunt replaced at Cook Children's Hospital, after the infected shunt from Gillette had been removed. It was a higher felony than endangering a child, and punishable by up to twenty years in prison. The twelve members of the grand jury voted unanimously to indict Mary on both charges.

ON JANUARY 1, 2015, the new district attorney of Tarrant County, Sharen Wilson, was sworn in. It was a holiday and swearing-in ceremonies were usually a simple process, but Mike was advised that New Year's Day or not, it would be politically wise to attend. The beginning of the ceremony was heralded by dramatic music as Wilson entered. It had the pomp and circumstance of a coronation, rather than the swearing in of a public servant. It was a harbinger of what was to come.

Sharen Wilson's reputation preceded her, and it wasn't a good one. In one notorious incident, Wilson was presiding over a child sexual abuse case where the prepubescent victim took the stand to testify, clutching a stuffed animal she'd brought along for comfort. Wilson ordered the stuffed animal removed, something court observers had never seen a judge do. She was also well known for playing Christmas music in her court during the holiday months as she sentenced defendants to long prison terms: a cruel bit of theater to drive home what they'd be missing while they were locked up.

During her first week on the job, Sharen Wilson strode into the office wearing one of her signature pantsuits, her no-nonsense gunmetal-gray hair feathered around her face—and called an all-office meeting: no excused absences, no exceptions. During this first meeting with her new staff—which consisted of criminal investigators like Mike, attorneys, paralegals, and various admin folks—Wilson told the attorneys, all of whom had chosen serving victims over the far more lucrative option of working in criminal defense, that if they were still with the DA's Office after five years of service, they were wasting their time. She clearly considered the work of the people under her as a mere stepping stone to more illustrious careers. Her message was clear: they were suckers if they stuck around.

Still, Wilson micromanaged the office to the hilt, seemingly more concerned about highlighter choice—only yellow and blue were acceptable—than getting back to her ADAs about a capital murder case. She blew apart a long-established office policy of having a committee dedicated to determining whether the death penalty should be pursued, and consolidated all decision-making power to herself. She had no respect for her team's time, sending emails to employees at five a.m. on weekends and calling them in on holidays. She berated employees for any and all mistakes, but also didn't take kindly to being asked questions. A month into her term—against the advice of her highest-level long-term staff, who knew that the policy would be devastating to morale and employee retention—Wilson instituted a rule that every attorney had to be at their desk by 7:45 a.m., and conducted "desk checks" to ensure compliance.

This was the breaking point for Letty Martinez. Letty's daughter attended a special school for autistic children and Letty usually handled drop-off (her husband, a judge, helped when he could, but couldn't do it every day), which could take time, because the school used the opportunity to help the kids learn social skills by greeting their teachers—an involved process that occasionally led to meltdowns. To appease Wilson, Letty arranged with her team of five for three of them to arrive at 7:45 to answer any incoming calls—even though the office was always dead at that hour. Letty asked that she and another attorney with young kids be allowed to come in closer to nine o'clock, which would give them plenty of time to get to court. Wilson refused, and that was it for Letty. She left in March 2015, along with much of the rest of the office. Between a spate of firings from Wilson and the turnover that resulted from plummeting morale, Mike suddenly found himself adrift, no longer surrounded by colleagues he trusted. Instead, there were multiple attorneys working in specialized units such as crimes against children and felony domestic violence who had never prosecuted *any* felony case, much less a case in their assigned discipline.

Shortly after Letty Martinez resigned, Wilson appointed ADA Patrick Mueller to take over as chief of the crimes-against-children unit. Mike was aghast at the choice. Mueller had previously handled child pornography cases, and it was well known throughout the county that he had rarely mustered the motivation to take a case to trial. Whether an offender had thirty or thirty thousand pictures of child pornography in their possession, they would be given ten years' deferred adjudication probation—more or less a slap on the wrist—by Mueller.

Some of the old-guard attorneys left in the office tried to reassure Mike that Mueller would be easy to work around; he was simply too lazy to be an obstacle. But Mike watched in horror as those attorneys were replaced one by one by Mueller's cronies, none of whom had experience prosecuting crimes against children. Mike tried to keep his head down and just do his job. So he had new attorneys to educate; he could do that.

MEANWHILE, THE WELCHES were in a holding pattern: the no-contact order placed when Mary was arrested had expired, and the family court had done nothing to intervene. Mike was shocked that even a criminal indictment hadn't gotten family court to take seriously the danger Mary posed. Mary once more had standard visitation rights with Gabriel, supervised by Rose.

After the initial separation from his mother, Gabriel had become quite the baseball star. Mike spoke to his coach during the investigation, and the picture he painted of Gabriel was very far indeed from that of the fragile boy who'd spent half his life in the hospital. Shawn saw Gabriel several times a week for practice and games and reported him to be not only healthy, but quite an athlete. "He was one of my top draft picks," Shawn explained. "He's one of my top players on the team." Mike asked him if Mary had ever said anything to him about Gabriel's health, and sure enough, Shawn noticed that Mom and Dad gave starkly differing reports of Gabriel's capabilities. "Mom seems real concerned about his health, like he could break at any moment," he said. Though Mary was always extremely pleasant, it struck Shawn that Doug seemed to have no such concerns—and he had certainly never observed any health issues himself in Gabriel. She'd also given Shawn the impression that his father, Doug, was a loose cannon, claiming in one email that he'd "threatened to beat me to death" with a baseball bat at one of Gabriel's games.

Shawn had also noticed that when Mary would come pick Gabriel up from practice, she'd make small sideways comments. "You're probably already tired, you're not thinking straight," she said once when Gabriel commented that he wished he could stay and play all night. This struck Shawn as odd, and he thought at the time, *This kid has more energy than I'll ever have.* Shawn told Mike that Gabriel was attentive and very coachable—in short, a coach's dream. None of his laundry list of alleged behavioral issues appeared to be presenting themselves. When Mike asked if Gabriel seemed to him in any way like a sick child, Shawn laughed. "No. Not at all. He's a little athlete, he's a fun kid, got a bright personality. Always respectful, has a good attitude. He's a little star."

In addition to sports, Gabriel also started to make up for lost time at school. Though he was behind in classwork due to all the days he'd missed, Gabriel was thriving academically, making good grades and quickly catching up to his peers. His alleged learning disabilities appeared to be nonexistent. Doug felt like he finally had his son back.

But perhaps not for long. The existing arrangement granted Mary one month of full custody during the summer. In July 2015, Mike learned that Mary was planning on taking Gabriel back to Gillette—her hospital of choice—for "adjustments to his shunt." Mike contacted the Gillette Hospital attorney, Dick Kaur, and informed him that he would need to interview Dr. Rahman and any other doctors Gabriel saw at Gillette again if Mary brought her son back for treatment. But Kaur refused to let Mike talk to the doctors under any circumstances. Mike was concerned that doctors would see Mary with Gabriel, assume nothing came of the case, and thus decide that Mary must be reliable—a conclusion that could be catastrophic. Mike knew he also couldn't trust Kaur, who had been an obstacle throughout the case, to tell the Gillette doctors about the criminal charges; he needed to tell them himself.

Mike relayed his concerns to the new Tarrant County prosecutor assigned to the case, Bucky Pear. A boyish attorney in his early thirties with no experience in child abuse cases, Pear was way out of his depth, but Mike tried to play nice and, as a courtesy, asked him if tracking down Dr. Rahman's home number presented any legal issue for the case. Pear assured him it didn't: Dr. Rahman was a witness, not a suspect; Mike should do what he needed to do. Pear would later deny, under oath in family court, that this conversation ever occurred.

Mike left a detailed message for Dr. Rahman, describing the improvement that Gabriel's teachers and baseball coach had observed in his health since his separation from Mary, and told him about the criminal charges that Mary faced. Mike also used some connections he had in the Minnesota area to back-channel his concerns to others involved in Gabriel's care. Mike felt relieved he'd been able to relay information that could protect Gabriel from more unnecessary surgery, and anxiously waited for Mary to return to Texas.

EARLIER IN THE investigation, Mike had asked Dr. Marc Feldman to review the Mary Welch case. Dr. Feldman spent months looking through the records. On August 2, 2015, he sent Bucky Pear his damning twenty-page final report.

"Gabriel has been victimized and endangered by his mother's medical deception and pathological lying that have spanned most of his young life. . . . At this point in the review process, I have found the evidence supporting my findings to be overwhelming. No other explanations for the child's overall course are credible."

In August 2015, the Brittany Phillips case returned a hung jury. Mike knew the prosecutor, Dawn Ferguson, was as torn up as he was about it—but even with the strength of the evidence against Brittany, what this outcome had shown Mike was that there was going to be no convincing some people that a mother could knowingly harm her child. That lone holdout juror—the dentist—had been one of them.

Fortunately, Sharen Wilson hadn't interfered with the Phillips case as it was well underway by the time she came into office. And while Brittany had a good lawyer, he wasn't the crusading type, and she had almost no supporters within her family. Brittany wasn't going to become a political albatross for Wilson. But Mary had hired some of the top defense attorneys in town, and her family had the deep pockets required for a lengthy legal battle.

Mike ran into DA Wilson at one of the ice cream socials she'd begun hosting at the office—a halfhearted attempt to combat plummeting morale from the draconian scheduling and management changes—shortly after the Phillips verdict came down. Wilson pulled him aside to ask what happened. Mike explained how they'd laid things out in the case, and how it had come down to one hold-out digging in his heels.

"Jury selection," she harrumphed, intimating that Dawn Ferguson had messed up by letting the holdout get through, as though she could have anticipated it. Mike stood up for Dawn and told Wilson how challenging these cases were. But his heart sunk. For Wilson, trials were about winning and losing, about the appearance of a flawless record. *It must seem simple to her*, Mike thought. She didn't have to sit with Alyssa in the hospital, or interview a half dozen desperate friends and family members who'd been watching Brittany starve her daughter in plain sight. She hadn't had to hear the anguish in Laura's and Bill's voices when they worried their beloved little girl might be returned to the woman who'd tortured her.

IT'S TEMPTING TO believe that when the evidence against someone is as strong as it was against Mary—especially considering that she'd already been indicted by a grand jury—the only choice would be to take the case to trial. But so-called prosecutorial discretion left a wide avenue, and Mike knew that the opinion of a cop didn't mean much to the new folks running the DA's Office. None of the evidence Mike had spent years collecting would mean a damn thing if he couldn't get any of the decision-makers to actually look at it. Mike felt like some freshman English teacher trying to get students to read *The Iliad*. But he had to keep trying.

One afternoon in late September, Pear's boss, Patrick Mueller—a big, balding, blowhard of a man—stormed down to Mike's office.

"You're off the Welch case! Your investigation stops now!" Mueller bellowed. Up until then, Mueller had been supportive of Mike. What had changed?

"Why?" Mike asked. This was a slap in the face.

Mueller would only say that he'd had a meeting with Gerald Nessman—Sharen Wilson's number two—and refused to elaborate further.

Mike caught his breath, knowing it wasn't actually Mueller's decision whether or not he stayed on the case. He went to talk to his investigative supervisor, Gary. Gary was a contradiction in terms: a burly six-feet-two vegan (which Mike didn't hold against him), and an investigator from the old faction of the DA's Office, who believed in doing what was right and protecting his people. Mike had always liked his boss.

Gary told him not to worry about Mueller, he was just blowing off steam. He told Mike to keep on with his work and he'd get them on the same page with leadership. But Mike was not reassured: he suspected Mary's attorneys had pulled a slimy move and gone over the prosecutor Bucky Pear's head. They were trying to make this go away. Gary informed Mike that he was arranging a meeting between Pear, Mueller, Nessman, Mike, and Gary.

"Relax, Mike, I'll let you know when it's scheduled," Gary assured him.

A week later, Mike walked into Bucky Pear's office to catch him up about a number of active cases. When he found Mueller also sitting there, he took the opportunity to bring them up to speed on the Welch case. Mueller told him they had a big meeting coming up about it with Nessman.

"Okay, I'll fill you in there," Mike said.

"Oh, you're not invited," Mueller snapped back snidely.

Mike saw red; Mueller had no idea what was going on in this investigation. "But I'm the one who knows the case and the facts."

"That's not up to me, Mike, that's Gerald's call," Mueller said, shrugging. But Gary had already told him he was invited to the meeting—Mueller was lying to his face. Was there anything this guy wouldn't do to protect his little kingdom?

Mike's stomach dropped: neither of them was taking the case seriously. "You know, if you drop this case, there's a good chance she could kill this kid," he said, not mincing words.

Pear looked aghast. "Are you saying that would be my fault?"

"Yes, I am, Bucky. Be accountable!"

Mike left the office, but he wasn't about to let them dump this case. He was going to attend that meeting; Gary had told him he'd be included. He went to check in with Gary.

But Gary told him Pear and Mueller had gone behind both of their backs. The DA's Office had already felt like a high school cafeteria, splitting off into factions—now the lawyers were deliberately subverting the criminal investigators? Mike got the sense that his opinion didn't mean a damn to them. Determined to make things right, Gary promised Mike that he'd get him his own meeting with Nessman.

When the time came, Mike laid out the case plainly and succinctly to Nessman. But once again, he was struck by Nessman's passive reaction to his detailed and harrowing account of the way in which Gabriel's life and well-being were at stake. Nessman was merely humoring him; none of what he was saying was sinking in. He felt the now familiar dread of trying to explain to a disbelieving listener that a nice-looking mom was a potentially lethal threat to her child.

Just like Barbour, Nessman thanked Mike for his time without asking a single question. The meeting had all been for show: his decision had been made before Mike walked into the room. Mike was sure not one of them had even read the case report.

Gary later told him that it was a call from Gillette Hospital attorney Kaur complaining about Mike's call to Dr. Rahman's residence—plus a visit by Mary's defense attorneys to Nessman's office—that had precipitated his removal from the case. Nessman simply trusted a fellow attorney more than some bullheaded cop he barely knew.

And as for Mueller? Mike felt he saw this man for who he was: a lazy prosecutor who would throw under the bus anyone who caused him the least amount of trouble.

LESS THAN TWO weeks later, on November 10, 2015, Nessman dismissed the charges against Mary Welch in Texas and deferred any further charging decisions back to Ramsey County, Minnesota, where Gabriel's surgeries had taken place. To Mike, this was a blatant cop-out: they already knew Minnesota wasn't going to charge her. Mary Welch was the hot potato that had been passed back and forth and, ultimately, tossed out the window.

Gary came to Mike's office to deliver the bad news. Mike was resigned; he shook his head as Gary explained the dropped charges.

"I'm sorry," Gary said. "I know you worked hard; they said it's just better prosecuted in Minnesota."

"Gary," Mike said, "Minnesota isn't going to do shit."

MIKE DROVE HOME to Granbury and pulled a bottle of Texas whiskey out of the cabinet: this called for something stronger than his usual can of beer. It was a mild evening, and he sat by the unlit firepit behind the house, overlooking the usually calming waters of Lake Granbury. He ran through the sequence of events in his mind: there'd been mistakes in family court, with the CPS attorney, with the lazy Minnesota detective. Yes, Mary had expensive lawyers and maybe it would have been too much to ask a jury to look at that sunny blond mom next door and believe she was capable of something as depraved as the evidence showed she was.

But they had *so* much evidence: piles of damning affidavits from doctors; hours of interviews with former friends, Gabriel's teachers, his baseball coach, his *father*. They had a report from Marc Feldman, one of the top experts on MBP and medical child abuse in the country. It wasn't nothing—far from it—and they owed it to Gabriel to try. Wasn't that their damn job?

But for Sharen Wilson, for Gerald Nessman, for Patrick Mueller, dropping the charges was a bit of paperwork off their desk, plus some goodwill with a powerful defense attorney. It was a headache of a case avoided, a possible loss pushed off the docket.

They hadn't seen what Mike had seen, because they had refused to even look. They didn't have to live with knowing what they were sending an innocent child back into. As Mike reached the halfway point in his whiskey bottle, he knew this case was going to haunt him forever.

And what about Doug? Mike and Brooke had walked him straight into hell: asking him to accept that the mother of his child was a mortal threat to the boy. And he'd been courageous enough to look at the evidence, to see the truth. Now it would cost him everything. Mike knew intellectually that it wasn't his fault, but he felt a guilt lodge itself in his heart that he couldn't shake.

MIKE COULD BARELY stand to drag himself back to the office, but he had other cases to work on, other kids who needed him to show up and do his job—especially as it appeared that the rest of the office wasn't going to do so. In late November, after a tense few weeks, Gary called Mike down for a chat. Mike felt his stomach drop as Gary asked him to close the door.

"Let me guess," Mike said. "I'm out of crimes against children."

Gary said he was so sorry, that Mueller was claiming a "personality conflict" made their working relationship impossible. *Well,* Mike thought, *that's one way to put it.* As far as he was concerned, the conflict was about right and wrong, about putting politics above the life of a child.

He would be transferred to the felony court team. Gary told him he had tried to keep him on, but the administration was adamant.

ONCE THE CRIMINAL charges against Mary Welch were dropped, the family court—which had never considered the investigation its purview—followed suit. Doug's fight with Mary was now seen as just a regular custody battle. Dropped charges—especially in light of an indictment by a grand jury—are hardly the same as an exoneration, but in this case, it gave fuel to Mary's claims that she'd been the victim of false accusations. "The judge in this particular case wouldn't listen to evidence about medical child abuse," Doug said about how things ultimately shook out. "As far as she was concerned, that was a criminal issue. And Mary was either guilty of it or not guilty of it. And if she was not guilty of it, then it didn't need to be brought up. And all the things that Mom had done were purportedly in the best interest of the child, because she was innocent."

It's an unfortunate reality that in our country, justice can very easily come down to who can afford to keep fighting and who can't. In this case, Doug was on the unlucky end of that spectrum. "The judge gave us the ultimatum of: you will either work this out through mediation, or you will go to a jury trial. Not having the funds to afford going to a jury trial and knowing I'm up against a family who has the funds, because Grandma and Grandpa come from a wealthy side of the street . . ." Doug felt he was screaming into the wind.

The only consequence Mary suffered was for Medicaid fraud—which was pled down to a misdemeanor charge—for continuing to receive and cash payments meant for Gabriel's care during the time he was not in her custody.*

The custody arrangement reverted to what it had been before the case, but everything had changed. Mary had cast Doug as the villain to her kids, telling them that he'd tried to take them away from her. Doug felt that Mary had made them so fearful that during his scheduled visitations, they simply refused to go near their father.

"It's cost me years of time with my children. It's cost me any relationship at this point with my children. It's been three and a half years since I've seen my children or communicated with them," Doug said in 2021 when I interviewed him for *Nobody Should Believe Me*, anguish on his face. "I even send them gifts on their birthdays and Christmas. I send them checks so that they know that Dad is doing something; none of the checks have been cashed. So as far as cost to me, it's ongoing."

Doug made the choice to see Mary for what she was, but because others chose to ignore it, he lost everything. Now he must live with not only the horror of knowing about the abuse, but the unyielding pain of knowing that some bureaucrats in an office made the choice to ignore it. They made the decision that Gabriel's life wasn't worth a challenging court case.

"Just doing this is difficult," Doug told me when he recounted his story on *Nobody Should Believe Me*, bravely choosing to share Mary's name after originally doing the interview anonymously. "It brings up a lot of past things that I have tried hard to bury that I suffer from. My dream life is not where it should be. I do the best I can."[1]

Estrangement is a different sort of loss than death: just as painful, but without the closure of finality.

---

* Mary's mother, Rose, also was charged, as she had been receiving a Medicare stipend for assisting with Gabriel's care.

MARY WELCH RAN a restaurant for a time, before being elected to her small Texas town's city council. The arrest came up during her election. She frames the dismissal of the case as proof of her innocence and blames the events on—in her words via a Facebook post—"a cruel ex-husband and a corrupt cop."

Gabriel recently graduated high school and for a time was running a barbeque joint—adjacent to one Mary owned.

I asked Doug what he hopes for in the future. "The kids to grow up and know the truth," he told me. "The kids to grow up and to realize that Dad wasn't trying to get Mom because Dad had some sort of ax to grind. Dad was trying to put my son first, my daughter first. And the system let me down. With that said, I wonder if that will ever happen, knowing the close-knit relationship that that family has."

Though many of Mary's former friends and extended family members obviously feel differently, those who've been allowed to remain in Gabriel's life appear united in the narrative that the trouble was Doug all along, that he's the villain in this story.

Even with this horrible outcome, Doug is grateful for Mike's efforts, and for the doctors and teachers who reported the abuse. "I think it saved my son's life," he told me. "It cost him greatly as far as family ties go, not being in contact with his father. But it changed the outcome of his life. Getting out of Mom's care for a short time, he saw then how the world could really be—what a normal child has, as far as opportunities. It put him in regular school, it put him in sports. Sadly, he is still called a special needs child by Mom. But it saved his life."

The cost of reporting someone for medical child abuse is undoubtedly high. It can jeopardize your career, as it did for Mike, and has for many of our MBP committee colleagues. It can lead to being excoriated in the press, as was the doctor who reported my sister. It can mean you forever lose some of the people you love the most, as it did for Doug and for my family. Yet the potential cost of inaction must always be kept in mind. Reporting can be the difference between life and death.

In 2020—not long after I first met Mike Weber, and following a two-year-long criminal investigation into my sister, this time concerning her younger daughter—the prosecuting attorney declined to file charges against her. This was following a juvenile court judge's decision to return her children to her, which came down in July 2019, four days before my novel came out.

Like Doug, I'm crushed by what I see as the failure of the system to save these children—and like Doug, I'm forever grateful to the people who tried.

We often use the term "survivor" to mean someone who has come through a terrible trauma, but in this case it's very literal. The system failed Doug Welch, but Gabriel is alive. Doug and I sit with this for a moment: this hard-fought and bittersweet outcome. "That's not nothing," I say to him finally.

"No, that's not nothing," he agrees. "It's what you hold on to."

Conclusion

In their own way, the cases of Hope Ybarra, Brittany Phillips, and Mary Welch are each shocking and distinct; these are stories of individual perpetrators whose actions reverberated in unique and harrowing ways throughout the lives of their children, families, and communities. Yet seen alongside other cases of medical child abuse, they hew so closely to an established pattern they become almost rote. They begin with premature births; graduate to feeding issues, unnecessary surgical procedures, and breathing trouble; and end up as rare, complex conditions alongside a cascade of unrelated diagnoses that combine to create a health history that numbers in the tens of thousands of pages. It is never one thing—it's all the things all the time—and only the mother can help their child. Often, the mother is the only one who even sees these symptoms.

Similarly, it's never *one* person who suspects something is wrong, but multiple friends and family members, multiple doctors, innumerable reports that too often go straight into a bureaucratic void. Hope's and Brittany's kids are the lucky ones: they were given back their childhoods and health by people who were brave enough to do the right thing. For too many others, the people with the power to act refuse to look at the uncomfortable evidence being placed before them.

Mike and I both understand that we are asking people to look at something they'd rather not see. Before he began taking on these cases, Mike moved through the world a little easier. He remembers the happy-go-lucky guy who took each day as it came, before stress had added years to his life and gray hairs to his head. This was before he lived in a world where that lovely, normal-seeming mom next door could be capable of the most heinous acts your imagination could conjure. Before he understood that the horror movie was real and that it was happening more frequently than anyone would like to believe.

In December 2015, reporter Deanna Boyd published a series of articles in the *Fort Worth Star-Telegram* about Mike's work on medical child abuse cases, including coverage of the three cases we've discussed in this book. Mary Welch's mug shot graced the front page.

At the time of the article's publication, Mike was dutifully working with the felony court team where he'd been plopped after the upheaval with the DA's Office, but he was keeping his eye out for other jobs. He watched from the sidelines as the office continued to bleed out their best people under Sharen Wilson's tenure. Though Mike was technically out of the crimes-against-children unit, he was already well known as the go-to guy in Fort Worth for medical child abuse cases, and the press coverage solidified that reputation. He continued to get calls from both CPS workers and desperate fathers in other jurisdictions.

In May 2016, Brent Kesler, a serious and motivated detective with the Fort Worth PD, rang Mike to tell him about the high-profile case of Danita Tutt. She had been pushing for her son to be entered into hospice care and had even purchased him a coffin. Mike assisted the investigation and Tutt was eventually convicted of attempted murder and sentenced to five years in prison. Thankfully, her son survived the abuse and is now a healthy young man. Tutt still has many impassioned defenders in Tarrant County; her defense attorney's argument was that Tutt had been falsely accused by Cook Children's.[1] Mike got calls about two other cases he felt were workable, only to watch them slip through the cracks in the hands of detectives less motivated than Kesler.

During the Tutt trial, Mike heard frequently from Bill Waybourn, who was by now both Alyssa's fully adoptive father and the newly elected sheriff of Tarrant County. He was also becoming a vocal advocate for victims of medical child abuse. When expressing his frustration about the two cases collecting dust at the Fort Worth PD, Mike made an offhand comment that Bill should let him know if he had any jobs available in his office.

A few months later, in November 2018, he called Mike with an offer. The sheriff's office made an arrangement with the Fort Worth PD that they would hand over any medical child abuse cases to Mike, which the already overburdened department was happy to do. The move meant Mike would take a voluntary demotion and sizeable pay cut in exchange for a much bigger workload. He jumped at the chance.

Mike's last day at the DA's Office was also—as fate would have it—the last day of his old nemesis Patrick Mueller, who'd fallen out of favor with Wilson and been told to resign or be terminated. Mike's work at the sheriff's office would encompass all forms of crimes against children, and he hit the ground running in December 2018 investigating the capital murder case of a two-month-old. During the writing of this book, that offender was sentenced to life in prison.

Mike quickly picked up the two medical child abuse cases he'd seen fall through the cracks at the Fort Worth PD and ended up arresting both offenders. Despite Mike's efforts and the severity of the charges, neither case saw a good outcome. One offender pled guilty to five years deferred probation and the other case was left to languish for five years before being dismissed by the Tarrant County DA's office, which cited "prosecutorial discretion" and told Mike they simply didn't feel they could secure a conviction. In both instances, the children were left in the offenders' care: where they were undoubtedly subjected to further abuse. This was an all-too-common outcome, even in Tarrant County, where the systems are arguably stronger than anywhere else in the county.* From January 2019 through December 2022, Mike would investigate over thirty-five reports of medical child abuse, making arrests on ten different offenders, with seven of them ending with felony child abuse convictions and three still pending trial as of May 2024. Mike suspected every one of them would have walked if he hadn't been able to take on the investigations, which only reinforced his commitment to this kind of work.

As for the Mary Welch case—which remains within the statute of limitations until ten years after the victim's eighteenth birthday—Mike has asked every subsequent chief of the Tarrant County Crime Against Children Unit to look into it. So far, none have.

While Mike's coworkers were initially leery of a political hire and skeptical of this seemingly esoteric crime, Mike just put his head down and let the cases speak for themselves, knowing that their respect was something he'd have to earn. He wouldn't have it any other way.

Sharen Wilson announced in 2022 that she would not seek a third term as Tarrant County district attorney. Judge Phil Sorrells—a longtime misdemeanor judge and former criminal prosecutor—won the election to replace her. Sorrells was well funded with West Texas oil money, and Sorrells's wife is the daughter of a highly influential Texas politician. Mike knew there were more qualified candidates in the field, but felt that money and influence won the day. His campaign highlighted his "tough on crime" approach and

* https://www.star-telegram.com/news/local/crime/article235483297.html

emphasized his support of law enforcement. Mike hoped that included law enforcement who were trying to protect children.

AFTER FIFTEEN YEARS of investigating medical child abuse cases, Mike knows how resistant systems are to change—and that systems are merely a composition of human beings, with all of their biases and flaws, right alongside their more admirable and protective instincts. Mike has been around long enough to remember the seismic change it took to move our societal conception of child sex offenders from "Uncle Johnny has a problem with children, so stay away from him" to "We need to call the authorities about Uncle Johnny."

In the fall of 2022, Sheriff Waybourn and Mike made their third attempt to get legislation passed that would apply a criminal law specifically to medical child abuse. The proposed legislation was dubbed "Alyssa's Law."

I had recently launched the first season of *Nobody Should Believe Me*, which featured—along with a bit of my own history—the story of Hope Ybarra, as well as interviews with Ryan Crawford, George Hunnicut, and Doug Welch. These were all people I'd met through Mike. It turned out that an aide to Congressman David Cook—who was supporting Alyssa's Law—was a listener of the show and asked if I'd come moderate a panel in support of it at the Fort Worth Club.

It was a few months after the birth of my son and about a month before the 2022 midterm elections. As I took my place on the panel between Congressman Cook and Sheriff Waybourn—two Republican politicians—I thought, *Well, this wasn't really on my bingo card.* The wide political spectrum within the coalition that has formed to combat this abuse is a rare and special aspect of the work. By then I was deep into production on the second season of *Nobody Should Believe Me*—which featured Alyssa Waybourn—and I'd developed a real affection for the Waybourns. Likewise, they'd trusted me—a liberal novelist from Seattle—to tell their daughter's story. It's all been a much-needed reminder that there are some things—arguably, nothing more so than the well-being of kids—that just shouldn't be turned into political footballs. The night before the panel, I had dinner with Nick Putscher—Hope's kid brother—and his fiancée. The next day, Doug Welch, Laura Waybourn, and Mike joined us at the tony Fort Worth Club, where the panel was held. We were all still battling with our demons over what had happened, but now we didn't have to do it alone.

The grassroots effort to pass Alyssa's Law had never gotten Sharen Wilson's support, which was no surprise to Mike. He was encouraged, then, when the new DA, Phil Sorrells, promised to back it. As Mike stood inside the criminal jurisprudence subcommittee meeting room, moments before testimony was set to begin, he spotted a dark-haired young woman whom he recognized as DA Sorrells's legislative liaison: he'd had several phone conversations with her about Sorrells's suggested modifications for the bill, and the DA's support for their efforts. He walked up to say hello and asked her if she was there to testify in support of the bill. She blanched.

"The DA's Office is staying neutral on this bill," she said evenly.

Mike shook his head and reminded her that she'd told him otherwise.

"I never said that," she replied, eyes darting around the room, perhaps looking for an excuse to exit the conversation.

Mike chuckled and shook his head. Another empty suit running the DA's Office. Perfect.

"Okay, I'm going to go tell that man right over there what you said and let him deal with this." Mike pointed to Sheriff Waybourn, who was standing nearby, waiting to testify on the bill named after his daughter.

Mike delivered the news and watched as Bill collected his thoughts for a moment before heading for the legislative liaison. Mike watched closely as Bill confronted her, a rare flash of anger crossing his face. She repeated that the decision was above her head, that she was sorry.

The sheriff called DA Sorrells the following morning. He equivocated and claimed it was a "misunderstanding," and that he still supported the bill. Conveniently, however, it was too late for this support to matter; the window for comment was closed. When Bill told Mike about Sorrells's backpedaling, Mike started to wonder if the DA wasn't worse than neutral, if he was actually trying to kill the efforts, behind the scenes.* That would allow Sorrells to have it both ways: he could save face with Bill and pretend that he had the sheriff's back, all while never having to go out on a limb to do the right thing.

Despite Sorrells's shenanigans, the bill was approved by the House criminal jurisprudence subcommittee and sent, at last, to the Texas House floor for a vote. But the bill was a late addition to the hearing, and was scheduled for a vote on the last possible day that it could be forwarded to the Senate. Evidently, the Speaker decided there were more important things that needed to go up for a vote—such as a bill allowing manicurists to get their certifications online rather than in person. Alyssa's Law died on the house floor waiting for politicians to pay attention.

It was devastating, and yet it had still made it further than any medical child abuse bill ever had before. It was a reminder that the victories in this fight are often measured in millimeters, and Bill and Mike would take every one they could get. They'd be back—and back again—until someone listened.

A few weeks after the fateful committee hearing, Mike and Dr. Jamye Coffman arrived at the Cornfield Room, in the building across the street from the Tarrant County DA's Office. They were

* Mike would later confirm that this was indeed the case when he viewed text messages from the chief of staff for a state representative explaining that the Tarrant County DA's office did not support the bill.

there to give an hour-long training to a crowd of forty attorneys who had shuffled into the mini-amphitheater. Mike's antennae went up as he noticed Rose Anna Salinas, chief of the criminal division, arriving with Teri Moore, who'd been brought in as her second-in-command only months before. Moore had not only been the defense attorney on the Danita Tutt case in Tarrant County, she was also a close friend of the Tutt family. Danita had spent her summers swimming in Moore's pool, and Moore told anyone who would listen that Danita had been wrongly convicted. This, Mike suspected, explained DA Sorrells's abrupt shift in support for Alyssa's Law—the call was coming from inside the house.

Salinas and Moore gave Mike the cold shoulder upon arrival and sat together scowling throughout Dr. Coffman and Mike's presentation, arms crossed over their chests, not taking a single note. The presentation covered the basics of MBP, with both Mike and Dr. Coffman sharing their professional experiences as well as the peer-reviewed literature on medical child abuse.

The moment Mike reached the last slide and opened the floor to questions, Salinas's hand shot up. She wanted to know why Mike didn't charge the *doctors* who'd done all of the unnecessary treatments. Mike recognized the argument: it was the same one Teri Moore had made in her closing in the Danita Tutt case. Salinas railed at Mike for several minutes, telling him that his advice was "scary" and risked sending innocent parents to jail. She said she was "offended" by Mike's comparison of medical child abuse and child sex abuse, a parallel Mike pointed out to her is not only apt but is recognized in the peer-reviewed literature.

"You're presenting it with commonalities with pedophilia so it can become a scarier topic," she reiterated. As though the specter of a mother making their own child ill needed any extra shock value. "Everyone here needs to understand," Salinas said, "that we're going to be careful as an office when we get these cases."

"I came up in a time when we were supposed to believe that baby shaking syndrome is a thing," she went on, recalling a conversation she'd had with a disgraced former medical examiner. "And I stood up and asked for people to go to prison. And then I found out that it is not."*

Dr. Coffman attempted to correct her, to no avail. Salinas was placing doubt on abusive head trauma, formerly referred to as shaken baby syndrome, a condition that is the subject of wide medical consensus.

The exchange solidified for Mike that while the previous DA's Office had been indifferent to pursuing child abuse cases, the new one was likely to be downright unsupportive.

Salinas's comments may sound confounding for someone who works in child abuse, but they reflect a growing pushback on not only the existence of medical child abuse, but the existence of *any* child abuse. This is at the heart of the conspiracy theory of "medical kidnapping" that has grown increasingly mainstream over the past few years. In addition to predictably stoking outrage in the media, these stories have proved a surefire way to appeal to constituents on both sides of the aisle: those on the right, who believe it's not the government's place to intervene in parenting in any way, and those on the far left who see all interventions by law enforcement as tainted by a deeply corrupt system, including those that happen in child abuse cases.

THERE IS NO doubt that everything in this arena has become even more complicated by recent global events. The Covid-19 pandemic isolated children in an unprecedented way via Zoom schooling and

* Dr. Nizam Peerwani, the medical examiner whom Rose Anna Salinas mentioned in her comments about abusive head trauma (or "baby shaking syndrome" as she called it), retired amid an investigation into his autopsies that revealed dozens of mistakes. A district court judge also found that Peerwani had given "false, inaccurate, or misleading" testimony during a murder case where the suspect ended up receiving the death penalty.[2]

telehealth visits with doctors. This was hard on all families, but for victims of medical abuse, it made an already challenging determination next to impossible. As the response to Covid became increasingly and hotly politicized, it also sowed distrust in the medical community, priming the public to be more receptive to the frequent claims of offenders that they are simply being falsely accused by arrogant, controlling doctors. As the political climate grows to a fever pitch on the issues of transgender healthcare, and abortion access after the fall of *Roe v. Wade*, physicians increasingly find themselves in the crosshairs of fervent political debates in a way they didn't sign up for when they went to medical school. Now, with an escalating panic about "false" accusations of medical child abuse, they're also being charged with kidnapping children for fun and profit.*

There is a widespread and deeply dangerous public misconception that child abuse pediatricians such as Dr. Jamye Coffman and Dr. Sally Smith—who was cast as the villain in the Maya Kowalski case—are simply trained to see abuse everywhere they look. But Dr. Coffman emphasized that of the suspected reports of medical child abuse that they see at Cook's, about a quarter of them receive a positive diagnosis of abuse. The bar is appropriately high. One recent study shows that child abuse pediatricians are actually *less* likely to come to a positive finding of abuse than their less well-trained colleagues.

And what gets lost in all of this are the victims. It's easy to forget in this political climate that not everything *ought* to be political, that there are some things that *should* unite us despite our other differences. Protecting vulnerable children from those who would harm them should be at the top of that list. Mike and I have seen people from the left and right step up and try to move this issue

---

* Not only is there no data to support the idea that child abuse pediatricians are kidnapping children, the existing data shows that they diagnose abuse in less than half of the cases they review.[3]

forward, and we've seen people on both sides successfully drag it backward. Both of us are jaded in our own ways, but neither of us are jaded enough to believe that one major political party or the other truly doesn't care about kids.

We recognize the intransigence of the interlocking systems in which these cases play out. And we also believe in the power of a few determined people to make change. Cook Children's Hospital—where the three cases in this book originated—continues to break ground in their prevention of medical child abuse. In fact, it is the first hospital in the nation to hire a dedicated employee to assist the hospital's child protection teams in reviewing records to determine if there is evidence of abuse. This work is costly, but it's often the first line of defense, the crucial tipping point that determines whether a case is properly investigated.

The issue of medical child abuse lives at the intersection of some of the most fraught institutions in the country: the healthcare system, the child welfare system, and the criminal justice system. And it's at the heart of perhaps the most fraught cultural institution of all: motherhood.

We live in a society that provides a baseline of exactly zero support for mothers. Even as motherhood is beatified and commercialized, venerated and fretted over, and used as a political pawn, it's not actually respected. Women receive this message loud and clear from the moment they are visibly pregnant: from the parade of strangers' observations about their body, to the condescending comments from men about how motherhood is the "most important job in the world." But women are still expected to do it all themselves. When I had my son, my husband was given one week of paternity leave before he was called back into the office. I "gave" myself six weeks, because as a freelancer, paid leave doesn't exist.

It's within this void of support—in a world where many parents may find themselves turning to GoFundMe to pay for a sick child's healthcare, in a world where we're all, to some degree or another, dependent on the goodwill of strangers—that offenders find a foothold. These very ad hoc, unregulated systems that many end up leaning on are ripe for exploitation. No one suspects a mom of lying about her child's health—until, that is, they've had to watch the abuse happen to someone they love.

In one of my numerous podcast interviews with Bea Yorker, a nursing professor who also has a law degree and years of clinical experience with medical child abuse, she made an apt observation: "As a society, we have a lot of laws that criminalize masculine forms of violence. That is bludgeoning, raping, strangling, gunshots, stabbing. We recognize it. We are much more aware as a society that it is abhorrent. We make laws against it, and we put people in prison. What we as a society are less aware of are feminine forms of violence: suffocating, poisoning, killing with kindness, infantilizing, and they're just as lethal as those other forms of violence."

Mike and I have seen this time and again—whether it's Mike arguing with ADA Salinas during a training, or me arguing with a clueless true crime podcaster. Regardless of what the evidence shows, some people are absolutely unwilling to believe a mom would hurt her child. And it is within this context that offenders get away with it, again and again.

The soft power of women looks very different from the power yielded by men, and yet it can be exploited in much the same way. Just as perpetrators of child sex abuse can find cover in organized religion, or in youth sports, or as troop leaders, medical child abusers can find cover in the guise of society's most sympathetic figure: the mother of a sick child. For though much divides us in this country, the plight of a sick child unites us. There is no one whose heart doesn't shatter when they see a seriously ill child. It strikes us as viscerally and horrifically wrong: a crime against nature. The idea of someone *purposely* exploiting this position is so distasteful that it doesn't even occur to most people to consider it. Once the possibility is brought to their attention, many push it away as hard as they can.

And in my experience, the last thing we let mothers be, in this culture, is human beings. Being a mother changes you forever, but it doesn't make you a saint. There's no qualifying test you have to take before you can get pregnant, no class you have to pass before you can bring your baby home from the hospital. Mothers are just people, and they're capable of the full spectrum of human behavior—including heinous, evil acts.

———

THIS SPECIFIC ABUSE takes place in the medical system, and part of the solution lies in educating doctors on what to look for. And in supporting them through their own emotional turmoil when abuse is suspected.

As Dr. Carole Jenny, an MBP expert and child abuse pediatrician, explained, pediatricians are taught from the very beginning of their training that their job is to work with parents to help their children. And doctors go into pediatrics because they love kids. "They've always been taught to trust parents and believe what mothers say. So it's really hard for a pediatrician to say, Oh, this mother's lying to me. When the mother breaks the contract and doesn't tell the truth, doesn't work in the child's best interest, it really makes the medical care system very rocky."

But while doctors may be vilified in the media for "falsely" accusing parents, a doctor's essential role is in reporting, and perhaps reviewing records, and testifying in court. This is part of their duty to the community, to the children they treat. And yet, as we write this book, stories of "falsely accused" parents are hitting a fever pitch. Take the case of Maya Kowalski, whose mother, Beata, was investigated after treating her young daughter's alleged pain disorder with high doses of ketamine—including a procedure in Mexico where she was put in an induced coma for five days. Beata died by suicide during the investigation, and much of the resultant media coverage, including the Netflix documentary of the case, veers into heavy conspiracy theory territory about the doctors and social workers conspiring to kidnap Maya. In Lehigh Valley, Pennsylvania, a city controller issued a report about alleged "overdiagnosis" of medical child abuse by the area's major healthcare providers. As these stories gather steam, one need only scratch the surface of these cases to see that the opposite problem is true: medical child abuse isn't overdiagnosed, it's underreported and underprosecuted. From Mike's perspective, there may be no easier crime to get away with.

And what these breathless advocates of "parental rights" fail to account for is what happens when doctors *don't* report.

In 2022, Colorado mother Kelly Renee Turner was sentenced to sixteen years in prison for killing her seven-year-old daughter, Olivia Gant. Turner had put her severely malnourished daughter in hospice care and pushed for a do-not-resuscitate order. Olivia endured years of unnecessary surgeries and other medical interventions, going to Children's Hospital in Aurora, Colorado, more than a thousand times in her brief life. The escalation of her alleged feeding issues will sound, by now, familiar to readers of this book: she suffered from a mysterious failure to thrive and was given first a feeding tube, and then TPN nutrition (administered intravenously). Ultimately, Olivia was transferred to home hospice care. Not understanding what was happening, the seven-year-old was pleased to finally be leaving the hospital and to have all of her tubes removed. Her paternal grandfather, Lonnie Gautreau—whom she called Paw Paw—was by her bedside in her final days. He'd always trusted his daughter-in-law to care for Olivia and believed her when she said hospice care was the best option. Once in hospice,

Olivia spent nineteen days with no food after her tubes had been removed. Her final words to her grandfather were "Paw, I'm hungry." She died two days later.

Turner wasn't reported to authorities until two years later when she attempted to take another one of her children in for cancer treatment. She was finally arrested in 2019 after a yearlong investigation. The hospital was sued by Olivia's grandparents, Turner's in-laws, for not reporting their documented concerns about abuse. The hospital denied any wrongdoing and ultimately settled out of court with the family.

While this is an extreme case, the idea of merely "charting" Munchausen by proxy concerns rather than reporting them to authorities is shockingly common. The Maya Kowalski case contains one such note from a doctor, who did not believe the child suffered from the severe asthma her mother had claimed, but never reported this to authorities. In fact, Mike has seen medical records from numerous hospitals where the term "Munchausen by proxy" is specifically charted by pediatricians, yet no report is ever made to law enforcement. When Mike presents to medical professionals, he highlights that if they are charting that term, they are charting abuse, and if they are charting abuse, they should be reporting abuse. Often, pediatricians feel they need to *prove* abuse before reporting. Mike stresses that proving it is the job of law enforcement and CPS, not the pediatricians—and while he acknowledges that police and CPS are often terrible at that job, reporting is still the responsible thing to do.

In all states in the country, CPS is the kind of organization tasked with keeping children safe. And yet they do not even have a box to check for medical child abuse on their intake form. These cases are impossible to complete in the standard two-month timeline CPS investigators are given; investigators are already overworked and underpaid. Furthermore, misconceptions about MBP being an issue of a mother's mental health loom large. The problem is at the root: we don't view a "sick" person the same way we do a well person.

Even if doctors and CPS workers do all the right things—the meticulous work of interviewing every friend and family member and teacher, of reviewing every page in the tens of thousands of medical records, of collecting evidence and affidavits—we will get nowhere if the lawyers and judges in charge of making the decisions to protect children do not understand what they're looking at.

It can seem impossible to make headway. But progress is measured by millimeters.

For me, it has always been the human stories at the center of these cases that are most likely to move people. To see the harm, you need to see the human cost. We need the voices of survivors, of fathers, of grandparents. Of sisters and aunts, brothers and uncles.

ONE FATHER, BRIAN, who's been fighting for his kids for years, told me something that I've never forgotten. We were at a child abuse conference where he and I were presenting to a packed room of professionals, along with Doug Welch and another father. This was Brian's first opportunity to meet other people who'd lived through a case. He said it was like meeting fellow veterans: it was a trauma that no one else could ever fully grasp. It was a perfect comparison: the way these stories fell on wide-eyed civilians when we told them. They were shocked—they didn't even know there was a war going on.

Or, worse, some of them told us we were lying. There was no war. We'd made it all up.

But those of us who've seen it know the truth: the war is real. The casualties as yet unaccounted for.

And no matter the odds, the fight continues.

ACKNOWLEDGEMENTS

We would like to thank the many colleagues who guided and informed our work on this book, especially Dr. Marc Feldman, who brought each of us into the American Professional Society on the Abuse of Children's Munchausen by proxy committee, and who has been such a champion for our respective work. Our deepest thanks also to Dr. Jayme Coffman and Bea Yorker for their support and for reading early versions of this manuscript and providing feedback. Thank you also to Dr. Mary Sanders, Jordyn Hope, Jim Hamilton, and all the rest of the our APSAC colleagues for their wisdom and support and for the work they do to protect children, often at great risk to themselves.

Thank you to our fantastic literary agent, Carly Watters, for her belief in this project from the beginning and her diligent guidance on both the proposal and the book itself. Andrea would also like to thank Carly for the decade of collaboration and friendship that preceded this, our fifth book together!

Thank you to our amazing team at St. Martin's Press, most of all Sarah Cantin, for championing this idea even before there was a hit podcast attached. Andrea would also like to thank Sarah for believing in her from the very first book they published together back in 2016 and for understanding the importance of this piece of her work for all these many years. Sarah, editors like you are one in a million! Thank you also to Laura Clark, Drue VanDuker, Josh Karpf, Danielle Fiorella, Katie Bassel, and Sara Beth Haring.

Our thanks also to Deanna Boyd for her excellent investigative reporting on all three of the cases in this book during her time at *The Fort Worth Star Telegram*.

We owe a deep debt of gratitude to the families who shared their stories with us. To Paul, Nick, and Robin Putscher, Fabian Ybarra, Bill, Laura, and Alyssa Waybourn, and Doug Welch: thank you for trusting us to help tell your stories. We are humbled by your courage.

Thank you also to Susan Rial, Faith Preston, Heather Harris, Dr. Karen Schultz, and Dawn Ferguson for taking the time to give us their perspectives.

From Mike

I want to thank Mom and Dad for providing an idyllic childhood and a safety net for me if I failed. I say all the time that I won the parenting lottery. Also, to my grandmother, Janie Pursley, for always taking care of three bratty boys. Thank you to Dr. Feldman and Dr. Coffman for helping me understand this abuse when I first started investigating these cases. To attorney Michael Trent (formerly of the Harris County DA's Office) for laying the legal groundwork and having the courage to prosecute some of the first cases in Texas. To Sheriff Bill Waybourn: without his unwavering support on this issue this book would not have been possible and I'm quite certain my investigative career would have ended earlier.

To Alana Minton, who always listened to my opinion on cases with an open mind and provided one of the best work environments I've had. To Rep. David Cook for advocating for an issue that is certainly misunderstood by many of his party colleagues in Austin.

To George Hunnicut and all family members of victims, especially for the courageous dads who have fought the abuser—and often the system that is supposed to protect their child—in an attempt to save their child. Thanks also to James and Connie Goochey, Mac and Stacey Bennett, Rico Lucero, Ray Morales, Don Pilcher, Jonathan Timpf, Rusty Yowell, Dr. Karen Schultz, Dr. Lazarus, Ashley Rader, Ashley Fourt, Kim D'Avignon, Eric Nickols, Letty Martinez, Mike Adair, Gary Willis, Danny McCormick, Paige McCormick, Deanna Boyd, Kim Garrison, Robin Chavez, Chief Venum, Amy Munoz, Candice Ferguson, Bill Foster, Stephany Garza, Jeff Gray, Dwayne and Ginger Ballard, Lynne Kovach, Kaley Johnson, Katia Gonzales, Brent Kessler, Stephanie Martin, Bryan Moody, Jason and Melinda Nag, Lynsey Nix, Lyndsi Price, Susan Rial, Rona Stratton, Linda Fash Bush, Lisa Gabbert, Donna Boswell, Ninfa Torres, Clara Holmes, and Suzy McCormick.

From Andrea

Thank you to my parents for supporting this work and understanding the importance of speaking up about what happened in our family. I love you both so much. Thank you to my husband, Derek, for your love and support, to my nanny, Kimberlee Brink, for helping keep the wheels on at home, and to my mom, Karen, and my mother-in-law, Susan Youngstrom, for saving the day during my increasingly frequent work travel. To my dear friends Christine Nancarrow, April Neubauer, and Kerri Hatfield and my ride or dies Monique Perlmutter, Sumako and Mayoka Kawai, and

Margaret Berend. A big thank you to my podcaster pals, especially Nora McInerny and Jordan Harbinger, who've supported me from the jump.

And lastly, thank you to my beautiful children, Fiona and Colum, for helping me understand the meaning of motherhood and for always making me smile on the hardest days.

NOTES

INTRODUCTION

1. Marc D. Feldman and Gregory P. Yates, *Dying to Be Ill: True Stories of Medical Deception* (New York: Routledge, 2018). Marc D. Feldman, *Playing Sick? Untangling the Web of Munchausen Syndrome, Munchausen by Proxy, Malingering, and Factitious Disorder* (New York: Routledge, 2004 and 2024). Marc D. Feldman and Stuart J. Eisendrath, eds., *The Spectrum of Factitious Disorders* (Washington, DC: American Psychiatric Press, 1998). Marc D. Feldman and Charles V. Ford with Toni Reinhold, *Patient or Pretender: Inside the Strange World of Factitious Disorders* (New York: John Wiley & Sons, 1993).
2. Richard Asher, "Munchausen's Syndrome," *Lancet* 257, no. 6650 (1951): 339–41.
3. Roy Meadow, "Munchausen Syndrome by Proxy: The Hinterland of Child Abuse," *Lancet* 310, no. 8033 (1977): 343–45.
4. "Cancer Faker Belle Gibson Reveals She's Fallen on Hard Times and Can't Afford Court Fine," news.com.au, https://www.news.com.au/entertainment/tv/current -affairs/cancer-faker-belle-gibsons-desperate-new-plea/news-story/87d8103c5d 7da3583b551bd0f3b84653.
5. "Confronting Belle Gibson—the Health Advocate Who Faked Cancer," *60 Minutes Australia*, December 11, 2018, https://www.youtube.com/watch?v=tCN2U vyz72k.
6. "Illinois Woman Who Lied About Having Cancer Sentenced to Prison," KSDK-TV, https://www.ksdk.com/article/news/crime/illinois-woman-who -lied-about-having-cancer-sentenced-to-prison/63–2cd588b3-f549–4253 -bc8a-0a4bc94475c3
7. Donna L. Hoyert, "Maternal Mortality Rates in the United States, 2021,"

National Center for Health Statistics (Washington, DC: Centers for Disease Control and Prevention, 2023), https://dx.doi.org/10.15620/cdc:124678.

8. Office of Research on Women's Health, "History of Women's Participation in Clinical Research," National Institutes of Health, https://orwh.od.nih.gov/toolkit/recruitment/history.

9. "The Untreated Syphilis Study at Tuskegee Timeline," Centers for Disease Control and Prevention, https://www.cdc.gov/tuskegee/timeline.htm.

10. L. Lewis Wall, "The Medical Ethics of Dr J Marion Sims: A Fresh Look at the Historical Record," *Journal of Medical Ethics* 32, no. 6 (2006): 346–50.

11. Feldman and Yates, *Dying to Be Ill.*

12. APSAC Taskforce, "Munchausen by Proxy: Clinical and Case Management Guidance," American Professional Society on the Abuse of Children's Practice Guidelines, *APSAC Advisor* 2018, no. 1.

13. Thomas A. Roesler and Carole Jenny, *Medical Child Abuse: Beyond Munchausen Syndrome by Proxy* (Elk Grove Village, IL: American Academy of Pediatrics, 2009).

14. "Children and Teens: Statistics," RAINN (Rape, Abuse & Incest National Network), https://www.rainn.org/statistics/children-and-teens.

15. Gregory Yates and Christopher Bass, "The Perpetrators of Medical Child Abuse (Munchausen Syndrome by Proxy): A Systematic Review of 796 Cases," *Child Abuse & Neglect* 72 (2017): 45–53.

16. D. A. Rosenberg, "Web of Deceit: A Literature Review of Munchausen by Proxy," *Child Abuse & Neglect* 11, no. 4 (1987): 547–63.

17. Mike Hixenbaugh, *Do No Harm*, NBC News and Wondery, November 10–December 15, 2020, https://www.nbcnews.com/news/us-news/do-no-harm.

18. Olivia Marble, "LVHN Tied to 'Systemic Overdiagnosis' of Medical Child Abuse in Lehigh County Report," *Lehigh Valley News*, August 23, 2023.

1. MEET HOPE

1. Deanna Boyd, "Munchausen Mom: I Didn't Want Her to Die," *Fort Worth Star-Telegram*, February 12, 2019.

2. Deanna Boyd, "Moms to Monsters," *Fort Worth Star-Telegram*, February 12, 2019.

3. Deanna Boyd, "Mommy's Little Secret," *Fort Worth Star-Telegram*, August 13, 2017.

4. Boyd, "Mommy's Little Secret."

5. Boyd, "Munchausen Mom: I Didn't Want Her to Die."

3. MEET MIKE WEBER

1. Yates and Bass, "The Perpetrators of Medical Child Abuse."

4. THE INVESTIGATION BEGINS

1. Katy Vine, "Mother, Heal Thyself," *Texas Monthly*, January 2010, https://www
.texasmonthly.com/articles/mother-heal-thyself/.

2. "Doctors: Texas Mom has Munchausen Syndrome by Proxy, Medically Abused
Kids," KHOU-TV, October 26, 2009, https://www.khou.com/article/news
/doctors-texas-mom-has-munchausen-syndrome-by-proxy-medically-abused
-kids/285-413270167.

3. "Doctors Believe Mother Has Munchausen Syndrome by Proxy, Has Medically Abused Children," WFAA-TV, https://www.wfaa.com/article/news/local
/doctors-believe-mother-has-munchausen-syndrome-by-proxy-has-medically
-abused-children/287-338908789.

4. One example of this is the Julie Conley case in Connecticut, in which the father
confessed to pouring a caustic substance into his daughter's unneeded feeding
tube. "Expert on Munchausen by Proxy Says Allegation in Conleys' Case Is 'More
Dramatic Than I've Ever Heard Before,'" MassLive, July 27, 2016, https://
www.masslive.com/news/2016/07/expert_on_munchausen_by_proxy
.html.

5. A FAMILY DIVIDED

1. Mary Sanders, "Can They Be Saved?," interviewed by Andrea Dunlop,
November 2022, in *Nobody Should Believe Me*, podcast, https://www.nobody
shouldbelieveme.com/can-they-be-saved/.

8. THE ARREST

1. There is only one case with a living child that led to a harsher sentence—fifteen
years—that of Houston mother Laurie Williamson. Dale Lezon, "Spring Mom
Gets 15 Years for Son's Needless Surgeries," *Houston Chronicle*, May 1, 2008,
https://www.chron.com/neighborhood/spring-news/article/spring-mom-gets
-15-years-for-son-s-needless-1762393.php.

2. "Nobody Should Believe Me"; Season One; https://www.nobodyshouldbe
lieveme.com/.

9. AFTERMATH

1. Boyd, "Munchausen Mom: I Didn't Want Her to Die."

2. Teresa Woodard, "Woman Suspected of Munchausen by Proxy Sentenced
to 6 Years in Prison for Injury to a Child," WFAA-TV, October 11, 2019,
https://www.wfaa.com/article/news/crime/woman-suspected-of-munchausen
-by-proxy-faces-judge-for-sentencing/287-ea628799-a6ef-484e-a9df
-8887bcf7c8f1.

3. "Hope," season 1, episode 1, *Something's Killing Me*, CNN, August 13, 2017.

4. "Can They Be Saved?," November 2022, in Nobody Should Believe Me
podcast.

18. JANE JUSTIN

1. This account is from a sworn affidavit that was part of the Mike Weber criminal investigation.

23. A SEISMIC SHIFT

1. "Can They Be Saved?," November 2022, in *Nobody Should Believe Me*, podcast.

CONCLUSION

1. Deanna Boyd, "Texas Mom Gets 5 Years in Prison for Injuring, Trying to Kill Son by Withholding Food," *Fort Worth Star-Telegram*, October 26, 2018.
2. Nichole Manna, "Medical Examiner Announces Retirement amid Investigations into Autopsies," *Fort Worth Star-Telegram*, April 30, 2021.
3. Katie L. Johnson et al., "Child Abuse Pediatricians Assess a Low Likelihood of Abuse in Half of 2890 Physical Abuse Consults," *Child Maltreatment* 27, no. 2 (2022): 202–8.

ABOUT THE AUTHORS

Andrea Dunlop is the author of four novels, including *She Regrets Nothing* and *Women Are the Fiercest Creatures*, and the host and creator of *Nobody Should Believe Me*, an award-winning investigative true crime podcast about Munchausen by proxy. Andrea is the founder of Munchausen Support, the nation's only nonprofit dedicated to supporting survivors and families affected by MBP, and a member of the American Professional Society on the Abuse of Children's MBP committee, where she serves alongside the country's foremost experts. She lives in Seattle with her husband and two children.

Mike Weber has forty years of law enforcement experience, including fifteen years as a crimes-against-children investigator. Detective Weber has consulted with numerous police agencies and district attorneys' offices nationally on cases of medical child abuse, and was awarded the National Center for Missing & Exploited Children's 2016 Texas Hero for Children Award. He currently lives and works in Fort Worth.